AZEING'S SIGNIFICANT PROPERTIES

	24
	9
	111
	50
	78
	59
	30
	77
	29
	75
	75
	115
The Nook or Ke...	13
36 North Street or White Hall Farm C	51
42 North Street or Northcroft C	52
60 North Street C	53
Northcroft or 42 North Street C	52
Northside & The Cottage, Back Lane C	118
Old House, Old House Lane C	72
The Old Post Office, Bumbles Green	100
Old Sun House C	16
Old Vicarage & Glebe House C	3
Orchard Cottage	87
Park Cottages C	117
Park View Cottage	101
Parkers Farm LC	64
Paynes Farm LC	41
2,4 Pecks Hill & 1 Maplecroft Lane C	54
Perry & White Cottages LC	119
Perry Hill Farm LC	79
Pillar Box Cottage C	28
Pindars Cottage C	103
Pond House LC	123
The Poplars & The Cottage C	83
Pound House C	40
Profits Hill Cottages LC	114
Queens Cottage C	112
Ravens or Rumbolds LC	110
Red House LC	21
Red Lion P.H. or The White House C	84
Ricketts C	124
Riddens View & Salem C	27
The Rookery or Shiree C	39
Rookswood	125
Rookswood Lodge, White House Farm or Windrush Lodge C	126
Rose Cottage, Back Lane C	113
Rose Cottage or 14 Elizabeth Close C	49
Rowing Club	46
Rumbolds or Ravens LC	110
St. Lawrence Farm C	26
St. Leonards Farm	36
St. Leonards House C	35
Salem & Riddens View C	27
Selways or Blacksmiths Shop C	22
Shadwalkers LC	73
Shiree or The Rookery C	39
Shottentons Farm, Pecks Hill C	57
Smalldrinks LC	74
Snows or Laun House C	31
Sturtsbury Farm C	90
Sun Cottage C	16
The Sun P.H. C	16
Tallis & Ashdown Cottages C	12
Teys Farm LC	109
Trevone	77
Upper Gate House & Cottage	15
Upper Town Cottage LC	7
Upper Town Post Office LC	7
Valley View & The Cottage, Colemans Lane C	34
Valley View, Waltham Road C	24
Vine, Heather & Clematis Cottages	10
1 & 2 Walnut Tree Cottages C	88
Warleys or Feltre C	80
Warwick House	102
Wheelers C	67
White & Perry Cottages LC	119
White Hall Farm or 36 North Street C	51
White House Farm, Rookswood Lodge or Windrush Lodge C	126
The White House or Camps Farm LC	63
The White House, Middle Street or Red Lion P.H. C	84
Whiteswood & Nonsuch Cottages	115
Windrush Lodge, White House Farm or Rookswood Lodge C	126
Wyndith C	25
Yew Tree Cottage	96

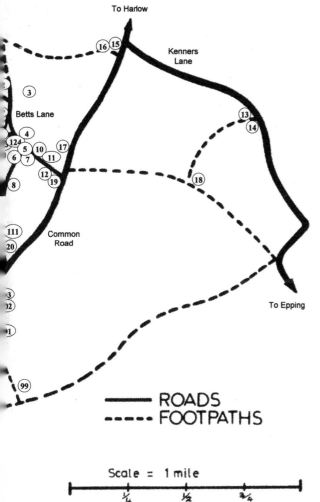

To Harlow

Kenners Lane

Betts Lane

Common Road

To Epping

ROADS
FOOTPATHS

Scale = 1 mile
1/4   1/2   3/4

...ottage C	94	Little End or Camps Cottages C	60	
...s Cottage, Nazeing Park LC	8	Little Profits C	116	
...e & Clematis Cottages	10	Lodge Farm L	18	
	122	Longyard Cottage LC	5	
...e House C	120	Mamelons Farm C	24	
	6	Mamelons House C	24	
...or Havenslea C	97	1 & 2 Mansion House C	71	
...ttages C	105	Mansion House Farm C	71	
...C	14	Maple Croft Cottage C	55	
...e Cottage or The Nook LC	13	Maplecroft, Maplecroft Lane C	56	
...Cottage C	106	1 Maplecroft Lane & 2,4 Pecks Hill C	54	
...s Head P.H.	104	38 Maplecroft Lane C	55	
...ock House	43	Marshgate Farm LC	48	
...near Kings Wood LC	20	Mayflower C	66	
...hase LC	20	Meadgate Farm, Sedge Green C	58	
...rm LC	42	Mill Bungalow	4	
...or Snows C	31	Mulberries C	37	
...age C	32	Namelons Cottage or Campions C	23	

...tion Society in 1987. More properties have been

Seventeen miles from Town

The story of Nazeing, part 2.
The twentieth century

The changing face of Nazeing. Above: Nazeingwood Common before 1941,
when it was ploughed up for wartime food production. Until then (below)
all the gates were kept closed to keep the animals from straying. On the left
are the King Harold's Head and the pound, 1930s

Seventeen miles from Town

The story of Nazeing, part 2.
The twentieth century.

David Pracy   John Garbutt   Colin Dauris

with

Doug Ball, Desmond Day, Valerie Day,

Nick Ellis, John Gervis, Paddy Hutchings,

Russell Martin, Tom Papworth, Mike Roos

Nazeing History Workshop
2002

ISBN 0 9537135 1 2

Nazeing History Workshop Publication no. 5

Printed by St. Edmundsbury Press,
Bury St. Edmunds, Suffolk, IP33 3TU

**Previous publications by members of
Nazeing History Workshop**

1. Not a better set in the country: the story
   of Nazeing Wood or Park 1778-1950.
   (David Pracy, 1995)

2. Nazeing Bury: the story of a house and its
   people.
   (John H. Gervis, 1997)

3. Nonconformity in Nazeing: a history of the
   Congregational Church 1795-1995.
   (Norman Bonnett and Paddy Hutchings, 1999)

4. Five miles from everywhere: the story of
   Nazeing part 1, from earliest times to 1914.
   (David Pracy, John Garbutt, Colin Dauris,
   Russell Martin, Valerie Day, Doug Ball, 2000)

CONTENTS

Page

LIST OF ILLUSTRATIONS

List of illustrations

List of illustrations

13

ACKNOWLEDGEMENTS

In addition to the organisations and authors listed in the bibliography, we should like to thank also the following people who helped by providing information and/or by lending documents and illustrations. Without their contributions this book could not have been published.

Peter Adams, Bill Aley, Derek Armes, Kathleen Atkins, Maureen Ball, Shelagh Ball, G.E. Bell, Marion Benton, Sheila Blake, Edith Boxall, Enid Brent, Peter Brent, David Brooks, Pat Camp, Robert Candlish, John Carr, Neil Chapman, Neville Cole, Brian Coleman, John Coleman, Maurice Coleman, Nance Coleman, Doris Cook, Connie Cordell, Joyce Crow, Peter Daniel, Prudence Dauris, Gordon Day, David Dent, Dorothy Dunster, Claude Faux, Brian Faux, Fred Finch, Bernard French, Sheila French, Margaret Gervis, John Graham, Janet Grove, Barbara Hargreaves, Margaret Harrison, Grace Harvey, Martin Harvey, Russell Haynes, Brian Hills, Michael Hills, Arthur Hollow, Pauline Hordern, Nancy Humphreys, John Hussey, Ray Hutchings, Steve Jones, Ken Judd, Elizabeth Kenworthy, Les Kimm, Elizabeth Lamb, Isa Lavis, Roy Leach, George Mackie, Catherine Macleod, Fred Mansfield, Joan Mansfield, Marion Manypeney, Frances Martin, Dennis Mead, Edna Miller, James Moncur, Rachel Montgomerie-Charrington, Fred Nash, Robin Pallett, John William Payne, Alan Peacock, Bernard Pegrum, Stephen Pollock-Hill, Mr and Mrs Alan Pond, Lucy Pott, Margaret Robinson, Phil Roos, Shirley Roos, Susan Ryder, Graham Saggers, Fred Sewell, Roy Sheppard, Harry Smith, Adelaide Starling, Brian Starling, Tony Stevenson, Marjorie Sykes, Joy Tizard, Eileen Vinther, Jeannette Wardle, Elizabeth Wells, Ken Wisdom, Dorothy Wood, Kenneth Wood, Mollie Wood, Gordon Wren.

Every effort has been made to trace and seek permission from copyright holders, and to acknowledge all contributions to the making of the book. We shall be glad to hear from anyone who has been inadvertently omitted.

PREFACE

Five miles from everywhere, Part One of *The Story of Nazeing,* described the development of the village until the outbreak of the First World War, concluding that "the 1920s were to mark the end of a long era and the beginning of a new one". A soldier returning from the First World War, magically able to travel in time, would have found Nazeing more familiar in many respects six hundred years earlier than sixty years later.

The most important reason for this was not a catastrophic war but the building of the humble tarmac road. Buses and cars were for the first time able to use the roads, so people could travel from Nazeing to the

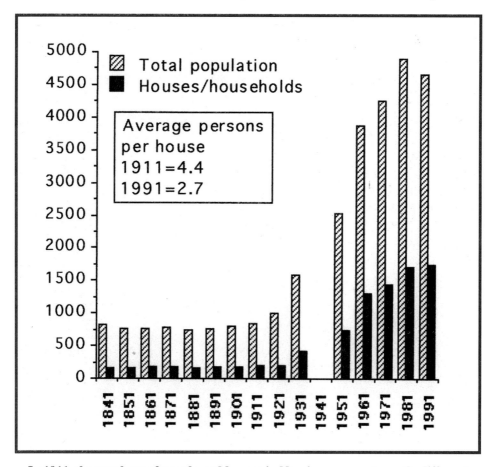

In 1911, the numbers of people and houses in Nazeing were not greatly different from those of seventy years earlier, whereas after another seventy years, there were nine times as many dwellings and nearly six times as many people.

surrounding towns or, on the railway, to London much more easily. This encouraged developers and individuals to build new houses and bungalows, which in turn made it worthwhile for utilities such as gas and electricity to lay mains to Nazeing. The basic infrastructure was in place by 1939 but the key decade was the 1950s, when car ownership became much more commonplace and there were on average 133 more people and 56 more dwellings in the village every year. After that the pace of development slowed down and in the 1980s, for the first time in a hundred years, the population dropped.

This book attempts to describe and explain those changes. Whereas the part one was broadly chronological, this part is organised by topic, an arrangement which demonstrates the ancient truth that "there is nothing new under the sun". History never repeats itself exactly but the same themes come round again and again in different forms. In most respects *Seventeen miles from Town* can stand alone, although we have referred to information that is in *Five miles from everywhere*, without repeating it.

Even across the watershed of the First World War there are continuities, so where appropriate this book begins in the 1870s. The

The barns and outbuildings of Wheelers have gone ...

16

Bumbles Green school, for example, opened in 1878 which makes a good starting point for the chapter on education. At the other end of the period we have taken most subjects to the end of the twentieth century, or even to the end of December 2001. This does cause difficulty. We have treated more recent years with caution because some subjects are inevitably still sensitive. On the other hand information is more readily available for the 1980s and 1990s than for earlier decades. We hope that some readers will not think that we have been indiscriminate about what we have included from that period.

Asked what he thought of the French Revolution, Chou En-Lai replied that "it was too early to tell". We would not go quite that far but, although we have described some of the most memorable episodes, we have made no attempt to pass final judgment on matters that are still in progress. We do not yet know, for example, whether the drop in population in the 1980s was a blip or a long-term trend. Much fascinating information about topics such as family size and origins of people coming into the village is locked up in census returns, which are only opened one hundred years after they are taken. It will be for future historians to use such documents to build on our work.

... but the house remains between the new homes in Middle Street.

We have used the reminiscences of many Nazeing people and obtained from them valuable comments on the first draft of this book. There was not time to speak to everyone who might have been able to help, so there must be many more who could have contributed. We hope that this publication will jog memories and shall welcome additions or corrections, and any photographs or other documents that readers would be willing to lend. We shall in any case add them to our archive. If enough material is forthcoming, we shall consider publishing a further book consisting mostly of reminiscences and pictures.

We have quoted extensively from original documents where spelling, punctuation, capitalisation and grammar are occasionally somewhat unorthodox. In order to preserve the spirit of the original, we have normally left these quotations unchanged.

One of the frustrations of using historical documents is that often there are references to place names that were familiar at the time but have since been forgotten. In most cases in this book, which was written at the beginning of the 21st century, we have used current names. For the benefit of present or future readers who may not know them all, we have tried to indicate where they are with maps, the index and an appendix listing road names.

One of the major changes in Nazeing during the twentieth century has been the replacement of horse driven power and transport by cars and commercial vehicles. Who in 1900, would have forecast the overwhelming effect that they now have on our daily lives?

CHAPTER 1

"GOOD WORK FOR THE PARISH"

Village leaders

The decline of the gentry

In 1900 Nazeing was, as described in *Five miles from everywhere*, still run by the gentry and the farmers. Together with the Wakes, who were the absentee lords of the manor, the Palmers and the Burys owned half of the village. Early in the twentieth century, the Hargreaves and Green families joined them. Between the wars these wealthy people ran the village in a generous, paternalistic way, but by 1970 none of their families was still living in Nazeing and their descendants owned very little property in the village. In 1912 the parish council described Nazeing as "a purely agricultural village" but by the 1950s this was no longer the case so that the farmers had lost their influence. Leadership became far more diffuse, often being taken on by incoming business and professional people. Such changes were commonplace in England but local circumstances had an important effect on the development of the village and need to be explained in detail.

The Wakes

The Wakes had moved to Courteenhall in Northamptonshire in the eighteenth century. When William, the 11th baronet, died in 1865, only a year after his father, their financial problems began. The publication of Charles Kingsley's *Hereward the Wake* had revived interest in the Saxon hero from whom the family claims descent but, for some reason, Sir William called his son and heir Herewald rather than the more familiar Hereward. Sir Herewald had to provide for several of his relatives and chose to meet his obligations by granting them the income from his Essex estates, while retaining ultimate ownership. This kind of arrangement, common among the landed gentry, was designed to ensure that one individual did not squander the family fortune, as might have happened had Sir William survived much longer. Sir Herewald inherited over 1,500 acres in Waltham Abbey and Nazeing but was soon forced, much against his will, to sell half of this land to the Corporation of the City of London. It became part of Epping Forest and now provides the splendid walk from

Epping Long Green through Harold's Park Farm and Galleyhill to Waltham Abbey. Although he always lived at Courteenhall, Sir Herewald continued to take an interest in his Essex estate; in 1916, only two weeks before his death, he dined with his Waltham Abbey and Nazeing tenants.

Sir Herewald was succeeded by his son Hereward, a career soldier who fought in the Boer War and the First World War, when he was awarded the Distinguished Service Order. Sir Hereward survived the war but many of his peers did not; the crippling death duties consequent upon the slaughter led the *Estates Gazette* to declare that "All England is changing hands". When such families fell into financial difficulties they tended to dispose of their outlying lands, as Sir Hereward did in 1919 when he sold the 300-acre Nazeing Bury farm and other smaller properties. After the Second World War Sir Hereward sold his remaining land in Waltham Abbey and Nazeing for housing and gravel extraction, some of it, like his father seventy years earlier, by compulsory purchase. Nothing remained of an estate once described as "a fair fortune in land".

In 1963 Sir Hereward died and was succeeded by his son Hereward, the 14th baronet, who served with distinction in the Second World War.

Sir Hereward Wake in 1998, entertaining members of Waltham Abbey and Nazeing history groups at his recently restored family home, Courteenhall.

Hereward has a great affection for his father and erected memorials to him in Waltham Abbey and in All Saints' Church. Although it is over 250 years since his family lived in Essex and they no longer own any land in the county, he still feels a strong affinity with the manors of which he is lord. He has visited Waltham Abbey and Nazeing and has invited local people to Courteenhall. In 1952 he married Julia Lees and they had a son, Hereward Charles, and three daughters. His son and family now occupy the main house at Courteenhall, while Sir Hereward and his wife live at the Old School House nearby.

"The Father of the Parish": Archdale Palmer (1865-1950)

Archdale Palmer, known to his close friends as Archie, was the last of his family to be born at Nazeing Park. Shortly afterwards financial problems forced them to leave the house that had been their home for seventy-five years. He was the fourth of five children and the only boy; his mother died when he was ten years old. He was educated at Winchester College, the motto of which, "Manners Makyth Man", might easily have been Archdale's own. His cousin William Waldegrave Palmer, later the second Lord Selborne and a senior politician, was a prefect who set a high moral tone which may have influenced Archdale, six years his junior.

Archdale never married but felt a strong loyalty to his family, so a period of ten years that saw a succession of personal tragedies must have affected him deeply. In 1905 his sister Charlotte (Lotta) and her husband Herbert Wellesley, a great-nephew of the Duke of Wellington, drowned in the wreck of the *S.S. Hilda* off the coast of France. Soon afterwards his father and another sister died. In 1910 his youngest sister's husband was strongly suspected of living with another woman and Archdale arranged to have the affair investigated. Then, in September 1914, his nephew Ronald Wellesley died in Canada of pneumonia while on his way to fight in Europe.

Archdale's last loss was perhaps the hardest to bear because it affected his niece, Violet, deeply as well. On 21st December, 1915, his nephew, Eric Wellesley, a 2nd lieutenant in the 8th Battalion of the Yorkshire Regiment, failed to return after carrying out an initially successful reconnaissance of the German trenches. On Christmas Eve Palmer received a telegram informing him that his nephew had been reported missing, although he had not necessarily been killed or even wounded.

Eventually the War Office concluded that Eric was dead and in March 1917 it proposed that the money in his account should go to his sister, Violet. She was convinced that he was still alive, so Archdale replied that it should be paid to him and another uncle as trustees because sending the money to her would inflict unnecessary pain, as it would involve explaining to her that the authorities had given up hope for Eric.

The Palmer family, like the Wellesleys, had a strong military tradition which Archdale continued. As a captain in the 24th Middlesex Rifle Volunteers and the Army Post Office Corps, he fought in the Boer War. At the outbreak of the First World War he joined the Essex Regiment and assisted in the training of the 9th Battalion. Being over military age and not in the best of health, however, he was unable to go overseas with them, to his great regret. After the war he devoted himself to organising the Nazeing branch of the British Legion, which provided the pallbearers at his funeral and formed a guard of honour from the lychgate to the church.

Another family tradition maintained by Archdale Palmer was its close involvement with the Mercers' Company. In 1918 he followed his forebears as Master and exercised his diplomatic skills at a potentially unruly meeting, where he headed off a "Bolshevist tendency" of younger members. From 1915 until his death he was a governor of St. Paul's School in Hammersmith, which was managed by the Mercers'. Towards the end of his life, when in poor health, his only regular outing from Nazeing was to attend the Court of Assistance at the Company.

Archdale Palmer's business success extended beyond the Mercers'. He had not attended university, preferring to go straight from school into a business career. In 1899 he became the paid secretary of the All-England Lawn Tennis Club at Wimbledon, where he had played as a gifted amateur player and had been a committee member. His successor considered his appointment "a lucky moment for the club", and described him as "...an ideal secretary. Bland but decisive in manner, of first-class business capacity, sanguine but not reckless, with many friends in the City, a man of the world with no known vices..." Having been in financial difficulties, the club began to make a profit immediately, but its affairs fell into confusion when Palmer went to fight in South Africa. He came back and, as with the Mercers' seventeen years later, averted disaster by skilful management of a turbulent meeting.

In 1905 he found himself at the centre of a scandal which had uncanny pre-echoes of similar episodes in the last decade of the twentieth century. He engineered a round robin of leading players, who requested that the contract to provide balls at Wimbledon should be taken away from the existing supplier and given to the firm of Slazengers. These balls were technically too small, so one of the Wimbledon referees resigned in protest and reported that, to keep him quiet, Slazengers had offered him £100 in an envelope. As soon as the contract was secured, Slazengers appointed Palmer as their general manager and he retained both jobs until in 1907 the conflict of interests became too great and he resigned the secretaryship.

Despite the scandal Palmer continued to play real tennis as an amateur; he competed in the 1908 London Olympics and in 1911, at the age of 45, reached the final of the national championship. For Nazeing people Archdale Palmer *was* Slazengers and retained an unsullied reputation as "a real gentleman". Having obtained the lucrative contracts for supplying balls to the two major tournaments, Wimbledon and Eastbourne, the firm was floated on the Stock Exchange as a public company and flourished under his leadership. In 1913 it made a profit of nearly £50,000 and Archdale benefited personally from this prosperity.

After the deaths of Herbert and Lotta Wellesley, Archdale Palmer moved into their home, Collyers, where he added brick-built extensions at each end of the old timber-framed house. Evidently he inherited from his great-great-grandfather William a keen eye for landscape when locating a new home (*Five miles from everywhere*, p98). He bought and demolished an old property called White House Farm, which faced on to Back Lane. In 1913, on a site behind the old farmhouse, he built Rookswood, a substantial red-brick house which commanded splendid views over Lower Nazeing and the Lea Valley. The house and its cottages were designed by Henry Inigo Triggs, most of whose work was south of the Thames and whose own house, Little Boarhunt at Liphook, is in a similar style. A nostalgic link between the old and new houses was provided by the staircase at Rookswood, which is a replica of the one in White House Farm.

Palmer's chauffeur, George Cordell, told his wife Connie that Archdale intended his nephews Ronald and Eric Wellesley to inherit Rookswood and Collyers. Until then they were to have two new cottages, which he built at the gateway to Rookswood. They became known as Rookswood Lodge and Rookswood Garage, later as Windrush Lodge and

Homefield. It must have been a great sadness to him that he outlived the boys by many years. The cottages were occupied instead by Cordell and Palmer's gardener, Mussell. Being built on the site of White House Farm, Windrush Lodge inherited its common right, somewhat to the displeasure of Palmer, who had expected to transfer it to Rookswood.

In the Second World War Palmer's niece Violet, the sister of Ronald and Eric, was an officer in the Auxiliary Territorial Service (ATS). One day she commandeered Cordell to show her how to dismantle and reassemble a car. Violet Wellesley often drove her ATS fellow-officer, Princess Elizabeth, who was photographed changing a tyre with Violet in the background, so it may be that Queen Elizabeth II obtained her considerable knowledge of car mechanics indirectly from George Cordell of Nazeing.

Rookswood became an important social centre, where garden parties and sporting events took place in the grounds. There were three tennis courts, two grass and one hard, where local children acted as ball boys. Among the guests was the first truly popular woman player, the flamboyant and graceful Suzanne Lenglen, who between 1919 and 1926 lost only one competitive match anywhere in the world. It is ironical that in later life Palmer, an enthusiastic participant in and patron of sport, suffered severely from gout. He often visited the spa of Karlsbad in

Garden party at Rookswood in the 1930s.

24

Czechoslovakia, although not always with the beneficial effects he hoped for. His frustration was expressed in a letter written in 1931: "I have just returned from Karlsbad a complete gout-stricken wreck". Palmer encouraged all forms of sport in the village; among the organisations represented at his funeral were the Nazeing Lawn Tennis, Cricket, and Football Clubs.

Curiously, Rookswood was located so that the drive past the front door followed the line of a public footpath. Perhaps this indicates the comfortable relationship between Palmer and the villagers, as normally such a situation would have reduced the value of the property. When the house was sold after his death, the new owner attempted unsuccessfully to have the footpath extinguished, as did the pop singer Cliff Richard who owned Rookswood in the 1960s. Finally, in 1997, Epping Forest Council diverted the path along a new route which has proved more satisfactory for all concerned.

Perhaps partly to avoid death duties, in about 1912 Archdale Palmer became joint owner with his uncle Ralph of the Palmer estate. Over a period of ten years he helped pay off the mortgage, a total of £25,000, which was roughly the amount he inherited from his father. Ralph died in 1923 and in 1924-5 Archdale put the bulk of the 800-acre estate on the market. He did not entirely share his uncle's enthusiasm for farming, which had in any case become unprofitable because of the agricultural slump. Annual rents from the estate are unlikely to have exceeded £1,000, from which he had to find expenses such as estate tax, tithes, and marsh rate totalling £240, and the salary of a bailiff whose services he no longer needed after the sale. By the end of 1925 he had sold most of his property, including Nazeing Park and five major farms, for some £40,000. There is a summary of the disposal of the estate in Appendix 2.

Any sentimental attachment Palmer may have felt towards property which had been in his family for a century or more must have been outweighed by his businessman's sense of economic reality. He did, however, retain some of the cottages and continued as a conscientious landlord until his death, when the sitting tenants were given the opportunity to buy their homes, which most did. He specified in his will that the remaining estate should be sold intact, a wish which was respected, technically. Almost immediately, however, the estate was broken up and sold again by four leading local figures, Col. Richard Andrew, his nephew Col. Peter Cane, Roger Frogley and Brian Meering.

There was a general belief in the village that in later life Palmer was very close to Mrs Mina Norris. There is some evidence for this in the sale documents, because he sold his late uncle's house, Hubbards, to her for £400. Archdale was warned by his solicitor that Hubbards had been valued for probate at £1,200 and that he might have to pay estate duty accordingly, but he replied: "I recognise that I shall be called upon by the Revenue Authorities to pay some fine for selling this bit of property at so low a figure." Whereas in most of the sales he drove a fairly hard bargain irrespective of individual circumstances, in the case of Mrs Norris he took a personal interest in the transaction and urged his solicitor to hasten it because she was "a little disturbed by the delay".

It was only when Ralph Palmer retired in 1921, aged 81, that Archdale began to play an active role in village affairs. Then, however, as Justice of the Peace and Chairman of the Waltham Abbey bench, rural district councillor, chairman of Nazeing Parish Council, chairman of the trustees of Nazeing Wood or Park, chairman and later president of the Nazeing branch of the British Legion, and churchwarden, his contribution was enormous. There had often been rivalry between the Palmer and Bury

**Archdale Palmer presenting mugs at the 1935 Silver Jubilee celebrations.
With him on the platform are his chauffeur George Cordell (right) and
Arch Coleman.**

26

families, but when Archdale Palmer died in 1950 it was Ralph Bury who suggested a suitable epitaph for him: "I loved Nazeing and I loved all the people of Nazeing."

A moving memorial address, given just ten days after Palmer's death by his friend and vicar James Sutherland, developed the theme of his love for the village and its people. Many such tributes have to be treated with a degree of scepticism but the memories of those who still remember him, half a century later, with great respect and affection leave little room for doubt that, in his case, it was fully justified. Too long to be quoted in full, the tribute emphasised four main qualities.

First was Palmer's helpfulness and desire to help people in trouble, with financial assistance and "by giving all his thought and attention and care and experience of life to those who needed it". Perhaps his own decade of personal sadness and his later infirmity were the source of his "warm-hearted thought for them when they were ill or suffered bereavement". Without going into detail, Sutherland cited the case of a war-time serviceman to whom "we both thought an injustice had been done, and he gave me all the help it was possible to give to try to remedy matters".

Second was his sense of kinship with the villagers. Enid Brent recalled how he took a direct interest in the affairs of his tenants:

> ...he was very good, a lovely old chap. If there was some fault somewhere he would always ask. If it was upstairs he would go and have a look, but as he got older he couldn't get up the stairs and he just had to take your word for it. Then in the very later time he got bad gout and he couldn't get out of the car...My cousin Harold [Starling] and his dad Harry used to be his employees who did all the jobs to the cottages...Anything you wanted done they came and did it.

During the Second World War, at a time of real danger from heavy bombing, his sister begged him to move to her home in the comparative safety of Somerset but "he would not leave his people".

Third was his thoroughness, which ensured that the annual Poppy Day collection was so well planned that "year after year records were broken and hundreds of pounds were sent to Earl Haig's Fund". The amount collected in 1939 was £52 8s 4d, in 1943 over £100 and in 1948 £179 5s 6d. Nowadays poppies are sold for a period before Remembrance Sunday but originally the collection was only on 11th November, the anniversary of the Armistice. Printed notices were distributed to all householders well

ROOKSWOOD,
NAZEING,
ESSEX.

11

Remembrance Day.

SATURDAY, NOVEMBER 11th, 1939.

Dear Sir (or Madam),

The Executive Council of the British Legion having announced that POPPY DAY will be observed on the 21st anniversary of Armistice Day, The Committee of the Nazeing Branch of the Legion have decided that substantially the same arrangements, which were made for the COLLECTION last year, shall be repeated, so that there will again be both a House-to-House call by Official Collectors, as well as Fixed Stations—as in the past—at certain conveniently-situated positions in the Village, where Poppies will be on sale at the hours indicated below.

I am, accordingly, desired to inform you that one of the Collectors will call upon you with a supply of Poppies on Poppy Day, Saturday, the 11th November next, during the course of the morning, when I trust it may be convenient for you to receive her.

If, however, this should not be the case, I would ask that you should endeavour to purchase your Poppy at one or other of the undermentioned Stations, between the hours named:—

I.	The County Council School.	8 to 11 a.m. 2 to 3 p.m.
II.	The "Coach and Horses", Waltham Road.	2 to 3 p.m.
III.	The Crown Inn, Keyser's Estate.	7.30 to 10.30 a.m.
IV.	The Fork Roads, leading to Broxbourne Station and to Keyser's Estate.	7.30 to 10 a.m.
V.	The Cross Roads at The Pound	8 to 12 noon.

Trusting that we may have a record collection,

I am, Sir (or Madam),
Your obedient servant,

ARCHDALE PALMER, *Capt.*
Chairman of Committee,
NAZEING BRANCH, BRITISH LEGION.

November 1st, 1939.

Facsimile of Captain Palmer's letter describing the Poppy Day arrangements for 1939.

in advance by George Cordell, whose daughter, Elizabeth Lamb, described the suitably military organisation:

Everything was arranged in great detail beforehand. Capt. Palmer chose his helpers very carefully and I think most people considered it an honour to be asked. All the trays of poppies were sorted out well in advance and then delivered with the collection boxes by his chauffeur, Mr. George Cordell. On the day itself Mr. Palmer would be driven around the village so that he could speak personally to each helper and encourage them in their task of calling at every door in their designated area. Sustenance was provided by his cook/housekeeper, Mrs. Stroyan, in the form of cups of hot coffee and soup. It was a very important day in the calendar and everyone had their contribution ready and no-one would have dreamed of refusing to contribute. In those days there were various grades and sizes of poppies and you received a poppy appropriate to the size of your contribution.

Brian Hills confirmed that it was "an honour to be asked":

Capt. Palmer had a large 20hp 1936 Vauxhall Coupé Drophead finished in a pale brown (reg. no. ADL 164), a really elegant limousine - the envy of all the village boys! Derek [Myson] and I were transported round the village in this magnificent motor car driven by... Mr. Cordell, delivering all the materials throughout the morning When we had finished ... we were given two half-crowns each - a small fortune to a youngster at that time, when Mars Bars were 2d and bottles of Tizer 5d. (with 2d. back on the empty!)

In 1948 Palmer wrote to his solicitor apologising that he had taken five days to reply to a letter because "all my time has been taken up with Poppy Day which I have organised since it was started many years ago".

Fourth was his devotion to All Saints' Church, where he was a churchwarden for over a quarter of a century. Even in his eighty-fifth year he braved the bitterest weather to attend the services he loved. "We have a nice church, Vicar, and we have very nice services," he told Sutherland the last time they spoke. He could not understand why more people did not attend church, although, to be fair to the parishioners, most of them lived further away from All Saints' than he did, and few of them even had a car, much less a chauffeur to take them there. It is said that in order to encourage churchgoing, he made attendance at church on the morning of his annual Sunday afternoon garden-party a condition of admission.

The vicar and the chairman of the parish council both described Archdale Palmer as "the Father of the Parish", and he was often paternalistic. Dennis Mead recalled: "When I wished to volunteer for the RAF as aircrew I was interviewed by Archdale Palmer who asked me, in his high-pitched voice, why I thought I was good enough." In a less deferential age, such attitudes, typical of their time, have largely passed away. Yet they seem to have aroused no sense of resentment because they were part and parcel of Archdale Palmer's devotion to "his people". After his death a collection organised by the parish council through boxes placed in the Post Office and shops raised £25 for a memorial plaque, which was placed in All Saints' Church on 3rd June 1953.

"I do not suppose," commented James Sutherland, "that in the long history of our village there has been anyone quite like him." Few would have disagreed with Sutherland, or with the verdict of "R.B." (almost certainly Ralph Bury) in the *West Essex Gazette*: "His death will be grieved for in many a Nazeing home and there will be a general feeling, 'We shall ne'er see his like again'."

Ralph Frederic Bury

Ralph Bury's family had been associated with Nazeing since 1769, but had been in Essex for many generations before that. The Nazeing branch was descended from the Burys of Bulphan, where Henry VIII had granted the manor to Edward Bury in 1540. The family fortune in Nazeing had been founded by an ensign who fought under Clive in India and, as was possible then, found soldiering quite profitable. His son bought property in Nazeing and gave Leonard's Green House to his son, James, who was Ralph's great grandfather. James rebuilt the house, renamed it St. Leonard's, and built up the estate, which remained in the family until after Ralph's death. Like the Palmers, the Burys took their responsibilities toward the villagers seriously. In the 1870s, for example, Charles Bury set up a charity which distributed hundreds of pounds in cash and kind to the needy.

Born in 1876, Ralph read law at Trinity College Cambridge, and was called to the Bar in 1901. He had inherited the family estate from his father, Charles James, in 1897 and had already become active in local affairs. Early in the twentieth century he became a member of the Board of Management of the Bumbles Green school and soon afterwards chairman, a post he held until 1950. He was a district councillor and Guardian of the poor in Nazeing from 1900 to 1910, and a churchwarden from 1906 to 1910 and again after the First World War. Ralph was appointed a Justice of the Peace and a Deputy Lieutenant when about thirty years old and in 1910 was "pricked" (chosen) as High Sheriff of Essex. Among his duties during his year in office was to proclaim the accession of George V at various centres in the county.

From a postcard of St Leonards, the home of the Bury family until 1963.

He started his connection with the Army in 1900, at the time of the South African War, by becoming an officer in a Voluntary Company at Waltham Abbey. Then in 1904 his keenness on motoring was recognised and he was asked to transfer to the Army Motor Reserve, in which he held a commission until 1907. Although he was still young, he must have been well thought of at the Bar, for in April 1909 the Bar Point-to-Point was held in Nazeing, presumably at his suggestion. The Lord Chief Justice was one of the eminent stewards.

When war broke out in 1914 he joined the Essex Regiment and raised half a company, which went to France in 1915, when Ralph was 40 years old. He remained there for 41 months, was mentioned in despatches and received the Croix de Guerre, as well as being wounded and contracting trench foot, which gave him difficulty for the rest of his life. On his return from the war and always afterwards he was known in Nazeing as Major Bury.

While he was DAAG (Deputy Assistant Adjutant General) to the 35th Division in France he happened to meet Bernard Montgomery, who was then a Brigade Major. In April 1945, when Montgomery had become a Field Marshal and was expecting to receive the surrender of all the German forces in north Germany, Holland, and Denmark, he received a letter from Bury recalling the occasion and asking whether he would be willing to stand as the Conservative candidate for Epping at the forthcoming General Election. Montgomery declined very politely, as he expected to have further military duties to perform. A legend that Churchill and Montgomery had a secret wartime meeting in the Bumbles Green school may have had its origins in this invitation.

Ralph Bury was always a keen supporter of the Conservative Party and, to judge from his file of press cuttings, was closely involved in the two General Elections of 1910. He was chairman of the party's Nazeing Branch for 25 years and chairman of the Epping Division.

He is best remembered, however, for his work for Nazeingwood Common. He was Parliamentary Counsel to Essex County Council for 32 years and was appointed King's Counsel in 1938 at the age of 62. This experience equipped him to draft the Nazeing Wood or Park Bill in 1947 and to pilot it through the House of Lords. Without his influence it is quite possible that Nazeingwood Common would have passed out of the control of Nazeing people (see page 269).

He died in 1954, at a Conservative dinner. He was recalled shortly afterwards as "one of [Nazeing's] outstanding and traditional characters of the old school." To meet death duties parts of the estate had to be sold. At that time there were some 300 acres in Nazeing, as well as land in Waltham Abbey and in Roydon. The rest was sold a few years later when Rachel, his daughter and heiress, moved from the area on remarrying. So the Bury connection with land in Nazeing came to an end and, Archdale Palmer having died just a few years earlier, so did an era.

The Hargreaves and the Greens

Born in 1865, Walter Ernest Hargreaves was educated at Merchant Taylors' School. Like his father, he became a Lloyds underwriter and, by the time he was forty, was one of the leaders of the profession, having been largely responsible for establishing the market for Lloyds' insurance in the United States. Walter and his wife Lydia had moved from Cheshunt to Nazeing by 1908, when he leased Nazeing Park from the Palmers. In 1924 he bought Teys Farm and Belchers Farm from Archdale Palmer for £3,700, and in 1925 paid £8,800 for Nazeing Park, where he lived until 1949.

Walter and Lydia participated in village affairs, particularly those of the Church. They were elected to the first Parochial Church Council, in 1922, she remaining a member until they moved from the parish and he being a member for nearly all that time. In addition they were considerable benefactors, paying for the installation of electric light at All Saints', among other things, and donating the lectern, screen, and bishop's chair.

In 1908 Walter made a donation towards the new Chapel Hall and a few years later he built the Princess Louise Convalescent Home in Middle Street. It is reported that this was in thanks for his missing the maiden voyage of the *Titanic*, because his chauffeur lost the way to the docks. The chauffeur was sacked on the spot but reinstated on the news of the sinking. From the early 1920s until her retirement in 1944 he funded Ruth Thrupp as district nurse for Nazeing, providing not just her salary but her uniform, bicycle, and equipment. It is said also that, in addition to these more public acts of philanthropy, he added ten shillings regularly to the pension packets of villagers. The story rings true but, as such action

Lydia and Walter Hargreaves at Nazeing Park with their daughters Elsie (left) and Molly, c1915. The large conservatory in the background stood behind the house.

would have flouted Post Office regulations, we are very unlikely to find written proof.

Walter Hargreaves was knighted in 1936 and made KBE in 1946, after he had served as chairman of the War Risks Insurance Office at the Ministry of Transport during the Second World War. He and Lady Hargreaves spent their last years in East Grinstead, where he died in 1954.

Frederick William Green moved to Nazeing in 1912, when he leased Collyers from Archdale Palmer. Harry Mead, known as Henry, was Green's butler and, in the First World War, batman to his son, Major Frederick Mason Green. Another son, Henry Edwin Green, a captain in the 22nd London Battalion, was killed in 1916. In 1924 F.W. Green paid Archdale Palmer a total of £6,430 for Collyers, the Golf House, seven nearby cottages and Bentons in Middle Street. He made a typically generous gesture in the same year, when there were concerns about the safety of the Golf House pond: Epping Rural District Council offered to fence it in provided the parish council found half the cost, so Green paid the whole of the parish's portion. A staunch Conservative and generous donor to the party, he was a district and parish councillor and a trustee of Nazeing Wood or Park for many years until his death at the age of eighty in 1937.

His wife, Elizabeth, was a member of the Parochial Church Council from its inception until 1947, when, aged 86, she was made "an honorary member". Their son, known as Major Green in the parish, was a member of the PCC in the twenties, together with his mother; from 1928 for two years, when Archdale Palmer said that he too busy, he was a churchwarden. During the Second World War Mrs. Green was the only person, apart from Palmer, to come to church in a chauffeur driven car. She died in 1950.

A shift of power

When the Palmers and Burys were in their heyday, it was clear where power and influence in Nazeing lay. They filled most of the significant posts, both within the village and representing it outside. Throughout the nineteenth century they were well supported by leading farming families such as the Pegrums and Standingfords but in the first half of the twentieth century the farmers' fortunes fell into decline.

George Church Standingford outside White House Farm c1870.

The Standingford family had owned White House Farm since 1798 and in 1838 the formidable Dinah Standingford bested George Palmer MP in a court case over carting rights (*Five miles from everywhere*, pp109-112). Soon after the death of her son George Church Standingford in 1904, however, his executors sold the farm to Archdale Palmer.

Bernard Pegrum was only three when his grandfather died, yet he remembered clearly that George was "in the last weeks of his life…carried downstairs in a Sedan Chair by two stalwart henchmen from the farm". George Standingford had been a leading figure in Nazeing and it was to him that George Palmer wrote in 1877 when he resigned as a trustee of Nazeing Wood or Park (*Five miles from everywhere*, p154). Standingford had belonged to the West Essex Yeomanry, of which Palmer was Colonel, and after his death Bernard "used to almost worship his old military tunic…and for many years his rusty riding stirrups were a treasured plaything".

Bernard recalled White House Farm vividly:

> The white paled fence separated the garden from the road, and the long path from the front gate was bordered on each side by lawn, until it reached the point near the front door where two huge drainpipes, set on end, stood

sentinel…The tall "Monkey Puzzle" tree outside the front-room window I remember well. Paths ran left and right of the front door, that to the left leading into the stack yard and farm buildings, that to the right led to a cluster of trees and shrubs known as "the Arbour", and beyond that the orchard.

The front door opened on a small, dark hall. To the right was "the parlour", a room which does not seem to have been used a great deal. I recollect that it had a musty smell, and contained furniture which oppressed me. To the left of the entrance was a large room which extended from front to back of the house, with large windows at each end…

I remember the long, low kitchen, with its large fire-place, with the "Dairy" beyond, and I can still smell the peculiar odour of the Dairy. I remember the long kitchen table…on which Grandma used to draw and dress fowls for the table, and in doing so explain to me the mysteries of a chicken's inside…

The state of the house symbolised the decline of the family. In 1912 it was described as a "very poor timber-built house much out of repair", and Archdale Palmer demolished it to make way for Rookswood and the neighbouring cottages (see page 23).

George's brother, William, was the Palmers' tenant at Mansion House Farm for over thirty years, until he gave it up in 1881. In 1907 David

Mansion House Farm, much as it would have appeared when William Standingford moved to Upper Town in 1881.

Standingford had to leave Meadgate Farm after an Inquisition of Lunacy, requested by his cousin Joseph Pegrum, found that he was "of unsound mind and not sufficient for the government of himself or his property". In 1919 John Standingford became pindar of Nazeing Common, not an insignificant post but one that earlier generations of the family had, as trustees of Nazeing Wood or Park, supervised rather than occupied. Other members of the family did prosper but had to move away from Nazeing to do so.

The decline of the Pegrums in Nazeing was more prolonged but equally drastic. Joseph Pegrum was for many years, along with Ralph Palmer and Ralph Bury, one of the three leading figures in Nazeing. He was a pillar of the Chapel, a trustee of Nazeing Wood or Park, a district and parish councillor and the owner of Wheelers and other properties. Having been the tenant of the largest farm in the village, Nazeing Bury, he seemed in 1919 to have sealed his position when he bought it and other property from Sir Hereward Wake. Three years later, however, he sold the farm and moved to Newlands, a much smaller property which he had built for himself, close to his beloved Chapel. His only son David prospered from farming during the First World War. He became one of the three chief landowners in the village but unwisely put his money into speculative building and left Nazeing in 1933. *Kelly's Directory* for 1926 lists five Pegrums as farmers but by 1940 all had gone. There were Pegrums in Nazeing until the 1990s but they lacked their former influence.

Some members of other long-established families have made important contributions in the twentieth century, not least Mick Welch who served as a district councillor for forty years and a parish councillor for twenty-seven. It would, however, be fair to say that most of the individuals who filled leading positions have been comparative newcomers to the village.

It is impossible to know what would have happened if Archdale Palmer or Ralph Bury had produced an heir able and willing to continue his prominent role. As the Second World War, more than the First, broke down old patterns of deference everywhere, it seems unlikely that things could have gone on as before. For a while a succession of former military officers were involved in village affairs and occupied positions of responsibility, much as they had had during the war. They combined an occasionally autocratic manner with a genuine sense of duty to the village and its people, yet none had the unquestioned authority exercised by Palmer and Bury.

Col. Richard H. (Dick) Andrew, who was educated at Haileybury and Cambridge, practised as a solicitor in London. He joined up at the outbreak of the First World War and until 1916 served in France, where he was mentioned in dispatches. When his uncle, Field Marshal Viscount Allenby, was appointed Commander-in-Chief in the Middle East, Andrew joined his personal staff and in 1918 was awarded the Military Cross. He retired from the Army at the end of the First World War but in 1940 Allenby's Chief of Staff, Sir Archibald Wavell, had been appointed Commander-in-Chief in the Middle East and sent for Andrew to become his Military Secretary. Col. Andrew was awarded the CBE in 1941 and finally returned home from service in the Middle East in 1944.

Dick Andrew played golf on the Nazeing Common course where he was for a while hon. secretary. Cycling out from his home in Hoddesdon, he fell in love with the village and in 1920 built and moved into Buttfield. His wife Aline, who was also active in village affairs, bought some of the adjoining fields from Archdale Palmer in 1924. They had two daughters, one of whom, Mary, spent her working life as a night sister at St. Margaret's Hospital in Epping. Andrew was an active member of the Parochial Church Council from 1926 to 1957 and more briefly occupied other posts, including those of churchwarden and parish council chairman. When Ralph Bury died, Col. Andrew became chairman of Nazeing Wood or Park. He saw long military service with the Ordnance Survey and, after his death in 1964, Aline presented a fine set of maps to the parish council, which eventually passed them on to Waltham Abbey Museum. The family also presented a leather bound lectern bible to All Saints' Church in his memory. Aline and Mary Andrew built and lived at Honeysuckle Cottage in Back Lane.

Col. Kenneth F. (Steve) May OBE succeeded Col. Andrew as chairman of Nazeing Wood or Park and as president of the British Legion. In the Second World War he had served with the 2/5th Battalion of the Essex Regiment, most of which was captured during the North African campaign. Taken as a prisoner of war to Italy, May escaped; later he wrote *Toothpaste for the Ass*, a privately published memoir of his experiences. He was a district councillor, whom Ray and Paddy Hutchings found helpful when they were negotiating with the council over the building of their bungalow at Mansion House Farm. He lived at

Old House in Old House Lane, to which he retired following service in the Indian Army, accompanied by his rather frail wife. May had a servant, Gomez, formerly his batman, who was devoted to Mrs. May and was allowed two weeks furlough each year to visit his family in India. Aided and abetted by Gomez, May was a keen gardener.

The last of the line was Major J.C. (Chris) Robinson. Born in 1910, he was educated at Marlborough and Pembroke College, Cambridge. While playing rugger for Richmond, he met Margaret Roberts and they were married in 1938. Fluent in French, he served in North Africa with the Rifle Brigade in the Eighth Army and received from the Americans the rare honour of a Bronze Star. Later he helped plan D-Day and was one of the first British officers to reach Berlin, where he remained for about six months. Before the war he had joined his father's insurance firm of Hogg Robinson in the City, but when he returned circumstances had changed. Therefore he used his experience in Europe to set up a new section of the firm, later to become a separate branch as Hogg Robinson Travel.

Chris Robinson presenting a cup at the Horse Show, which for many years was run by the Nazeing Conservation Association at what became Clayton Park.

Chris and Margaret moved to Camps in 1941; after the war he became involved with many aspects of life in Nazeing and west Essex. He was a JP on the Epping and Ongar bench and at the time of his retirement was deputy chairman. He served on the Council for the Preservation of Rural England and represented it on the Essex Farming and Wildlife Group. He was a member of the Parochial Church Council and its secretary for sixteen years. A founder member and first secretary of Nazeing Conservation Society, he later became a vice-president. His activities also included the parish council, the Royal British Legion, and the cricket club, for which he played until he had to have a hip operation. In the 1991 Queen's Birthday Honours he received the MBE for his community services.

A keen Conservative, Chris Robinson was treasurer and vice-chairman of the Epping constituency association, and later vice-president of the Harlow association. He helped re-form the Nazeing branch after the Second World War and became its first chairman. He was greatly involved with the horse shows run for many years by the Conservatives at what later became Clayton Park. One of the cups for the shows was presented by Major Ralph Bury, who was described by Chris as "clever as a barrow-load of monkeys". He was commenting on one of the most remarkable episodes in the history of Nazeing, a conflict between Ralph Bury and Winston Churchill.

Parliamentary politics

In 1924 Churchill became Conservative MP for the Epping constituency, of which Nazeing was part. He enjoyed the hurly-burly of electoral campaigning and, in the days before sanitised television soundbites, spoke on several occasions at the Nazeing Chapel Hall. He had been elected as a Conservative in 1900 but, in his own words, "ratted" to the Liberals in 1904 and "re-ratted" to the Conservatives in 1922. As Chancellor of the Exchequer from 1924 to 1929 Churchill was a loyal member of the Government. During the election campaign of 1929, his son Randolph made his first political speech at the Chapel Hall, with Winston in the audience. According to *The Daily Mail* of 16th May 1929 Winston said afterwards: "From what I heard, I think I can see, at no great distance, a moment when I shall be able to sit at home in comfortable retirement and feel that the torch which falls from my exhausted hands is being carried boldly forward by another."

Randolph never fulfilled his promise. For a while his father's political judgments seemed misguided too. In the 1930s, no longer in office, Winston attacked the government's policies on India and German rearmament. Thereby he fuelled the suspicions of those who regarded him as an unstable turncoat, including Ralph Bury who had initially supported Churchill but was alarmed by his apparent disloyalty to the party. On 2nd February 1935 the Nazeing Branch, of which Bury was president, passed a resolution deploring "Mr.Churchill's consistent opposition to the National Government in the House of Commons". Despite Churchill's fury Bury was unrepentant but, as most branches of the party admired Churchill's stand, Bury resigned as president of the West Essex Unionist Association.

In 1938, following a dinner held by the Nazeing Branch at the Chapel Hall, the split within the party deepened and opposition to Churchill grew. The dinner took place shortly after the Munich Crisis, when in effect the Prime Minister, Neville Chamberlain, surrendered Czechoslovakia to Hitler. It was skilfully chaired by Ralph Bury, described as "a real old-style Tory who...seemed to enjoy using his powers of eloquence to bait...Mr. Churchill". The guest speaker, Colin Thornton-Kemsley, was Churchill's chief critic in the West Essex Unionist Association. He welcomed the invitation to "such a citadel of orthodox Conservatism...which...has expressed its loyalty to the premier". Churchill's support in the constituency was at its lowest ebb. Less than a year later, however, his warnings were vindicated when Germany invaded Poland. Britain declared war and Churchill was recalled to the Government. In May 1940 he became Prime Minister and what he described as Britain's "finest hour" was also his.

In 1945 the huge and scattered Epping constituency was split up and Churchill opted for the safe seat of Woodford. Since then the constituencies of which Nazeing has been part have always been marginal, usually but not invariably going with the Government of the day.

The Labour landslide of 1945 made the new smaller Epping seat into a marginal, which was won for Labour by Leah Manning with a majority of 987. She spoke in the Commons on three topics that affected Nazeing, bus services, flooding, and sanitation, and opened her 1950 campaign in the village. Labour hung on with a greatly reduced majority and Leah Manning was one of the casualties, losing to the Conservative Nigel

Davies by 4,000 votes. In 1951 there was another election and her campaign included a passionate anti-war speech at the Cadet Hut but, perhaps because her rhetoric was out of touch with changing times, she lost again. After a third successive defeat in 1955 she retired. She remains the only woman to have represented Nazeing in Parliament.

From 1951 to 1964 the country had a Conservative Government and Nazeing had a Conservative MP, Graeme Finlay. He was a conscientious MP, who usually took up issues brought to him by the parish council and others, but perhaps he lacked Leah Manning's understanding of the less well off in society. In 1955 and 1959 his Liberal opponent was John Arlott, best known as a cricket broadcaster, and for a while the local party was quite active. In the 1959-64 Government Finlay was appointed Vice-Chamberlain of the Royal Household, a post in the whips' office which meant that he had to present to Her Majesty a regular report on proceedings in Parliament. The job automatically carried a baronetcy.

The rapid growth of Harlow and the villages meant that Epping was

A trip to the Houses of Parliament arranged in 1947 by Leah Manning MP for Standards III and IV of Nazeing School. The adults in the back row are from the left: Leah Manning, Gladys Hills, Marcus Hills (headmaster) and Miss E. Wooley, a student teacher. On the far left is Miss Harding, also a student teacher.

again one of the largest constituencies in the country. In 1964 Labour won a narrow majority and one of its gains was Epping, taken by Stan Newens. He held it in 1966 but was defeated by Norman Tebbit in 1970, when the Conservatives gained a surprise victory. The huge Epping constituency was once again broken up and when Labour gained a narrow victory in 1974 both men were elected for new seats, Tebbit for Chingford and Newens for Harlow, of which Nazeing was part. The new Harlow constituency based on the predominantly Labour town seemed safe for the party and even when the Conservatives won the 1979 election Newens kept his seat. Yet it included solid Conservative areas like Nazeing and so, from his point of view, was vulnerable.

The early 1980s were catastrophic for Labour, while Conservative policies designed to appeal to disillusioned Labour supporters resulted in the phenomenon of "Essex Man". Harlow was the type of constituency where he thrived and in 1983 Jerry Hayes, somewhat to his own surprise, took the seat for the Conservatives. He won easily in 1987 and again in 1992, when Harlow was the type of constituency Labour had to capture if it was to obtain a majority in the Commons. The late 1990s were as bad for the Conservatives as the early 1980s had been for Labour, so it was no surprise in 1997 when New Labour's Bill Rammell defeated Hayes by over 10,000 votes.

Nazeing Parish Council

In 1936 a resident named W.C. Portman spent a good part of the Annual Parish Meeting complaining about the parish council. He then moved a vote of thanks to Archdale Palmer as chairman, adding that "the Council had done good work for the Parish". The parish council is the lowest and least regarded tier of local government and Portman was neither the first nor the last to complain about it. Nevertheless, it could be argued that without its activities Nazeing would have become a less pleasant place.

When Ralph Palmer retired in 1921, Archdale Palmer was co-opted on to the parish council and immediately elected chairman, an office which he held for almost twenty-five years. He was something of a benevolent dictator: the council met only two or three times a year and often he took decisions on his own, faithfully reporting them to colleagues who invariably gave their approval.

Until 1946 parish councillors were elected normally by show of hands at the Annual Parish Meeting, a secret ballot being necessary only if five electors disputed the initial poll. The meeting had to be chaired by someone who was not standing in the election, a responsibility that from 1922 onwards was always undertaken by Ralph Bury. The voters took their civic duty very seriously. In 1925 there were seventeen candidates for seven vacancies and an estimated 250 voters were present. This was about one third of those eligible; the equivalent in 2001 would be a thousand people. The meeting was held at the Bumbles Green Council School and many were unable to get into the room, so it was agreed that the result "might not be a true record of what the village would have voted had there been greater available space" and it was left to the district council to decide what to do about it. At the next election, in 1928, about a hundred people attended, but there were only seven candidates for the seven vacancies and so the proceedings were rather more straightforward. For some unexplained reason the turnout in 1931 was fewer than twenty, even though there were eight candidates, but in 1934 and 1937 it was again around a hundred.

The first woman parish councillor in Nazeing was Emily Drane, who taught at the council school and was secretary of the Women's Institute. Elected in 1934, she was not overawed by the wealthy businessmen who were her colleagues and made some valuable contributions, for which they expressed their appreciation. After a year, however, she moved away and was replaced by Alfred Barratt of Westfleet in Riverside Avenue, the first Keysers resident on the parish council.

There were no elections in wartime so the councillors who were elected in 1937 saw Nazeing through the Second World War, apart from Arthur May who moved away in 1940 and was replaced by Charles Judd. The council included most of the leading men in the village. Captain Archdale Palmer was chairman and Sir Walter Hargreaves vice-chairman, until 1944 when Col. Richard Andrew returned from service in Egypt and elsewhere and took over. The other members were Alfred Barratt, George W. Chapman of Langridge, and Edward J. Fowler of Mamelons. Many of the matters normally dealt with by the parish council were either taken over by specially created wartime institutions or fell into abeyance for the duration. The council met therefore only once or twice a year, usually at Rookswood. In December 1945 Archdale Palmer, having just turned eighty, announced that because of ill health he intended to resign with immediate effect; his colleagues presented him with a heart-felt tribute.

To **Captain Archdale Palmer,**
J.P. (Essex)

he members of the
PARISH OF NAZEING
have heard with regret that you have decided
not to seek re-election to the Nazeing
Parish Council and that you have relinquished
the office of Chairman of that Council
which you have filled with such ability for
the past 23 years.

During the years of your Chairmanship
there have been great changes in the parish
and a large increase in the population, but
you have never hesitated to give your personal
attention to the many problems that have
arisen, and your prudent guidance and advice
have gone far to overcome difficulties and
to promote good feeling.

Your unfailing courtesy and fairness
have won the respect and esteem of all
members of the parish who wish to assure
you of their continued affection and regard
in your retirement.

March 1946

**Illuminated address presented by Nazeing Parish Council to Archdale
Palmer in 1946.**

In 1946 the council was elected at a parish meeting for the last time; this was once again attended by over a hundred people. There were nine members rather than seven, reflecting the rapid growth of the parish, and no fewer than twelve unsuccessful candidates. This contrasts strikingly with the experience of the twentieth century's last parish council, which had to co-opt three members to make up the numbers. Meetings were held at the council school and for the first time members of the public were admitted, though "only as spectators". By contrast with the continuity provided by Ralph and Archdale Palmer in the first forty-five years of the century, there were four chairmen in the next six years, Andrew, Barratt, Leonard Archer, and L.F. Tucker.

Although even in the nineteenth century there had been a perception that the village was divided into three distinct areas, for the 1945 General Election only one polling station was provided, rather than three. The village was not yet split into wards and in 1948 a suggestion that this should happen was resisted successfully. In 1954 the Ministry of Housing and Local Government ordered that Nazeing should be divided up, even though the parish council had objected. As there had only just been an election however, the order did not come into force until 1958. Then, as a result of the 1957 Parish Councils Act (and, probably, the increase in population), Essex County Council advised that the total number of parish councillors should be thirteen. Seven were elected for Nazeingbury ward and three each for Riverside and Bumbles Green.

In 1952 the choice of chairman for the newly-elected parish council was perhaps a pointer to the future. In the first ballot A.J. Nicholls obtained four votes, F.B. Radford three and F.A. Widdicombe two. Widdicombe then stated that under the Local Government Act of 1933 the chairman should have a clear majority of all votes cast, so a second ballot was held between the two leading candidates and Widdicombe's two votes were apparently transferred to Radford, giving him a 5-4 win. When, however, Nicholls pointed out that the council's practice of having cheques countersigned by the clerk also contravened the 1933 Act, the council voted to disregard the legal niceties and to continue as before.

Arthur Nicholls was a farmer from an old Nazeing family who might well have gone on to contribute much more to village life but tragically in 1953 he was killed in a freak shotgun accident. Frank Radford was a businessman and comparative newcomer, who lived at Riverside. He served as chairman of the parish council for the next twelve years and as a member for thirty. He proved a wise and conscientious chairman who helped guide the village through the most rapid period of growth in its entire history. His successor as chairman, W.G.A. (Jack) Bilton, paid tribute to his "hard work, long service, and devotion to duty".

Although much of the parish council's business is conducted in a non-partisan way, it has usually been dominated by the Conservatives, who sometimes used their majority for party political purposes. On three occasions in the 1950s there was, as a result of death or resignation, a vacancy for a parish councillor. Each time the Labour Party proposed a replacement and the Conservatives argued that, having a majority of elected councillors, they "had a perfect right to nominate another". Some parish councillors were known to be Freemasons and others sometimes felt that the real decisions had been made before the council met.

In 1970 Margaret Gervis stood as a Conservative but came to feel that "parish councils should be for the people...I am not a political animal and the parish council is political. It is in fact completely Tory controlled and it would be hypocritical of me if I stood for the Tories again". The parish council denied that there was any political bias and claimed that "the present situation was forced on it by the Socialists some years ago". Mrs. Gervis was uncertain how much support she would get but topped the 1974 poll as an independent. Not until the national decline of the Conservatives in the late 1990s did the party cease to dominate the parish council.

In 1976 Nazeing Parish Council discussed the American Bicentenary of Independence, and the minutes note that "after a statement from the Chairman it was agreed". One wonders what would have happened had the council not agreed, since two centuries of history might have been rather difficult to undo.

The parish council helped lead the campaigns against Harlow and other proposed developments which could have ruined Nazeing as a village. These activities are described in chapter 5. The days when a collection of apparently leisured gentlemen met two or three times a year are long past. The powers of parish councils, though still limited, are considerably greater than they were then. Most of the men and women who serve on the parish council work full-time and have to fit their unpaid duties into busy lives. No councillor since Frank Radford has come anywhere near matching his record of twelve years as chairman and thirty as a member, and there is no immediate prospect that anyone will. To pick out any individual from the recent past would be unfair on the rest, but it would certainly be true to say that many of our councillors have continued to do "good work for the parish".

Parish clerks

When parish councils were created in 1894, they took on the

responsibility of assessing and collecting rates for relief of the poor. Two parish councillors were elected as Overseers of the Poor but an Assistant Overseer did the actual collection under their supervision. Often, as in Nazeing, the post was combined with that of parish clerk. George Lipson served faithfully as Assistant Overseer of the Poor and Parish Clerk for twenty-four years. Despite severe wartime inflation which saw the doubling of wages and prices, his annual salary stayed at £36 10s from 1904 until 30th March 1920, when it was raised to £45. Sadly he did not enjoy even that modest increase for long, for he died a month later. The parish council expressed its appreciation of his "valued services...carried out with such conspicuous ability", and invited his son Arthur to take on the duties at the same salary. Arthur accepted the offer, but stated from the outset that he considered the salary inadequate "in view of the exacting nature of the duties". He stuck it out for a year but despite the offer of an increase to £60 resigned because "from his experience of the duties £100 was the lowest salary he could accept".

Charles Judd was appointed but resigned after three years because he was "unable to devote sufficient time to his duties". A year later his successor, Leonard C. Smith, resigned for the same reason. When Smith was appointed the unsuccessful candidates included two women, so in seeking a replacement the parish council made it clear that "ladies would be ineligible" because "owing to the character of the business of Assistant Overseer the appointment should only be open to male members of the Village". Among the applicants were Arthur Lipson and George Sinclair, who was a former parish councillor and overseer; both demanded a higher salary than that on offer and the council "unanimously resolved that they be non-considered".

In the summer of 1925 the post of Assistant Overseer and Parish Clerk was offered to Arthur Coleman. Given the problems of recruitment and retention in the previous five years, it is ironical that within a year the parish council chose to increase his salary from £60 to £80 because of the "capable and efficient manner in which Mr Coleman had been carrying out his duties". In 1929 the Government abolished the Poor Law and the post of Assistant Overseer disappeared. Clearly the duties were considered important, for Coleman's salary was cut to £35. In 1946 it was increased to £52, with a further £8 maximum as travelling expenses.

In 1950 Arthur Coleman retired after twenty-five years of "very good service" and Eric Reynolds was appointed. His salary was raised to £75 in 1953 and to £104 in 1958, the latter because of the increased duties resulting from the installation of street lighting. His father, Arthur, had been sexton and verger at All Saints' for almost forty-five years, and Eric was a member of the choir and secretary of the cricket and football clubs. In 1933 he married Connie Goodacre and they moved to Coulsdon in Surrey. Towards the end of the war they returned, to become prominent members of the Nazeing community. Interviewed when the family left Nazeing for the second and final time in 1959, he commented: "There are occasions when I'm Connie Reynolds' husband, and there are other times when she is Eric Reynolds' wife."

Connie claimed to be "Nazeing's first squatter". In 1944 there was no accommodation to be had and Trevone stood empty so she simply moved in, although Eric later legitimised the arrangement by buying the house. It became the centre for a wide range of social events including dances in the orchard, tennis tournaments on the lawn and fêtes for various charitable causes. In 1946 she was elected as one of the first Labour parish councillors and campaigned tirelessly on behalf of groups and individuals whom she thought had been unfairly treated. When Eric was appointed parish clerk, Connie's offer to resign from the parish council was not accepted, but she decided that "the position was a little embarrassing" and did not stand in the 1952 election. She threw her energies into other organisations and had, in her own words, a "finger in every village pie". After their departure Trevone continued to be adorned with posters at election time but they were blue ones, for Eric and Connie sold their house to Conservative stalwarts John and Bessie Downes. Bessie served for many years as a district and parish councillor.

When Eric Reynolds announced that he would be moving away, Maurice Coleman resigned as a parish councillor and was appointed "without remuneration" to the post formerly held by his uncle Arthur, although it was soon agreed that his expenses should be paid. In October 1960 he was awarded £104, the same salary that Reynolds had received, and a year later the new council increased his salary to £175. In 1965 Coleman was given a further £45 in recognition of additional administrative duties, especially street lighting, and six years later his salary rose to £317. In 1966 he suggested that the parish council should publish a booklet giving new residents information about the village. Entitled *Nazeing Round and About*, it met a need, so that six editions have been published, the latest in 1997. He was a founder member of the National Society of Local Council Clerks and first chairman of its Essex branch. He retired in 1982 and became a parish councillor again.

Maurice Coleman often described himself as Mr. Nazeing. Though very few other people used the phrase, it is true that, like Connie Reynolds, he had a "finger in every village pie". Apart from his long involvement with the parish council, he was also, at various times, auditor to the ill-fated Nazeing Village Association, clerk to Nazeing Wood or Park, president of the Nazeing Common Cricket Club, and a governor of Nazeing County Primary School. Born into a leading Chapel family, he retained his allegiance to that church all his life.

An aerial view of Nazeing Park in 1935. It was the home of the Hargreaves family from 1908 to 1949.

Above: The Princess Louise Convalescent Home shortly after it opened in 1914. It was financed largely by Walter Hargreaves. Below: the last Court Leet in 1925. Standing from the left: Henry Weare, unknown, Joe Pegrum, George Sinclair, Fred Cook, William Graham, George Crowe, John Nicholls, Edward J. Fowler, Alfred Pulham, Alexander Frogley. Seated: James Selway, Arthur Reynolds, William Moore, F.C.E. Jessopp (steward), Mansfield, Smith.

Above: the Congregational Church, c1920. The Chapel is in the centre with the hall to the left. At that time, Middle Street had not been surfaced. Below: the first flower festival at All Saints' in June 1965, with (from the left), Doreen Thornborough, Sheila Blake and Joy Gomes.

CHAPTER 2

"THIS VAST AND SCATTERED PARISH"

The churches

Before the First World War most people living in Nazeing had a regular, if not invariably frequent, association with either the Church of England or the Congregational Church and were very conscious of the differences between the two. As the century progressed, the number of regular worshippers and the influence of the churches in the village declined. At the same time the wariness with which the two congregations had viewed each other evaporated, most markedly after the Second World War.

The Church of England

The first Parochial Church Council

The Anglican Church might have seemed little changed since the latter part of the nineteenth century. The times of services were according to the usual Church of England pattern, with Matins at 11.00 and Evensong at 6.30 every Sunday. Holy Communion took place sometimes at 8.00 and sometimes after Matins. The vicar and churchwardens would have appeared all powerful in church affairs at the local level. Yet from 1920 there was a major change. From then onwards representatives of the laity other than just the churchwardens were brought into the government of the church in Nazeing, as elsewhere, with the formation of a Parochial Church Council (PCC). The members of this council are elected only by members of the congregation who are on the parish's electoral roll (not to be confused with the register of electors for civil elections, which includes almost all adults). The first roll for Nazeing, comprising those who qualified because they were resident in the parish or worshipped at the church regularly, was compiled by Ralph Palmer.

In April 1920 Thomas Goddard, the vicar, presided over the meeting at which the members of the first PCC were elected. When the council met for the first time, two years later, he was too ill to attend. Connie Cordell recalled that Goddard insisted on officiating at her wedding to George, and had to be in a bath chair at the altar. He retired in 1923, at the age of 87, and died shortly afterwards. He had been inducted as vicar in 1890; his was the longest resident incumbency ever.

The PCC does not seem to have met before there was a fresh election of its members, in 1922. The names as minuted started with "R.C. Palmer Esq., Major R.F. Bury, Mrs. A.L. Bury, W.E. Hargreaves, Mrs. Hargreaves". Of these only Mrs. Bury had been elected previously. Evidently the squirarchy had decided that the PCC might be important after all. Indeed, until the death of Ralph Palmer in 1923, he and his nephew Archdale, Ralph Bury and his mother Anna, and Walter and Lydia Hargreaves made up half the membership. Ralph Bury presided at the first PCC meeting in absence of the vicar.

At its second meeting the PCC discussed the vacancy created by Thomas Goddard's retirement. One possible replacement, a young ex-army chaplain, decided that he could not undertake the responsibility of renovating the Vicarage, which was in a deplorable condition. After

Church choir with W. Stewart Fossett, c1930. Women and girls had not yet been admitted to the choir.

discussion the PCC agreed instead to recommend to the parish's patron, the Lord Chancellor, that W. Stewart Fossett should be appointed. They stipulated that Fossett should give a written undertaking to resign after five years if required to do so by the council. Why there were misgivings about Fossett is not explained. The undertaking, if it had been obtained, would have been unenforceable at law, as Ralph Bury, a barrister, surely knew. Anyway, Fossett was inducted to the living and stayed until his death in 1933.

The next vicar was James Sutherland, a bachelor, who came to Nazeing from Torquay. In his early years in the parish, his relationship was not always easy with the established parishioners, particularly with Aline and Richard Andrew, as Cecil and Margaret Mansfield left their employ to become chauffeur and housekeeper at the Vicarage. Sutherland was tireless in his work for the village and its people in the dark days of the Second World War and was remembered with affection by the members of the post-war Church youth group. His writings and sermons suggest a great directness and simplicity that seem to have struck a chord in many people. He died, greatly mourned, on 29th May 1950, less than four months after Archdale Palmer. Sutherland admired the choir and left £10 to its members in his will. A memorial window to him was installed on the south side of the nave.

Maintaining the church and its buildings

All Saints' is the only Grade 1 listed building in Nazeing and, from the outside, it appeared much the same throughout the twentieth century. No external alteration was made until the Pilgrim Room was built on the north side of the vestry in 1999. Inside, however, several changes and improvements were made. Lighting continued to be by oil lamps, which needed fairly frequent repair or replacement, until 1934. Then electricity reached the area and the original installation in the church was paid for by Walter Hargreaves, whose wife had already, in 1926, presented a silver chalice and patten. The Hargreaves' great generosity towards the church did not extend as far as helping the parish to make its contribution to the Diocesan Family Purse, or "Quota", when it pleaded poverty throughout the twenties.

The lordship of the Manor of Nazeing and the rectory of the church, which had belonged to the monks of Waltham Abbey, had passed to laymen at the Dissolution and eventually had been inherited by the Wake family. In 1872 Sir Herewald Wake, the twelfth baronet, had paid £120 for the internal restoration of the chancel, apparently with good grace. About sixty years later, however, his son Sir Hereward disputed such claims on his funds. In the spring of 1929 the PCC learned that the whole church floor was rotten and so requested from the lay rector a contribution to the cost in respect of the chancel. He, in reply, asked to be relieved of all responsibility in consideration of a grant of £100. The PCC replied firmly that it had no power to relieve him of future responsibility for repairs and that it would look to him to refloor the chancel. Sir Hereward's answer led the PCC to ask counsel's opinion, which was that the obligation on the lay rector to repair was generally confined to the structure of the chancel and did not extend to the pews or the fittings.

In the autumn of 1934 the PCC was discussing repairs to the chancel once more and sought further counsel's opinion on the lay rector's duties. A lay rector receives the rectorial tithes of his benefice and by custom enjoys the right of the chief seat in the chancel for himself and his family. He has the freehold of the whole church, but this gives him no right of possession or of entering it when it is not open for divine service. He has also the duty to repair the chancel. The PCC was well aware of this, as repairs to the fabric were necessary continually and money had to be found to pay for them. Counsel's view was to the effect that Sir Hereward was responsible for the repairs to the chancel and that he should ensure that results were in keeping with the rest of the church. Sir Hereward disagreed, so the PCC issued an ultimatum, receiving in reply an offer to carry out essential but not "extensive" repairs. The dispute went to the County Court at Waltham Abbey, where the Judge found against the PCC. Sir Hereward seems still to have contributed £15 or £20, but he insisted that this should not be taken as any precedent whatsoever as to his future responsibility towards repairs to the chancel. There the matter rested.

The heating of the church was a constant problem. In the early years stoves were fuelled by coal or coke; the advent of electricity did not help appreciably because there was insufficient power. In 1938 the PCC agreed to the installation of a new coal fired system at a cost of £250. In spite of this there were complaints about the cold during the winter of 1940/1941 and more electric points were put in. The use of these was superseded in 1952 by the introduction of tubular heaters under the pews.

All Saints' was not the only building for which the PCC was responsible during the twentieth century. It always held possession of Church House, later called Church Cottage, at the entrance to the churchyard, where vergers and, later, caretakers lived. It was responsible for the maintenance of the Betts Lane church school, which is described in chapter 8. Until the 1950s there were outbuildings of the Vicarage on the right of the approach to the lychgate. When the new Vicarage was built, the old one was sold as two dwellings, called the Old Vicarage and the Glebe House, and the outbuildings were demolished, their site becoming a car park.. There was also, opposite the gate of the old Vicarage, a church hall known irreverently as the Tin Tabernacle or Tin Hut; it was taken over by Nazeing Parish Council in 1936 and is described in chapter 9.

The Sunday Schools

The Sunday School had been started, or possibly revived, by Mrs Goddard soon after her arrival in 1890. By 1910 this Sunday School met at the Tin Tabernacle and another, run by Ralph Palmer met at the church school in Betts Lane. There was some animosity between Palmer and Thomas Goddard (*Five miles from everywhere,* p149), which may explain the existence of two separate organisations within a few yards of each other. Palmer and Goddard died in 1923 and apparently the two Sunday Schools merged, for during the twenties Gladys Fossett, the wife of the vicar, was in charge, aided by the Misses Hargreaves. During the Second World War it met in the tack room of the Vicarage, where a small harmonium had been installed. After the war it moved to the north aisle of the church; it was then run by Phyllis Goff, with help from Dorothy Mansfield. Then in 1951 it moved back to the Tin Tabernacle and Kenneth Bell, a churchwarden, took over. When that building was demolished in 1959, it returned to the church, where it remained until it closed in January 1964, just before the dedication of the new church in Lower Nazeing. There had been a break during the interregnum of 1933, between the death of Stewart Fossett and the induction of James Sutherland, and other brief ones during the Second World War. Otherwise a Sunday school had continued in the Upper Town for at least three quarters of a century.

With the increase in the population in Lower Nazeing there had come a need for a second Sunday School. This met for the first time in February 1949, with Bea Catton in charge, at the Cadet Hut. By the end of April nearly 60 pupils had been enrolled, some of them transferring from the Chapel Sunday School to save a long walk. Another advantage was being able to avoid the dung deposited in Middle Street by the cows from Mansion House Farm, an indication of how remote and rural Nazeing was still. When the "military authorities" gave up the Cadet Hut, the Lower Nazeing Sunday School moved to "Mr Compton's garage", on the site of Elizabeth Close, where it stayed until St. Giles' was opened in February 1964.

Before the war there were Sunday School outings to the Kursaal at Southend, to Thorpe Bay, and to Westcliff. There were summer treats in the orchard and garden at the Vicarage, and indoor treats at Christmas. James Sutherland used to hide coins for the children to find; in his later years these were half-crowns, worth considerably more than a week's pocket money to most of the seekers. From the start the Lower Town and Upper Town Sunday Schools shared an annual outing, the first being to Clacton in August 1949. Teas and prize-givings were organised too. The success of the Lower Nazeing Sunday School gave great pleasure to Sutherland, who died just over a year after its foundation.

Changes after the war

James Sutherland was succeeded by Harold Hawkins, whose period as vicar marked a break from the pre-war and wartime years. The squirarchy, which had dominated the first Parochial Church Council and whose influence and benevolence had helped the church for many years, ceased to exist in Nazeing. Sir Walter and Lady Hargreaves moved away in 1949, Archdale Palmer died in 1950, and Ralph Bury in 1954. Further, Samuel Martin, who was vicar's warden from 1937 to 1958, had become the PCC's secretary and treasurer as well from 1942 until 1954, taking over from Jimmy Savage, who had been only the second holder of those offices.

In 1929 the church had started to publish *Nazeing Parish Magazine*, with Molly Hargreaves as editor. This contained information about the activities of the Congregational Church, as well as those of the Church of England, and articles about the history of Nazeing by Alfred Perkins, who wrote under the pseudonym A. Sojourner. It ceased publication early in the war and was revived as *Nazeing Church News* in 1947, post-war austerity necessitating a much smaller magazine, which contained news about just the Church of England. There has been no break since then.

The name was changed to *Parish Church News* and later to *Nazeing Parish Magazine*; most recently *Nazeing Parish News*. The size increased gradually and from the mid-1980s articles on local history appeared again.

Nazeing was never a well-endowed parish so that the vicar's stipend was comparatively low. When Harold Hawkins was about to arrive, Richard Andrew proposed the establishment of a fund to which parishioners would contribute for the augmentation of the vicar's stipend. Initially the PCC was wary but by January 1951 the fund had been started, and a year later was valued at £181 per annum. Hawkins's

Harold Hawkins at Nazeingbury crossroads in the 1950s, collecting towards the £1,750 needed to eradicate Death Watch Beetle. Standing from the left: Dennis Hutchings, David Hawkins, Louie Welch and Flossie Welch.

59

successor, David Read, recalled that when he was considering coming to Nazeing he saw some figures "on the back of a cigarette packet" to explain how "the Col. Andrew Fund", added to the stipend of £900 a year, would help to provide a moderate income. The levelling of stipends in the Church of England while Read was the vicar removed the necessity for supplements directly from the parishioners.

As early as 1931, when the Keysers Estate was being developed, the PCC became concerned about the distance to All Saints' for increasing numbers of parishioners. A special bus service to take people to church was arranged in 1937 and continued until 1943. When more building started in the village in the 1950s, buses were introduced again from time to time. In February 1951 midweek evening services were started in the Cadet Hut but two years later, when a hire charge of 12s 6d per evening was requested, the venue was transferred to the Princess Louise Convalescent Home, where they continued until 1960.

At the end of 1953 the PCC considered whether the 11.00 service should be held at the Cadet Hut on alternate Sundays. The matter seems to have progressed slowly until November 1958, when the secretary was asked to write about hiring the hall in the new school in Hyde Mead on Sundays. This initiative met with a response after some delay and by the summer of 1960 there was a service at the school at 6.30 pm on one Sunday a month.

The building of St. Giles'

As Lower Nazeing was becoming the main centre of population in the parish, it was causing concern that the Church had no premises of its own there. Back in 1942 the PCC had noted "the lack of facilities for children in the areas of St. Leonard's Road and North Street" and considered the building of a hall, although there was no possibility of doing anything at that time. In 1957 the increasingly cramped conditions of the new Sunday School at George Compton's garage were used to support the suggestion to the Bishop of Chelmsford that he send a special investigator "to inspect this vast and scattered parish". A reply came from the Bishop of Barking, the suffragan for the area, who explained that the diocese was putting every available penny into the New Towns so that it could offer no help to Nazeing. Undeterred, Harold Hawkins wrote to Chelmsford again in October about the lack of accommodation for the Lower Nazeing Sunday School.

The terms of the response are not recorded but may be guessed, as it was not until a visit by the ecclesiastical secretary of the Lord Chancellor, the parish's patron, in March 1960, that the Church authorities showed that they were aware of the problem. Kenneth Bell, a church warden,

David Read at All Saints' in 1964.

reported that the secretary had been very surprised at the growth of the population in the parish and thought that an all purpose hall would be helpful in the lower part of the village. At the suggestion of Ken Wood, the PCC's secretary was asked to invite the Bishop of Barking to visit the parish to assess its requirements. He did not come but the Archdeacon of West Ham did. As a result of his visit the PCC was able to pass a resolution that set in train the building of St. Giles'.

Harold Hawkins, who had been unwell, moved from Nazeing to a small parish near Reading at the end of May 1961 and David Read was inducted two months later. Under his chairmanship the PCC discussed

The evening service for the laying of the foundation stone of the new church by the Bishop of Barking on St. Giles' Day, 1st September 1963, with Dorothy Wood at the harmonium. Top left is Rose Cottage and "Mr Compton's garage".

the site and the type of building required in Lower Nazeing and in October 1962 it approved plans for a church to be built near the crossroads, on land bought from George Compton. David Read promoted the idea of a hall for the whole village, and so there was a moveable screen between chancel and nave which enabled the nave to be used as a hall, thus providing valuable funds for the church and partially satisfying the need for a village hall. The construction started in the following year and was completed at a cost of £13,000, about half of it raised locally. St. Giles' was dedicated by the Bishop of Chelmsford on 23rd February, 1964.

Since then services have been held regularly there as well as at All Saints', with the worshipping members of the Church of England considering themselves one congregation with two buildings. The Roman Catholic congregation in Nazeing began to meet every Sunday for Mass at St. Giles' as soon as it was open, making it one of the first churches in this country to have been used jointly.

Vergers and organists

Like most other churches All Saints' had a verger, who lived in Church Cottage. Arthur Reynolds succeeded George Smith in 1901 and held the post from 1902 until his retirement in 1947; until 1933, he looked after the church hall too. He was succeeded by Phyllis Goff, who had the pleasure of seeing mains water laid on in 1950, at the same time as to the Vicarage. After she died in November 1958 there was a succession of appointees, none of whom stayed long. From 1968 caretakers, who were not expected to take part in services, were employed instead. They were responsible for keeping the church clean and the churchyard tidy.

In 1942 the vicar reported that the space for burials in the original churchyard would probably be taken up within two years. After negotiations two acres of adjoining land were bought from Mr C. Burton of Chickney Hall, Broxted, in 1944. The old churchyard was closed for burials in 1954.

The church needed an organ blower, who would pump the bellows by hand. In 1943 Arthur Reynolds undertook this as an extra duty, for an additional payment of 2s 6d per Sunday. By 1947 it had become difficult to persuade him or anyone else to do the work, so an electric blower was installed. The hand pump proved useful even in the early 1990s on an occasion when the electricity went off.

The organist in the 1930s and 1940s was Edward Booth. Since the departure from the parish in 1923 of H.G. Verrall, who had been the organist as well as the first honorary secretary and treasurer of the PCC, there had been three organists in fairly quick succession. Ted Booth led a dance band which came to play at the church hall and was asked whether he played the organ. He said that he did, accepted the post, and bicycled from Rye House two or three times each week. There were complaints from time to time that he failed to turn up for choir practices and that was ostensibly the reason for his departure in 1952. Unofficially the reason was Harold Hawkins's unhappiness that he played for dances on Saturday nights before attending services on Sundays.

His successor was Dorothy Mansfield, who had been assistant organist. She was the daughter of the vicar's housekeeper, Margaret, and his gardener, Cecil. Dorothy was employed provisionally, perhaps because the PCC was uncertain about having a woman in such an important post.

Indeed it was another twenty years before Nazeing had women as sidesmen or reading lessons regularly, and twenty-seven years before Sheila Blake became the first woman to be elected as a churchwarden

Isobel Baillie with the church choir and the vicar, Harold Hawkins, 1954. Women and girls were first admitted to the choir when James Sutherland was vicar.

since 1741. Dorothy Wood, as she was after marriage, played for services until she and her husband Ken moved away in 1976. After another period in which no organist settled for long, Malcolm Songer, who had played the trombone in the Salvation Army, joined the Church in Nazeing and was appointed with a new title, director of music, in 1980.

Many concerts have been organised at All Saints'. One created a great stir in April 1954 when Isobel Baillie came to sing, accompanied by Douglas Rogers, organist of Hoddesdon Parish Church. There were at least two visits by the Salvation Army National band from Nottingham. In later years there were several visits by groups of young musicians from the Royal Academy.

Nazeing church bells

Nazeing has what is known as a light peal, the tenor bell weighing 9¼ cwt and capable of being rung by an average man or woman quite easily. Five bells originally made in 1779 by the Whitechapel Foundry were re-hung in 1900, when the first recorded peal on the bells was rung. Only five peals were rung before 1952, but over the next 48 years there were 33, all having been recorded on a board in the ringing room.

The ringing of church bells for services was banned during the Second World War, as ringing was intended to be a warning of invasion. Because of this hiatus, in 1948 Charlie Sams and some ringers from Roydon helped to train Nazeing young people who had come forward to learn to ring the bells at All Saints'. In the December parish magazine the vicar wrote:

> Some people imagine that it is quite easy to ring bells but those of us who have visited the tower during practices have discovered that it is not so easy and may be a perilous business. Considering the short while they have been practising, our team of ringers have done well and we look forward to the time when we shall have the bells rung at least once a Sunday.

Evidence of some 170 years of "perilous business" can be seen from grooves worn by the ropes into the walls of the tower, as until 1952 there were no guides for the ropes, which could therefore fly about almost unchecked. Bill Aley became a ringer in Nazeing at that time and in 2001 celebrated half a century of ringing in the All Saints' tower.

In 1952 the bells were rehung again, this time by Gillett and Johnston of Croydon. The third bell was recast and a new treble bell added to give a ring of six bells, enabling many different peals to be rung. The new bell was donated in memory of Archdale Palmer by the Mercers' Company; many of its senior members attended the service of dedication. It was rung for the first time half-muffled, following the memorial service for King George VI.

In 1903 Thomas Goddard had urged Ellis John Webb to leave Nazeing and seek his fortune in Canada. Sixty-five years later Webb bequeathed £300 to provide Christmas dinners for the bellringers of his old parish, who considered, however, that they were not wanting in this respect. They decided that the money would be better spent on providing a first floor some ten feet above ground for their ringing chamber, thus making ringing easier and enabling the choir to use the ground floor as a robing room. The large congregation at the dedication service in 1971 included Doris Pegrum, niece of Ellis Webb.

Nazeing Church Handbell Ringers

A set of twelve handbells came into the possession of Ben Burton, who was a tower ringer at both Roydon and Nazeing churches and had rung handbells since the twenties. Unfortunately he died very soon afterwards. His family donated the bells to All Saints' Church and on 4th November 1973 David Read dedicated them to the memory of Ben and his wife, Elsie.

Only Bill Aley had any previous knowledge of ringing a handbell, so he faced a somewhat daunting task when the vicar stipulated that the bells should be rung at the Christmas services. Much to the surprise of the ringers they did manage to play two or three carols, which fired them with enthusiasm. So that was really the start of the Nazeing Guild of Handbell Ringers. The majority of the first group was male but by 2001, when only Bill remained of the original band, all the others were women.

Eventually Alexander Henry ("Jimmy") James evolved as leader of the Guild, which was renamed the Nazeing Church Handbell Ringers in 1977. Jimmy arranged several traditional pieces for twelve handbells and in 1981 published them as *The Nazeing Collection*, which became a standard among handbell ringers. To raise money for further bells the team rang at local venues, and by 1991 had bought 20 to add to the original 12. With a further three from another set belonging to the church, the number reached 35. Latterly they rang at rallies and represented the East Anglian Region of the Handbell Ringers of Great Britain.

The handbell ringers at Harlow Museum in 1987: Marcia Seymour, John Seymour, Jenny Slater, Jimmy James, Janet Crabbe, Bill Aley, Howard Kimber, Ron Seymour.

When Jimmy was no longer able to carry on through ill health, Marcia Seymour, who had officiated as secretary, treasurer, music archivist, and general factotum for more than 20 years took over the leadership. Jimmy died in September 1997, leaving a bequest to the Nazeing Church Handbell Ringers, which enabled them to obtain four fitted bell cases. When Marcia died only two years later, it had become possible to augment the set with two more bells to make a complete run of 37.

Recent times

In Nazeing, as in other parishes, church fêtes were well attended in the years after the Second World War and helped greatly towards balancing the books. In 1951, for example, £210 was raised in the Vicarage garden on one Saturday afternoon but, as social habits changed, support for fêtes declined. A main fund-raising occasion, as well as an evangelistic opportunity, for the Church became its Flower Festival. The first one was held at All Saints' in June 1965 and was organised by Sheila Blake.

Raymond Hodson (second from right) is seen here after his induction in November 1977. He was the first vicar to come to Nazeing with a young family for at least a century. He is holding Katy with Linda holding Lucy, and Jenny standing beside James Adams, the Bishop of Barking. Far left and right are the churchwardens, Colin Dauris and Alan Peacock.

Another was held at the August Bank Holiday weekend in 1967, since when it has become the major event in the village calendar, taking place biennially and involving many other groups and organisations. From 1969 onwards the flower arrangements had a Christian theme. Since 1983 an art exhibition has been held at the same time, initially at Dormarlyn Hall and latterly at St. Giles'.

David Read retired in 1977 and was succeeded by Raymond Hodson. Under his guidance the modern language Holy Communion service was introduced for family worship. After he moved to Ampthill in 1984, the interregnum of 21 months before the induction of Martin Webster was by far the longest on record. Coincidentally, both men were graduate physicists and came to Nazeing with young children. From 1987 Alan Peacock assisted as a lay reader and in 1996 Gay Ellis, a non-stipendiary deacon, was appointed to be the parish's first curate to assist a resident vicar. A year later she was ordained to become its first woman priest.

Martin Webster was possibly the last vicar with responsibility solely for Nazeing, for on his departure to Waltham Abbey in 1999 the Bishop of Chelmsford suspended the power of the patron to appoint a new vicar. Instead he appointed a priest-in-charge so that the Bishop of Barking, who has responsibility for the area, might consider whether the benefice should be amalgamated with that of the adjoining parish of Roydon.

The congregation of All Saints' and St. Giles' marked the year 2000 by reading continuously the Old and the New Testaments in St. Giles' Church during 83 hours at the Spring Bank Holiday weekend. The readers included members of other Anglican churches, and of the Roman Catholic and Congregational Churches in Nazeing.

The Congregational Church

Nazeing Chapel was, as described in *Five miles from everywhere*, founded in 1795 as a result of open air evangelical preaching by John James and other students from the Countess of Huntingdon College at Cheshunt. In 1876 the present building, accommodating 150 people, replaced a smaller chapel, and in the early 1900s the Chapel grew rapidly as a result of local evangelism influenced by the Welsh Revival. The little Sunday school at the back of the chapel was overflowing with children and necessitated the building of the present Sunday School Hall.

Although the influence of religion on people's lives has declined dramatically in the last fifty years, things were different in the first half of the twentieth century and the impact of the Chapel on village life should not be underestimated. Most people attended church at least occasionally and religious institutions were still held in high regard. The Chapel had a major role in both the spiritual and social life of the village and several of its leaders were men of influence. Joseph Pegrum, John Davies Welch, John Banks and, later, James Gray were parish councillors. All but Welch were trustees of Nazeing Wood or Park and Pegrum was also a district councillor and an overseer of the poor. Thus the chapel was possibly, at least until the 1930s, the dominant religious force in the community, reflecting the strength of non-conformity throughout the country.

Leadership was undertaken by part-time students from Cheshunt College, called deans. With the outbreak of the First World War most of the students dispersed and in 1916 the Chapel appointed a minister for the first time. The Reverend C.V. Williams came at a less than generous

John Banks and family at Coburg (later Warwick) House, c1890.

salary of a guinea a week (£54 12s 0d per annum) "to be reviewed as the financial prospects of the church increased". Evidently this did not happen, for chapel records imply that dissatisfaction with his salary led to Williams' departure a year later.

Many men went from Nazeing to the Great War in 1914. The people left at home applied themselves to sewing, knitting, sending parcels, and raising funds to support the boys at the front. After the war, when the village scheme for a war memorial fell through, it was the Chapel that organised welcome home celebrations held on its premises and took over arrangements for the memorial, which is on the front wall of the Congregational Church.

Between the wars

Chapel life returned to normal and much emphasis was placed on creating a social structure within the church, offering something for all ages. Thus there was a renewed and greater emphasis on youth work, with badminton added to the football, cricket, and tennis already on offer.

The Chapel Brass Band, c1905. Back row from the left: Bandmaster Barnet (holding baton), David Pegrum, a Mr Starling, Arch Coleman, Percy Baker, Charles Judd, unknown, Thomas Nicholls, George Francis, a Mr Crowe, "Bottle" Starling, "Tractor" Smith and Bert Hills. Front row: Tom Crowe, Sam Pegrum, George Judd, John Welch, unknown, Joe Pegrum, unknown, John Coleman, Ted Coleman, Jim Pegrum. By the drums: Fred Ashby and Ernest Coleman.

Poetry, Bible studies, drama, and social events catered for those who preferred quieter pursuits. A choir was formed and coach outings for the whole church were organised.

At the suggestion of Harland Brine, co-dean at the time, the Chapel Brass Band had been formed in 1903. The cost of the instruments and the Bandmaster's salary were defrayed by a weekly subscription of 1s 6d and practice meetings were held in the little schoolroom at the back of the church. The band seems to have been a great success and played at village events as well as special Chapel occasions. It was disbanded and re-formed several times before its final demise in the late 1920s.

There seems to have been a good relationship with the Anglicans, as the vicar came to preach at Chapel anniversaries on several occasions. Women's meetings flourished, the Sunday School prospered and new members joined the church at an average rate of nearly five per year. In 1930 the membership figure of eighty was the highest at any time in the

The Chapel Deacons c1930. From the left Mr Sebry, Ted Coleman, George Judd, Joe Pegrum, John Coleman, Sophie Pegrum, Hubert Janische (Dean), Mr Jackman, Mr Martin, Mr Payne, Mr Francis.

Chapel's history, and did not include those who attended services without becoming church members.

Despite this success the Chapel was perpetually hard up, offset to some extent by numerous sales of work (a fundraising event for which church members made and donated items), hiring of church crockery and, in 1925, the sale of 300 tickets at 9d each for the anniversary tea. The congregation nevertheless raised funds for outside causes such as hospitals, children's homes, and missionaries. Several Sunday collections and harvest produce were donated to the newly built Princess Louise Convalescent Home and £100 was raised for a fund to provide superannuation for ministers and their widows.

The Chapel was affected by modern attitudes and progress within the village. Delegates to the Herts Congregational Union annual meeting in 1927 were allowed to go by motor car at the Chapel's expense. In the same year Sophie Pegrum was elected as the first woman deacon and oil lamps were replaced by electric lighting in church and hall; when removed in 1950, four lamps retained for emergencies still contained solidified oil. In 1929 water was laid on at the hall and a sink was installed, although it was not until the 1960s that electric heating replaced the old coke stoves.

Joseph Pegrum, a successful farmer with a finger in most village pies, was a remarkable character who displayed a strange mixture of meanness and generosity. He was loathe to part with money unnecessarily and always suggested a lower figure if salaries were being discussed. An episode in which he was prosecuted for failing to stamp the National Insurance Card of his employee, Frank Hales, is probably typical of the man. When in 1926 Hales left after three years' work as a cowman and wages of £1 5s 6d were due to him, Pegrum not only refused to pay him but asked for a refund of 1s 6d, saying that he owed it for National Insurance contributions. Hales had asked Pegrum to stop the money weekly but Joe "could not be bothered with all that", preferring to stop it every six months. The Bench found that Pegrum had had no intention to defraud but that he had committed an offence; he was fined accordingly. Tight-fisted in his personal dealings, Pegrum was nevertheless generous to the Chapel and stood surety for it on several occasions.

To the young Bernard Pegrum "Uncle Joe" and the Chapel were inseparable:

> When we arrived he was always there at the front door, greeting everyone with a smiling "Good Morning" and a handshake. I was quite sure that no-one could enter the place unless Uncle Joe was there to let them in, and I had a hazy notion that he used to get there early to open the door to let God in, of course with the inevitable handshake and "Good Morning God"...

> Uncle Joe was on the "large side". He always used to usher in the preacher from the vestry, and had a peculiar method of coming through the vestry door sideways. I used to think that it was because he carried so much before him that he could not get through any other way...

Like his niece Sophie, Joe always had faith at the centre of his life. Church minutes are full of Sophie Pegrum's work on committees, organising teas, setting up sales of work and, not least, teaching in Sunday School for over thirty years.

For many years the Pegrums dominated the membership but early in the twentieth century the Coleman family challenged their position. Alfred and Sarah Coleman, sub-tenants of the Pegrums at Darmers, had had ten children, six of them boys. Most of the children joined the Chapel and all the boys became enthusiastic workers in the church and Sunday School. Although some tensions arose between the Pegrums and Colemans, it is clear from the records that both families contributed enormously to the life of the Chapel.

Rent receipt "for House called Darmans [Darmers]" dated 1890 given
to Alfred Coleman and signed by David Pegrum senior, brother of Joe.
For many years, the Pegrum and Coleman families dominated the
membership of the Chapel.

Until 1939 there were about 100 children on the Sunday School
register, meeting morning and afternoon with an average attendance of 66
per cent and 75 per cent respectively. This was a creditable effort,
considering most scholars had to walk some distance to the school. Many
teachers had three journeys to the chapel on a Sunday, often their only
day off work. They worked without modern teaching aids, organising
Scripture exams, competitions, and the annual Sunday School
Anniversary, at which the children performed special songs, dramas, and
readings for parents and church members. The teachers organised (and
often paid for out of their own pockets) prizes for attendance, races,
games, and teas for the summer and winter treats. They supervised sales,
sideshows, and other events to raise money for Sunday School funds.
They were a hardworking, dedicated band of people who cared
passionately about the spiritual welfare of the children in their care.
Occasionally hostility arose between church and Sunday School, mostly
because the teachers felt that non-teaching members were not interested
in the work among young people and did not appreciate the problems they
faced.

Bernard Pegrum, a distant cousin of Joe, was a controversial figure in many ways but a gifted teacher who gave unstintingly of his time to the Sunday School. On Sunday afternoons after the war, he could be seen making numerous journeys in his tiny 1936 model Y Ford, picking up as many as eight children per trip, dropping them at the hall and taking them home afterwards. In the 1950s he was joined by Ray Hutchings, who could get fifteen or more children in his old Austin van. Marjorie Ashby also devoted many years of her life to the Sunday School and, like Bernard, taught from the late 1920s until they both suffered strokes, Bernard in 1964 and Marjorie in the early 1970s.

The Trust Deeds of Nazeing Chapel had remained vested in Cheshunt College, so the Chapel, as part of the Huntingdon Connexion, had little or no autonomy with regard to its affairs, in theory at least. This was fine as long as there were deans to act in a pastoral capacity and church members were unschooled in the business of management. As men like Joe Pegrum, John Banks, and John Welch became influential in the village, however, they were prepared to take more responsibility for their church and saw that lack of autonomy might eventually compromise the work. The matter was first raised by John Welch in 1900 and rumbled on unsatisfactorily for many years. It came to a head in 1927, when the Chapel was thinking about calling a minister; Henderson from the College pointed out that under the Trust Deed, this power was vested in the trustees of the college. Furthermore, there remained only one of the original trustees and "he of a greatly advanced age", so clearly something needed to be done. The matter was settled in 1932 and although the Chapel was no longer part of the Huntingdon Connexion, the deeds did lay down that it must abide by certain articles of the Connexion's beliefs. Except for a part time pastorate from 1934 to 1937 the Chapel continued to rely largely on Cheshunt College to provide preachers.

During the Second World War the Chapel struggled on, holding the evening service at 3.00 pm to avoid the black-out. The Sunday School split into three local groups, which met at Mayflower, the chapel, and Long Green to minimise travelling and the danger from air raids. The Home Office evacuation authorities commandeered the chapel hall in 1939 and later the senior day school was held there. It was also used as emergency accommodation for families whose homes had been hit by the V2 rocket in November 1944.

A breath of fresh air

After the war student pastors from New College in London replaced the deans and after nearly 150 years the last link with Cheshunt College was severed. Billeted at Netherdown, next door to the chapel, home of Miss Annie Pegrum, they brought a breath of fresh air into the fellowship, doing much to dispel any lingering notion that enjoying oneself was somehow sinful. The work of the Chapel was furthered by evangelical meetings, socials, a highly successful Sunday School (140 on the register in 1948), and a popular women's meeting. There were fund-raising events like the chapel bazaar, which became an annual feature, raising £200 in 1964 and £239 in 1973. After the war, when social activity increased generally, there were in the village, drama groups, women's groups, youth groups, and clubs for the elderly. Many of these groups met in the chapel hall, which was also the venue for most concerts and meetings and, together with the "Tin Tabernacle", was effectively the village hall until St. Giles' was built in 1964. In 1951 the old school at Bumbles Green could no longer accommodate the post war baby boom, so Essex County Council hired the chapel hall for a schoolroom and provided the building's first flush toilets.

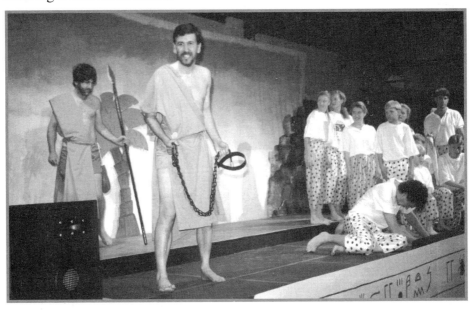

Joseph and the Amazing Technicolour Dreamcoat, **performed by the Chapel Choir in 1990. From the left: Johnny Huggins, Robin Sinden, Vicky Stretch, Jenny Featherstone, Nicky Huggins, Laurence Brown, Susanna Snow, Clive Hutchings. In front: Tobias Spencer, Francis Brown, Phil Knudson.**

In 1952 Jim Sparkes was the last student pastor from New College and after his departure the Chapel congregation joined with Hoddesdon Congregational Church to call Reg West to a joint pastorate in 1955. In March 1957 the Chapel joined All Saints' under Harold Hawkins to hold an evangelical campaign led by George Duncan, well known for broadcasts on the BBC. A united evening service at All Saints' opened the campaign and there was a week of well-attended nightly meetings at the chapel hall.

When Reg West left in 1959, the Chapel members wanted a pastor of their own but needed accommodation for him, so they set up a fund for a Manse (the home of a nonconformist minister). In 1962 they bought Lanshaven, a house in Middle Street, but the mortgage put such a strain on church finances that they struggled to find the minimum stipend. Eventually they resorted to lay preachers, renting out the Manse from 1968-1977 in order to do essential repairs. After 1977 it was occupied by successive ministers and finally was paid for in 1987. In 1997 the Chapel sold Lanshaven and bought 20 Middle Street for a Manse.

Having achieved autonomy, the Chapel retained a fierce spirit of independence and in 1972 opted by a large majority to remain Congregational instead of joining the United Reformed Church (URC). For Congregationalists the church meeting is traditionally the authority under God for all decisions affecting the affairs of that particular fellowship, whereas the URC is governed by a central synod and Chapel members wanted to retain the right to make their own decisions. Subsequently, on a more contentious issue, the members voted by a narrow majority to join the Evangelical Fellowship of Congregational Churches and eventually the trust deeds passed into their keeping.

In the early 1960s afternoon Sunday School was discontinued and the children were encouraged to come with their parents to morning Family Church. This led to shortage of space since congregation and children needed separate rooms. The Scout hut across the road was used for a time but was not very satisfactory and in 1974 a prefabricated building known as the Cabin was erected, remaining in use until 1992. In 1985, during the ministry of Keith Holder (1980-88), the evening service was replaced by informal House Groups, held in members' homes. Keith was a gifted youth worker, especially with teenage boys, and organised a successful 5-a-side football team.

Under Norman Bonnett's leadership (1989-98) the church buildings were extensively enlarged and improved with a complex integrating church and hall. House Groups were revitalised and Alpha Courses, aimed at introducing non-Christians to the Christian faith, were started in 1996 with great success. A choir was formed and put on several Christian musicals.

The Chapel celebrated its 200th anniversary in 1995, with a number of events scheduled throughout the year to mark the occasion. Chief of these was an open air service at the crossroads with pastor and congregation in period costume, commemorating the preaching of John James to a handful of village people who were sufficiently moved by the power of his message to form the small group of dissenters which eventually became the Congregational Church as we know it today. The anniversary also inspired minister Norman Bonnett and member Paddy Hutchings to publish *Nonconformity in Nazeing*, a detailed history of the church on which this brief account is based.

Norman Bonnett with wife Ruth leading his congregation to the open air service at Nazeingbury crossroads in 1995, celebrating the two hundredth anniversary of the Chapel.

CHAPTER 3

"CONSTANT WORRY AND ANXIETY"

Nazeing at war

Even a remote community like Nazeing was never entirely immune from the influence of war. In the nineteenth century, for example, the economic dislocation of the Napoleonic and Crimean wars caused hardship in the village. The two world wars, however, had a far greater impact. Over fifty Nazeing people were killed and many more were left to grieve for their loved ones. Those who escaped such direct losses were affected as well, by the greater regulation of daily life and, in the Second World War, the ever present danger of bombing.

The First World War, 1914-1918

Marjorie Sykes, whose mother was a member of the Pegrum family, related an incident from early in 1914 which was perhaps a foretaste of things to come:

> Another outing which we enjoyed was made when quite by chance a plane came down on the Common. I had heard about aeroplanes but I had never seen one. Then one day in the school holidays, when we were staying at Nazeing, suddenly a great rattling sound was heard and there was a plane. All at work or play left everything to gaze in amazement. Excitement increased as we saw the thing rolling, falling, getting up again, and eventually descending somewhere that couldn't be very far away.

> Then the trek from the village began; from field and garden, from cottage and house they came, eager to be in on whatever there was: visitors, schoolchildren, babes in prams, and odd characters and anyone who had time to spend. And there on the Common, in all its glory and downfall, a small bi-plane and a worried young naval officer puffing anxiously at a cigarette.

> The young man was offered hospitality at Mr. Green's [Collyers] and the plane was left to the interested bystanders, guarded by two of the local police force, who were fully aware of the national importance of their unusual job…It is impossible in these days to imagine how excited we were. Planes had seemed to us so unusual that we had never expected to see one.

As Nazeing people enjoyed the sunny Bank Holiday of Monday, 3rd August 1914, most would have known that Germany had invaded

Marjorie Sykes wrote "Dad took a picture of the scene in which two of us appear but it is so faint a print that it is impossible to decide which two. All the same you can see the plane and the two policemen." The Royal Navy bi-plane that made an emergency landing on Nazeing Common in 1914.

Belgium, making Great Britain's involvement in a major war almost inevitable, but few could even have guessed the extent to which it would affect their own lives. Most of the young men went away to the front, so women and older men took on their jobs. For the first time there were identity cards and rationing cards. In 1917 Epping Rural District Council asked the parish council to establish a Food Control Subcommittee, which soon claimed that it received little support from Epping so that "complaints are frequently received from Parishioners who have not received food cards or emergency food cards, which neither the subcommittee nor this Council have any means of satisfying".

There is no record of any bombs falling in Nazeing although some dropped at Broxbourne, where the stationmaster usually gave a warning if planes were flying over. An anti-aircraft gun was sited at the top of Colemans Lane, where its concrete base can still be seen. In the Second World War there was a searchlight on or near the same site.

Before and during the war there was fear of German invasion. Defences for London were situated in Nazeing. A record of compensation paid to W.J. Hollow of Brewitts Farm shows that a camp, a roadway, and trenches were built there. In 1918 the pindar of Nazeing Common was paid 6s by the War Office for "cutting thistles on the trenches". Trenches across Tinkers Lane (between Hoe Lane and Roydon Hamlet) were not filled in until three years after the war, when the Government paid £130 for the work to be done.

At All Saints' Church there is a pair of brass candlesticks, one engraved "And the light shineth in darkness", and the other "And the darkness comprehended it not - 1917". Dorothy Wood explained their significance:

> In 1917 some soldiers were billeted in Nazeing for training before going to France. Part of their time was spent practising the digging of trenches in the field below the church. The officer in charge stayed at Church Cottage with Mrs Reynolds, the verger, caretaker, gravedigger etc. being away in France. When the soldiers were posted to the Western Front the officer gave the candlesticks to our church.

Unfortunately we know neither the officer's name nor even his regiment. Ridges in the field below the church are still visible.

Marjorie Sykes painted a vivid picture of wartime life:

> Country customs and agricultural methods that had been almost unchanged for centuries already before the 1914 war were showing signs of change. The bicycle had arrived and soon became an essential of country life. This proved to be a good thing and just in time, as in the early days of the war, farm horses were commandeered for the Army; most of the young men joined up, and the older men and women, left to fend for themselves, were thankful that they had bikes.

> Kaiser Bill and little Willie, his son, were the arch villains, and they had their spies everywhere, even in Nazeing. 'What would they want in Nazeing?' asked the ignorant outsider, to be greeted with a knowing 'Ah Ha? What indeed, but what about the Common?' Some thought he had plans to set up a headquarters there: it was big enough. If a stranger was seen to pass through the village, his errand unknown, he was immediately suspected of being a spy; if he chanced to write in, or consult a notebook, suspicions were confirmed...

> During one of my visits, we had a zeppelin raid; these enormous death traps could only come over when there was a full moon. On this occasion, Uncle and Aunt's first thoughts were for the animals and we three growing girls were left to the care of May's Aunt Clara, who was very deaf and consequently liable to mispronounce words. The aircraft and anti-aircraft guns must have been very close, and deaf as she was, Clara must have felt

the vibrations. There were also vibrations from May who had one of her giggling fits, which Clara mistook in the darkness (no lights were allowed) to be fits of terror and distress. So she petted and stroked May and tried to comfort her by repeating: "There, dear don't cry, they're only on the coach." She meant coast. This only made the giggles worse and spread to us.

But the war was not funny to most of us. Uncle Will's three boys were in Flanders and Uncle Joe's Florrie had lost her husband, and had to bring up her little daughter Eleanor on a very limited pension; and Uncle Bert had gone into the Army and was sent to Egypt. Most of the older people were horrified at this great catastrophe and old ladies like Aunt Susan found passages in the Bible which foretold these events; even younger people thought there might be something in what they said.

The war seemed endless. When it began, many said it would be over by Christmas, but it actually landed us in a weary drag for over four years that seemed like an eternity...When it did come to an end in November 1918, we could hardly believe that we were no longer at war, without the men folk, with constant worry and anxiety. But peace brings problems and the old days and scenes were over. Bicycles, cars, even aeroplanes had come, and the role of women had changed.

Nance Coleman recalled that

Father worked at the Munition Works - the gunpowder factory, at the experimental place and he had some terrible experiences during the war - explosions and one thing and another... Father was most particular, probably because of his work. If we had anything in our fingernails he would call us ebonytips. We never saw anything in his because the least little bit of grit would have caused an explosion. He walked to work and back. In the summer holidays and after school we children would meet him with a picnic tea up from Waltham Road, just opposite Monkhams...He used to have his tea and go back to work - no sleep - just took half an hour for his tea while we were haymaking or something - sit back and then 'back to work'.

John William Payne remembered his war service, which began at the end of his first year at college.

Then came the war and many people were of the opinion that it would end by Christmas 1914 and it was thought that 6 months in the Army would do me no harm! I joined up on 4th September 1914 in a London regiment, transferred to the London Electrical Engineers, and in 1917 was granted a commission in the Royal Tank Corps. On Boxing Day 1918 I arrived home on leave from France and discovered that students would be given immediate release from the Services.

The men who returned were changed. Marjorie Sykes told of Willie Tilbrook whose family lived at Bentons:

> The eldest son was away in the Army. He had a great artistic gift and we were shown some of his paintings. He was later taken prisoner by the Germans and for a long time that's all I knew of him. When he returned to the village at a time of release from the worry of the war, in spite of renewed expectations and hopes, it was also a time of difficulty in the readjustments that were necessary in the new state of affairs. He was a sensitive person and the years of trench warfare, and prisoner of war camp, must have been a severe trial to him; but he seemed so happy in the new life before him [working for Welch's and getting engaged], and was busy making very beautiful furniture for his and May's new home."

At the end of the war there was a Welcome Home meal at the Chapel Hall (see page 148), where Ralph Palmer, Walter Hargreaves, and Joseph Pegrum were prominent on the top table. All were parish councillors and probably contributed to the expenses. When, however, Essex County Council suggested more long-term provision for the returning soldiers in the form of cottages, land, and employment, the parish council declined to help. It claimed that these needs were being met by "private negotiation with Landlords" and by grazing rights on Nazeing Common, adding pointedly that "the employment of ex-servicemen would necessarily be restricted owing to the high rate of wages sanctioned by the Wages Board".

"An armistice for twenty years", 1918-1939

When the war ended in November 1918, it had brought dramatic changes. Men who had seldom left their villages had been abroad and had endured experiences which had been unimaginable previously. Women had played a vital part that helped to ensure them the vote, although initially only for those aged thirty and over.

At the signing of the Treaty of Versailles, in 1919, Marshal Foch of France commented: "This is not a peace treaty, it is an armistice for twenty years". With the rise of Hitler the fulfilment of this remarkably prescient prophecy seemed increasingly likely; from 1935 onwards Civil Defence planning took on an unparalleled urgency in Nazeing, as elsewhere. In 1936 the Lord Lieutenant of Essex asked Major Bury to help in raising a squad of volunteers to make good the shortage in the Essex Anti-Aircraft Unit of the Royal Engineers. Bury thought the Nazeing Branch of the British Legion might suggest suitable personnel and suggested a note to all members, calling attention to the serious threat of air-raids. On 7th May 1939 Archdale Palmer, as Branch Chairman, referred to a letter in the local press suggesting that British Legion members should join the County Police Reserve which was being formed, provided they were not already committed to other services of a national character.

The Second World War, 1939-1945

On 2nd September 1939 the *West Essex Gazette* wrote perceptively: "War means today as much to the civilian population as to the military forces in the way of danger."   Maurice Coleman recalled the following day:

> The sun was shining on Sunday, September 3rd, and I was at home at the crystal wireless set fiddling with the cat's whisker trying to get a better reception. I heard the thin, cool voice of Neville Chamberlain: "This morning the British Ambassador in Berlin handed the German Government a final note, saying unless the British Government heard from the German Government by 11 a.m., that Germany was prepared at once to withdraw its troops from Poland, a state of war would exist. I have to tell you no such undertaking has been received. We are at War."

> I immediately thought "Thank God. At last someone has the guts to tell that ****** what to do, and without thinking or considering my own responsibilities I was…saying to myself, here I am, take me." Gradually the reality of the situation dawned upon me, and…my thoughts wavered somewhat. But, again to myself, and before consulting anyone else I thought "Wait and see but do whatever you are called to do for your King and Country, and end all thoughts of Wars."

John Graham was only ten years old on the day war broke out, but forever etched on his mind was the fact that "Messrs Charles Judd and Fred Ashby were installing the bathroom in Lodge Farm". Daisy Nettle also remembered that day:

> When war was announced my baby son, John, along with other babies from Bumbles Green was being taken out for a walk, as they often were, by the young girls in the road. They were away for ages and we were all very worried about our babies. Usually they walked up the Common but when we went to look for them they had disappeared. Had the Germans got them already? Eventually we discovered that when the Common air raid siren had gone off, dear old Mrs Standingford who lived in the Red House on the Common, had taken them all in for safety.

This war, in Britain at least, was very different from the previous one, in that civilians were affected to a much greater degree. As the site of a major defence line and two airfields, the quiet country village of Nazeing found itself in the thick of things.

Defences in Nazeing

When in May 1940 Winston Churchill replaced Chamberlain as Prime Minister, he set up a Home Defence Committee, which considered that landings could be expected at any suitable beach along a 500 mile stretch of coast in southern and eastern England. It drew up plans for constructing defensive stop-lines, including the Outer London Defence Line, which followed a 120-mile course similar to that of the present-day M25 and passed through Nazeing. It consisted of concrete pillboxes and blocks, steel "hairpins" (a WW2 anti-tank obstacle consisting of a length of steel bent back on itself and stuck in the ground), and an anti-tank ditch that was up to eight feet deep and up to twelve feet wide.

In 1998 Essex County Council's Archaeology Section said of the Outer London Defence Line that

> the Nazeing to Copped Hall section retains the highest concentration of
> surviving pillboxes and anti-tank obstacles along the entire length of the line.
> In this five-mile section there are sixteen FW3/27a pillboxes, the only ones
> of their type in the county. There are seven concrete anti-tank barriers
> totalling over 60 three-foot-square blocks and two of the only three anti-tank
> 'hairpin' sites so far recorded in Essex.

The Defence Line entered the village on the east bank of the River Lea upstream of King's Weir where there are two anti-tank blocks, and a pillbox, clearly visible from the towpath on the west bank of the river and accessible from the footpaths on the east bank. This pillbox and the others within the village are constructed of concrete, with eight sides approximately eight feet long, and with a blast wall linked to the roof protecting the entrance. Each side has a loophole, so giving the pillbox a 360 degree field of fire for riflemen, and there is a cockpit in the roof, accessible from the interior, with a mounting for a medium machinegun. The line continues eastwards with the remains of a pillbox and blocks at the south end of Green Lane, then a concrete block and some steel hairpins in Paynes Lane, near Langridge Cottage.

The anti-tank ditch went over Clayton Hill and down to St. Leonards Road, crossing it north of Laundry Lane, and up towards Perry Hill. Just before the summit, and overlooking St. Leonards Road, there are a pillbox and twelve concrete blocks in two rows of six. There are then three more

Second World War defences: above, the pillbox by the River Lea and below, 34 of the original 36 concrete anti-tank blocks at Bumbles Green allotments.

pillboxes, one in a field at the top of Old House Lane, one at the junction of Perry Hill and Cemetery Lane with three anti-tank blocks, and one some way along Cemetery Lane facing north-east. This overlooks six concrete blocks in two rows of three, which covered a crossing of the anti-tank ditch, and there is a similar crossing in a field north of St. Lawrence Farm. The line continues to Bumbles Green where there were concrete blocks between the council houses and thirty-six at the allotments, of which all but two remain. There was a pillbox at the

Second World War defences: above , the demolition of the pillbox at Bumbles Green around 1970 and below, the pillbox at the top of Old House Lane with Perry Hill Farm in the background.

corner of Bumbles Green Lane, but the ditch continued behind the school, telephone exchange and Welch's garage, going on to Belchers Lane and eastwards up the hill from the King Harold's Head. The trustees of Nazeing Common were paid an annual rent of £5 for the 295 yard section passing through their land. The last pillbox within the village is on the brow of the hill east of Harold's Park Farm, beyond which the line continued southeast to Parvills Farm and down to where the M25 is now.

The evacuation of Bumbles Green

In May 1941 Parish Invasion Committees were formed for rural areas and throughout the country plans were earnestly drawn up for local action in the event of invasion. In Nazeing the parish council worked closely with the invasion committee and, in August 1942, circulated to all householders a leaflet entitled *What To Do If Invasion Comes*, of which it was rather proud. Councillors were therefore angered when the chairman received from the Air Raid Precautions (ARP) controller for Essex a petty-minded and ungracious letter, which suggested that the circular, if sent at all, should have been issued in the name of the Parish Invasion Committee. Archdale Palmer, who was doubtless courtesy itself in telling the controller what he thought, was left to put together a reply.

The War Plans for Nazeing referred only to the evacuation of the area around Bumbles Green, which would have been necessary because the anti-tank ditch isolated that part of the village. On 30th October 1942 the Invasion Defence Officer of the Waltham Holy Cross Civil Defence Service sent the Nazeing Parish Invasion Committee a letter headed MOST SECRET:

> ...at the meeting of the 10th September we discussed the probability of the evacuation of a portion of the Nazeing population owing to their isolation by anti Tank lines, and it was generally agreed (subject always of course to military situations) that the best method and route would probably be by walking from Bumbles Green along the Green Lane to the top of Galley Hill Green, thence to Aimes Green and via Galley Hill Road to Waltham Abbey. With this in view I have already provided for a reception post at Aimes Green, where I have erected an emergency cooking stove at the White Cottage (Mrs. Maloney) where I am also providing for an iron ration of tea, sugar and milk for about 300 people for a passing drink whilst resting. Also I am making arrangements for a certain amount of first-aid requisites to be lodged there. I have it in mind to provide from that point, transportation by car if at all possible.

In this connection there is a small point of very considerable importance which I would like you to take up, and that is to make some arrangements that people to be evacuated should not fail each to bring a knife, fork, spoon, cup & plate. In the present supply position this is a matter of prime importance.

The Invasion Committees all received secret instructions from the Minister of Home Security to support organised resistance to any German occupation, although how effective such resistance would have been is debatable. Early in 1945 the Nazeing Invasion Committee was stood down by order of the regional controller.

Digging for victory

The authorities tried to minimise the hardships caused by shortage of food. District Food Offices were responsible for ensuring fair distribution of food and for enforcing rationing control. In the summer of 1944 the arrangements for distribution of ration books and clothing cards and the location of the station in the ARP post at the Crooked Billet were said to have been "smoothly run and excellently organised". Little else is recorded about this aspect of the war in the village, but there were at least two ways in which Nazeing people contributed to the war effort by

Nazeing women helped the war effort by making jam. Standing: unknown, Vida Nicholls, unknown, Lady Hargreaves, James Sutherland, Rachel Geary, Mary Bailey and unknown. Seated: Mrs Garner and daughter, unknown, unknown, Joan Baker, Nancy Humphreys and Connie Cordell.

producing their own food, by growing it on allotments and by making jam.

Women who were not in paid employment were encouraged to take part in various kinds of home production. In Nazeing medium scale jam-making was organised at the Parish Hall ("the tin tabernacle") in Betts Lane. The organiser was Joan Baker, who lived at Roydon Hamlet. She had received a strict training at the Ministry of Food and Agriculture's College for Preserving and Canning. Miss Baker's twenty to twenty-five assistants came from Upper and Lower Nazeing, Broadley Common, and Roydon Hamlet. When the Upper Nazeing Women's Institute applied for free use of the hall "for the purpose of Jam making etc. under the scheme of the Ministry of Food", Archdale Palmer negotiated with the "Lady Chairman of the Institute" a special rate of 3s 6d per session, and offered to "store any of the jams etc, pending their disposal, in his own game larder".

Almost all the fruit used was grown locally. As sugar was rationed, supplies for the process were provided specially by the Ministry and kept in a storeroom at Rookswood under lock and key. When required a load was put into a tin bath by George Cordell, Palmer's chauffeur and was then taken along to the hall in a wheelbarrow by his wife, Connie. The jam was distributed by the Ministry, some through Jimmy Brent's shop at Bumbles Green. Being good and home-made, it was very popular.

After the Enclosure Award of 1861 the parish had set aside part of the Lower (Bumbles Green) Recreation Ground for use as allotments. In 1921, on a site deliberately chosen to be next to the new council houses, the parish council provided a new "Allotment Ground" behind Long Green, which was to be "solely for the purpose of cultivating gardens". The rent was usually 5s a year for each plot; at first no individual had more than two. When, however, John Nicholls applied for five vacant plots, councillors felt that it would be a "dangerous precedent to allow anybody to have as many as five allotments...in case other applicants came along", although eventually they decided to let him have them, provided that he gave up all but one if necessary.

As war approached, the Ministry of Agriculture urged parish councils to encourage the use of allotments, but this was sometimes easier said than done. In 1939 Nazeing Parish Council told the district council that the Town Planning Scheme (see page 159) should have identified more land in the Pecks Hill area, but apparently nothing happened. Four existing allotments were unlet because of the "character and poverty of the ground". Those to the south of Middle Street, behind the Long Green council houses, were blocked off by the anti-tank trench and were inaccessible to residents, while those on the Recreation Ground were only too accessible to rabbits and had to be wired off. Six Upper Town residents asked the parish council to find additional allotment space in their area and the field next to the Parish Hall was laid out at a cost of £26 9s 6d. By that time three of the applicants had withdrawn, one by leaving the village, one by having a son in the forces, and one by death.

During the war the parish made a small profit on the allotments but afterwards they ran at a loss. Only the site at "Brimmers Green" (Bumbles Green) was said to be in good condition, despite the 36 anti-tank blocks, of which 34 are still there. The Ministry of Agriculture and Fisheries asked that adequate land should be made available for allotments and it was agreed that there was enough to meet demand. This proved to be a sound judgment, as in 2001 not all the allotments were taken.

The dummy airfield: Nazeing Common

An important strategy in the early part of the war was the creation of around 200 decoy airfields, designed to divert the attention of the enemy away from real aerodromes nearby. K sites were intended to replicate the appearance of a normal operational aerodrome as seen from the air; Q sites were the night-time equivalent, designed to represent the working lights of an airfield after dark. The Common became one such dummy airfield, which was both a K site and a Q site. It was laid out with dummy aircraft and a flare path, as a decoy for the major operational fighter station at North Weald, four miles to the east. It was protected by a searchlight situated opposite Back Lane, anti-aircraft guns manned by the Royal Engineers, and a contingent of the Observer Corps.

John Graham recalled that

> The airmen from North Weald used to bring their beacon and flare path when the wind was in a certain direction to distract German bombers from the aerodrome target on to the dummy aerodrome on the Common. One used to stay out on duty with the wireless (R.T.), while the rest used to come in the farmhouse to play cards, or help us boys make our Meccano models or play with our Hornby Trains. Through them we received several extra rations of sugar, tea, etc.

91

The Royal Air Force (RAF) had laid out the same lighting pattern for approach and landing as a conventional airfield, and Les Kimm remembers seeing plywood Hurricanes and other aircraft dotted around with a few military type huts. The huts housed personnel who would move the aircraft around during the day to make it look more convincing to over-flying German aircraft. Soldiers guarding the dummy airfield lived in huts near the road to Lodge Farm, and one of the officers was billeted with the Grahams at the farm.

As elsewhere, the daytime K site was less effective than the night-time Q-site, when plywood planes were lit up. It was so realistic that in late 1940 the Germans dropped fifty high explosive bombs and hundreds of incendiaries in the area. Les Kimm and Nance Coleman, however, remembered a subsequent German propaganda broadcast in which William Joyce assured the villagers of Nazeing that they were perfectly safe because the Germans knew the airfield was a dummy. Joyce was better known as Lord Haw-Haw from his supposed manner of talking and Nazeing people, like most of the country, regarded his broadcasts more as a comedy show than as a serious threat.

Nazeing members of the Observer Corps (from 1941 the Royal Observer Corps), whose role was to look out for enemy aircraft. Standing from the left: Freddie Weir, Fred Myson, George Crowe, Mr Tilbrook then unknown except far right Ted Coleman. Seated: Fourth from left Mr Savage then Mr Cousins, George Cordell, Frank Kingham, George Rogers and Sid Myson.

A plywood dummy aircraft at the decoy airfield on Nazeingwood Common.

The decoy deceived the crew of a British bomber aircraft too. On 17th May 1940, whilst returning from an operational flight, a Vickers Wellington from 9 Squadron found itself short of fuel and dogged by a thunderstorm as well as by the enemy. Flight Lieutenant Rivett-Carnac, presented with a fully lit flare-path on an unidentified airfield displaying a degree of laxity in the black-out, brought the aircraft down towards the "runway" unaware that it was a decoy. The aircraft made a near perfect landing between the lights and came to a halt at the end of a line of flares after hitting a hedge at fairly slow speed. The aircrew were picked up after the resident RAF personnel made the necessary arrangements. Very little damage was done, even though they had landed in a shallow valley on agricultural land.

The aircraft could not be flown out of the confined site, so a crew came to dismantle it and send it to No. 9 Maintenance Unit for repair, where it was converted to a freighter and used as such until it was finally scrapped in 1947. Peter Brent, who lived opposite, remembered that part of a wing or tail-plane bridged a ditch, and that scrap metal dealers took away other parts. Dennis Mead later joined the RAF and was on a course when he requested weekend leave from the instructor, who asked him where his home was. Dennis told him that it was Nazeing, a little village in Essex that he would not have heard of. The instructor replied that he had heard of Nazeing because he had been the navigator of the Wellington bomber.

At first some Nazeing people felt that the military was prosecuting war more vigorously with them than with the Germans. Roy Leach recalled that movement was restricted: Nazeing Gate was manned by soldiers who challenged him and his father when they stopped to look at some lambs. The Air Ministry encroached upon the Common without reference to the trustees and was responsible for "the wrongful destruction of 45 willow trees at Cup and Saucer Pond". The ministry eventually paid the trustees £80 as compensation, but only after the Stuart Surridge Company, suppliers of cricket materials, carried out a survey to establish the extent of the damage. Archdale Palmer, games enthusiast and managing director of the Slazenger sports company, aptly described this as "The Air Ministry's Invasion of Nazeing Common". David Graham of Lodge Farm in turn made a compensation claim of £37 against the trustees for "damage caused to the grass in 3 meadows by the encroachment of Sheep and Lambs making their way through the hedges between the Common and his land". An investigation by Palmer revealed that much of the alleged damage had been caused by "the military and their lady friends" and the trustees offered Graham £5 "without prejudice".

The Allan-Williams turrets, like this one formerly on Nazeing Common, could be concealed more easily than conventional pillboxes.

In the southeast corner of the field opposite the King Harold's Head there was a prefabricated steel Allan-Williams gun turret, one of over a hundred issued to Eastern Command for use as strong points in defended positions. They were operated by two men, one to rotate the turret and one to fire the gun at enemy aircraft through a hatch in the top. The turrets were both intimate and private, and local gossip suggested that when two people occupied the one on Nazeing Common they were not always military personnel. By 1995 it was one of the two best preserved in the country so it was removed to Duxford and in 2000, repainted in what may have been its original colours, was part of the *Spitfire Summer* exhibition at the main Imperial War Museum. For many years buildings used by RAF personnel and for storage were a reminder of Nazeing Common's war effort but by 2001 the only visible remains of the dummy airfield were the two control bunkers east of Common Road, above the cascades.

The real airfield: Broxbourne Aerodrome

As well as the dummy aerodrome Nazeing had a real one. The Herts & Essex Aero Club airfield, which operated from 1930 to 1953, was one of many converted for wartime use. It was located on the north side of Nazeing New Road, on the site of the present Hillgrove Industrial Estate.

The establishment of the aerodrome began on 13th November 1930, when the Ministry of Civil Aviation granted a licence for flying. The fields there were farmed by Gerard Frogley whose two sons, Arthur (always known as Buster) and Roger, were leading speedway stars who made good money from the sport. They first appeared at the famous High Beach circuit, which was opened in 1928 on a site that later became the Epping Forest Conservation Centre. Within a year Roger was British champion and a household name in England and Australia. Flying was another of the Frogleys' passions, so they acquired their licences and adapted the farmland for it. Then they met Edward Darlow, who had been instrumental in forming a gliding club which flew from Fairlop Plain. He suggested that they might finance their hobby by forming a club and became the first Secretary of the Herts & Essex Aero Club, while the Frogley brothers developed the flying. In 1929 Buster married Hetty Wrighton, who obtained a pilot's licence and helped in the running of the business. In 1930 a clubhouse and hangar were added to existing buildings and W.R. Bannister became Chief Flying Instructor. He was killed in 1935, when he crashed in the English Channel, so Roger Frogley, who had obtained his "B" (advanced) licence, took over the CFI post with Buster as Managing Director. Doris Cook remembered watching Buster and Roger Frogley loop the loop and that she and her friends used to pick up wallets and combs which fell during the display.

From the outset the directors developed the enterprise energetically, realising the value of good publicity. Amy Johnson and the film star/comedian Will Hay performed the official opening ceremony on Sunday, 14th June 1931. A few years earlier Amy had become famous as the first woman to fly solo to Australia and as the first to obtain a Ground Engineer's Licence from the Air Ministry. She married the famous pilot Jim Mollison and the couple became Joint Presidents of the Club, remaining associated with it until the outbreak of war. The friendly atmosphere at the club encouraged private owners to base their aircraft at Broxbourne; other personalities associated with the Herts & Essex were Victor Ercolani, aerobatic champion in 1935 and founder of the Ercol furniture company, and show business stars Ben Lyon and Bebe Daniels, Clapham and Dwyer, and the Western Brothers.

It was not only the rich and famous who enjoyed the facilities of Broxbourne Aerodrome but also groups and individuals. One of the

The official opening of Broxbourne Aerodrome in 1932. Left to right: Roger Frogley, Fred Mockford, Amy Johnson, Jim Mollison, Hetty Frogley and Buster Frogley.

largest groups was the London Busmen's Flying Club, a separate entity with its own aircraft and instructors. Local youngsters who were members included Clive Darlow (son of Edward), his friend Derek Harvey, and Les Kimm. For a fee of 6d a week they were entitled to thirty minutes dual instruction for 4s and an hour of solo flying for 8s. At these rates most members gained their "A" licences for about £5 to £10.

The high standard of instruction became well known at home and abroad, so many students expressed a wish to stay at the aerodrome during their flying courses. As a result a large clubhouse was built, incorporating sleeping accommodation together with additional hangars and workshops. Nearby fields were purchased, and trees and hedges were taken down to extend the aerodrome and make it one of the finest privately owned flying clubs of the 1930s. Membership grew rapidly and by 1937 the fleet had grown from one aeroplane to eight. The D.K. Aircraft Corporation, which had its office and works at the airfield, designed and built a low-wing two-seater aircraft but production ceased at the outbreak of war.

The aerodrome was the venue for various notable events. In 1935 it was on the course for the King's Cup air race and a demonstration was given by the designer of the Flying Flea, a £70 build-it-yourself midget aeroplane, which created a lot of interest but was discontinued owing to the number of fatalities world-wide. In 1936, 21 year old Josephine Anne Nadin, having completed her ten jumps needed to qualify, became the youngest professional parachutist. In July 1937 the RAF organised an Open Day and the *Mercury* recorded that huge crowds arrived by bus, train, and cycle to watch, amongst other things, a dazzling display of aircraft handling by Roger Frogley, who took up a lady passenger who had paid ten shillings for the flight. This did not meet with the approval of Ralph Bury and the parish council, who complained to the Air Ministry about the whole event, in particular what they regarded as dangerously low flying and unnecessarily noisy engines. Such was the interest that there were also complaints about motorists who stopped to watch the displays at summer weekends and blocked the road.

With the approach of war a Civil Air Guard unit for flying training was established; by the end of 1938 it boasted a fleet of 24 aircraft accompanied by 13 instructors and 50 ground staff. Eventually the Herts & Essex trained up to 400 pilots to "A" licence standard, 75 of whom joined the RAF, 17 the Fleet Air Arm, and 18 the Air Transport Auxiliary

(ATA), while 30 became Instructors. Among the pilots was Hetty Frogley, whose guests at the aerodrome included many West End stage personnel, some of whom went on to become ATA pilots delivering aircraft of all types to aerodromes throughout the country.

At the outbreak of war in 1939 all private and club aircraft were grounded and many considered not suitable for military purposes were left to rot. Broxbourne was taken over by the Ministry of Air Production and run by the Civil Repair Organisation. It became a repair and maintenance base for light aircraft and the Frogley brothers formed a new company called Herts & Essex Aviation Ltd. In 1942 a new hangar and dope shop were built for the covering of wooden framed aircraft with sheets of fabric. Two or three coats of dope (paint) were then applied, followed by topcoats of coloured paint or camouflage. Former Herts & Essex employee Harry Smith explained the value of a work force drawn from local firms such as T.M. Gardner, who were skilled in the handling of wood for cricket bats and tennis racquets. They were ideally suited to repair wooden aircraft, as were cabinet makers from bombed out premises in Shoreditch and elsewhere in London.

Peter Ayles instructing an Air Training Corps cadet, c1950.

As Broxbourne Aerodrome retained this role throughout the war, a number of operational aircraft landed at the tiny airfield. Les Kimm, who worked and flew there, reckoned that there were about 400 employees, mostly arriving on bicycle or bus from the surrounding district. Such was the labour shortage that "girl fitters", recruited from London and given about six weeks Government training, worked alongside the older hands and did an excellent job. Most damaged aircraft arrived by road on low loader transport but, when the company was awarded a contract to modify Canadian-built Harvards to RAF standard, some fifteen aircraft flew in on the same day. This was a vital contribution to the war effort. The variety of aircraft which were kept in flying condition for training and communication roles included French planes brought over after Dunkirk and renovated for use by the Free French Air Force.

On 13th September 1940 two high explosive bombs landed close to Monty's Café, which was used by people from the aerodrome and passing lorry-drivers; roof tiles were blown off and windows were smashed but the aerodrome employees were still able to use it for their refreshment. According to a good though unconfirmed story, a man waiting for the bus was tipped head-over-heels by the blast but picked himself up unscathed.

1947 floods with the aerodrome buildings in the background.

One RAF Hurricane pilot from North Weald used to fly in to spend weekends in Broxbourne. He was allowed to borrow his CO's aircraft but on one occasion, to get back to his own station, he took off in thick fog and crashed into a glasshouse. When the aircraft was being recovered the propeller caught the glasshouse frame and the engine started. On another occasion Doris Cook and friends "saw a large aircraft try to land, go through the hedge and end up near Three Quarter Mile [Dobbs Weir] Road".

Roy Leach said that after the Battle of Britain his family's house and garden in Nursery Road, which backed on to the airfield, were requisitioned and they did not return until after the war. When the anti-aircraft guns were brought to the airfield, without prior notice, two soldiers walked through their garden. His grandfather was most suspicious because people were on the look-out for fifth columnists. He told another story of some First World War veterans who believed that there was someone signalling to the enemy; this turned out to be a cowshed door swinging to and fro during milking after dark.

The Tiger Moth which in 1951 crashed into trees at the aerodrome.

After the end of the war, when the Air Ministry offered aircraft to flying clubs at £50 each, the club acquired three of them and reconstituted itself as Herts & Essex Aero Club (1946) Ltd. Gradually the old members returned and there was an influx of new people, as the armed forces reduced their numbers. With charges at £3 per hour, in 1947 the total number of flying hours was 2,898. This revived activity was not universally welcome and the parish council complained to the Minister for Civil Aviation about low flying, especially on Sundays. They asked that flying should be reduced to a minimum because leisure flights, advertised to members of the public at ten shillings upwards, were "a serious nuisance which was interfering with the amenities of the district".

Disaster struck on the night of 22nd/23rd June 1947 when fire engulfed a hangar, destroying eleven planes. Club members, roused from the dormitories, pulled a few aircraft from the blazing hangars. These and three replacements kept the club flying. Recovery was such that in July 1949 the club received official recognition from the Minister of Civil Aviation, so pupils needed only 30 hours to qualify for their licences rather than the 40 hours for non-approved clubs. The club attracted new faces, among them the racing drivers Roy Salvadori and Stirling Moss.

Harry Smith recalled a number of crashes and incidents. As Under-Secretary of State for Air, Herts & Essex member Geoffrey de Freitas waived petrol tax for light aircraft, thus providing a subsidy for flying clubs. On one occasion he was flying solo and brought his Tiger Moth down to earth slightly more quickly than was prudent, so that it had a politically appropriate lean to the left as he taxied to the hangar. An Air Training Corps cadet on a pre-solo flight made an inept descent and landing approach, so he and his instructor landed in the trees at the edge of the aerodrome. It was lunchtime and the ground staff were in Monty's Café, so Margaret the cook, in great agitation, announced that there was a Moth in the trees. Lunch was abandoned and the ground staff retrieved the Moth for repair.

In 1953 the directors decided to move to Stapleford Tawney, initially with the intention of setting up a subsidiary club. There were massive amounts of sand and gravel under the Nazeing site, so the directors sold the land for extraction and the move became permanent. Flying all but stopped at the end of 1953 and the airfield closed officially in March 1954. The buildings were bought by the Wrightons, relatives by marriage of the Frogleys and members of the club. They built their kitchen furniture factory on the site. Even though the airfield existed for less than 25 years and no trace of it survives, the bend in the road there is still known as Aerodrome Corner.

Civil defence in wartime

Nazeing had its own civilian defence corps, which included Air Raid Wardens, Civil Defence rescue workers, the Fire Service, and the Home Guard. In the early part of the war the Bumbles Green Post Office was the village control centre. Harry Mead stayed up all night to receive telephoned reports of incidents and then organised a postal delivery at seven before getting to bed. There was another defence post at Poona Lawn in Nazeing Road.

Air Raid Precautions (ARP) for Nazeing were discussed first in 1936, when the parish council returned a twelve-page questionnaire on the subject to Essex County Council, although at that time it was thought more applicable to urban areas. In 1938 specimen gas masks were available for inspection and 94 men and twenty women volunteered to train as wardens. Theirs seems to have been an unusually democratic organisation, for in November 1938 they resolved unanimously to suspend their voluntary services pending the publication of a new

Home Guard, Civil Defence services and the Church Choir at All Saints', on 13th May 1945, the first Sunday after VE Day. The now demolished outbuildings of the Vicarage are on the right.

The Parish Council

NOTICE is hereby given that A.R.P. WARDENS are URGENTLY WANTED to fill existing vacancies in

Section B 10

Applications for Enrolment should be made to :-

THE SENIOR WARDEN, B 10,
(Mr. ARTHUR CORDELL)
OAKLEY, ST. LEONARDS ROAD

or at

THE A.R.P. HEADQUARTERS,
THE CROOKED BILLET INN

Between the hours of 7 and 9.30 p.m.

IT WILL BE APPRECIATED THAT THE PRESENT SHORTAGE OF WARDENS IN THE ABOVE SECTION INVOLVES A HEAVY STRAIN UPON THE EXISTING WARDENS

For The Parish Council,

ARCHDALE PALMER,
Chairman

April 12th, 1941

Printed by Thomas Knight & Co., Ltd., The Clock House Press, Hoddesdon.

By 1941 there was a severe shortage of air raid wardens in the Nazeingbury area, and Archdale Palmer published an urgent appeal for volunteers.

Government scheme transferring control of the ARP service to the police. The Western Area ARP Committee, the police, four representatives of the parish council, and the Nazeing wardens themselves attended a rapidly convened meeting. Evidently the wardens' concerns were resolved, because at a meeting in January 1939 they elected chief wardens and deputies for the three sectors into which the parish was divided, with Leonard Archer as the senior of the three chiefs.

**The Crooked Billet before the Second World War. In 1940 the cart shed on the
left was repaired so that it could house air raid wardens and fire equipment.**

In 1940 Nazeing Parish Council bought three stirrup pumps and six
buckets for fire extinction and paid £12 12s for 24 helmets for the
Wardens and Wardens' Messengers. Shortly afterwards Essex County
Council started paying for these helmets and over the next two years the
parish council made persistent but unavailing attempts to get a refund on
its outlay. Essex had recently acquired the piece of land where
Nazeingbury Parade was built later, so the parish council asked to use an
old barn there to provide accommodation for the ARP wardens and for
"the Parish Car with its Trailer, Pump and Pulling Vehicle". This request
was turned down and so, at a cost of £19 19s 11d, the parish council
carried out "trifling repairs" to a cart shed at the Crooked Billet. By 1941
there was a severe shortage of wardens in the Nazeingbury area, so
Archdale Palmer published an urgent appeal for volunteers.

The Nazeing Fire Brigade was a unit within the National Fire Service,
which was set up by Herbert Morrison, the Minister of Home Security, to
consolidate 1,400 local fire brigades. Its equipment was housed in a shed
behind Whitehall Farm, near the junction of Highland Road and Western
Road. The appliance was a Dennis fire engine, of the sort that was used
during later emergencies and acquired the nickname of "green goddess".

In addition the district council provided a two-man manual pump for protection of the council houses at Bumbles Green.

In May 1940 the Local Defence Volunteers were inaugurated. Self-deprecatingly they called themselves "the Local Duck and Vanish Brigade". In the following month, however, they received Churchill's more inspiring title, the Home Guard, and soon had more than a million men under arms. Consisting chiefly of First World War veterans, they prepared to combat the awaited invasion of the regular German army by uprooting signposts, patrolling tank obstacles, and lying in ambush with pikes, pitchforks, shotguns, home-made petrol bombs, and any more effective weapons that could be issued. That splendidly affectionate TV tribute *Dad's Army* may do the real thing something of an injustice, for later it was well equipped and professionally organised.

The three Deputy Lieutenants of the county, all military men, raised no. 10 Battalion of the Essex Home Guard. In classic *Dad's Army* fashion the Battalion headquarters was the Windowlite offices in Harlow; B Company was based at Passmores in Harlow and later at The Corner

Highland Road in 1927, when the pair of large wooden gates on the left led into the apple orchard of Nazeingbury Farm. For much of the war Sidney P. Taverner, who lived at Oak Porch House on the left, was the Home Guard Commander. The Home Guard and the Army Cadet Force used a nearby hut as a training base and drill hall.

Shop, Netteswell. Nazeing men belonged to no. 3 Platoon of B Company, which was led initially by Commandant A. Watts. He offered to donate a hut for use as an Action HQ by the Home Guard, provided that the parish council defrayed the costs of dismantling and reassembling it. Once again Archdale Palmer used his influence and the Mercers' Company contributed £20 towards the total cost of £25. The hut was erected near the Fire Brigade shed behind Whitehall Farm but, judging by various unflattering references in the parish council minutes, was rather an eyesore, so its removal soon after the war was unlamented. The observation post was All Saints' Church and standing patrols were located at the high points of Perry Hill and Maplecroft. As late as November 1941 the Home Guard instructed police to warn people in the area of the aerodrome to evacuate in the event of invasion, so evidently the threat was still being taken very seriously.

From Home Guard records and personal reminiscences we know something of the men who served in the Nazeing Home Guard. In 1941 Sidney P. Taverner of Oak Porch House was Commander of no. 3

Platoon, first as a civilian and later as a lieutenant; by 1944 Lt. J.T. Willats had taken over. Dennis Mead, who at the age of sixteen was a motor-cycle despatch rider before going into the RAF, said that one member, a Mr. Moore of St. Leonards Road, had served in the Boer War, forty years earlier. Doris Cook and Dorothy Dunster recalled that their fathers, Fred Dale and James Jones, were often on look-out on the tower of All Saints', along with the resident bats. Sgt. L.F. King, who owned the building firm in North Street and according to Doris Cook wore size 12 boots, was one of eighteen officers, NCOs, and men in no. 10 Battalion to receive a Certificate of Good Service.

Fred Dale senior in Home Guard uniform at Nursery Road in 1940.

Some auxiliary units of the Home Guard were trained to organise resistance with the aid of secret hideouts and arms caches. In 1941 there

106

were in Essex 169 such men in 28 groups, each with its own hideout. Although the secrecy means that there are no detailed records, it is possible that one of these units operated in Nazeing because of its aerodromes and its strategic significance on the stop-line.

Bombing

Initially Nazeing, like most of Essex, was classified as an area to which evacuees could be sent safely from London. The district council was responsible for sharing out among its parishes an allocation of 4,400 evacuees. Even before the war, however, the parish council expressed concern about unspecified "vunerable [sic] features presented by Nazeing to enemy Air-Craft". In April 1940 Col. Richard Andrew, as chairman of the Nazeing ARP Committee, wrote to Epping "deprecating the sending of any further Evacuees to the Nazeing area on the grounds of its vulnerability to enemy aircraft in consequence of the...Dummy Aerodrome". Evacuees who were to have been billeted in Nazeing were accordingly passed on to Ware but, as Essex was re-classified as a neutral area, those who were already in the village stayed. The district council used the Chapel Hall to give the evacuees a Christmas party which, with the help of the Women's Institute, was a great success.

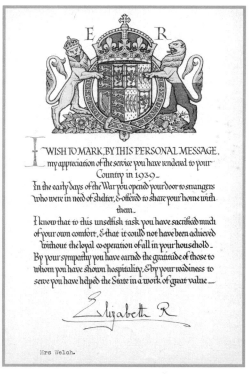

The Queen's certificate of thanks to Flossie Welch for housing evacuees.

Nance Coleman recalled that

> we were going to take two boys but they were diverted elsewhere and we had expectant mothers and tiny children"...Ministry people came and had a look round and said 'You're for evacuation' and we said 'But we've got evacuees here. Where are we going to take them then?' It was all laid out that we were supposed to go to Scotland with Mr. and Mrs. Gray. 'Oh

well, Mrs. Gray will know the way there. We'll be all right.' It never came off. We were glad because they were going to put holes in the house to put the guns through and the little cottage on the common was camouflaged. I was glad I didn't have to go - you have to leave your stuff - but I know people who left and went along to the country and when they came back there was nothing wrong only a little damp.

All over the country people were building air-raid shelters. In Nazeing the RAF gave eight Standard Shelters to homes near the dummy aerodrome. By 1941 the district council had supplied 23 brick and concrete shelters, capable of housing over 800 persons altogether, but there were complaints that they were not being maintained in a "proper and sanitary condition". Towards the end of the year private table-top Morrison shelters, which were erected inside houses, began to arrive in the village; by November 1942 147 had been delivered.

It became apparent that, in the event of a raid during school hours, children needed to be protected. Soon after the outbreak of war Col. Andrew visited the Bumbles Green school to discuss provision of shelters; work was started on them in August 1940. The Essex Education Committee provided two brick and concrete shelters for the Bumbles Green school and one for the Betts Lane school, each of which held about 100 children. Essex refused, however, to provide a shelter for children at the Chapel Hall school on the grounds that it was a hired building. Archdale Palmer regarded this "differential treatment" as "preposterous" and fired off telegrams to the county council and to the President of the Board of Education. Initially his intervention was unsuccessful but later a large brick shelter was built in front of the Hall.

Within a few week of completion the Bumbles Green school shelters were in use during daytime air raids. During the first winter they must have been very unpleasant, as there was no heating or lighting until two Davy lamps were delivered. Before repairs were done, the roofs leaked, floors were under water, and seat supports became broken due to frost. Once, in 1943, children had just returned to the classrooms after a morning alert when gunfire was heard and another alert sounded, so they had to crouch under their desks until it was thought safe to go to the shelters. Bus children who went home to dinner were detained until 1.45 pm and given barley sugars, presumably to appease their hunger. Paddy Hutchings remembered singing *She'll be coming round the mountain* in the shelter during one raid. The shelters were used frequently again during the flying bomb attacks, which started in June 1944. One shelter at Bumbles Green housed controls for the air-raid warning siren erected on two poles next to it. It was demolished in 1996, because it had become unsafe, but the other shelter remains on site.

The Senior Air Raid Warden, Leonard Archer, calculated that hundreds of incendiaries, 215 high explosives, and 28 other bombs fell on Nazeing. His list was published in the Reverend James Sutherland's *History of Nazeing* and reprinted in *Nazeing Parish News* of September 1987. This prompted many responses including one from G.E. Bell of Hyde Mead, who thought that Archer may have underestimated the number of bombs which fell, at least on Chapman's farm and nursery at Langridge, as he and friends had counted over thirty craters beside the banks of the old Lea, south of King's Weir.

Mr Bell added that he was in the Wormley Home Guard until he joined the Essex Regiment in August 1942. He spent a vast amount of time on night patrol during the early blitz and was a witness of attacks on the aerodrome on 13th September 1940:

> I actually saw this plane, a Junkers 88, dive out of the mist at 8.30am on that day dropping its bombs and could hear it machine-gunning the aerodrome. That evening I cycled from Wormley to see the bomb craters, one being in

Bomb damage at Langridge Nursery, 18th September 1940.

109

the middle of the road, the turning into Keyser's estate, the other being in the ditch which used to skirt this road.

He recalled that when the high explosives fell at King's Weir on 9th October 1940 Mr Snooks, the lock keeper, was winding up the gates and lost two finger tips, never recovering properly from the shock.

Not surprisingly, Nazeing people remembered the bombing more vividly than any other aspect of wartime life. Margaret Robinson recalled that a bomb destroyed a little cottage behind Camps, although the main house only lost some tiles. Roy Leach said that a bomb at the end of the Old Nazeing Road "made a crater big enough to hold a bus". He also remembered a Hurricane fighter crashing at Jacks Hatch, and that a V1 flying bomb was taken away on a lorry. Martin Harvey described a V1 in Crooked Way which blew out all the windows of the Little House in Middle Street, where he lived at the time. Several people remembered another V1 which landed in the branches of a tree in Hoe Lane; when the Bomb Disposal Squad opened it, they found not explosives but sawdust inside.

Nance Coleman said:

It used to be a wonderful place here - quiet, very quiet but unspoilt. Birds in the coppice and nightingales in Back Lane common - that's the sort of thing I remember. When the war was on and they dropped the incendiaries, that was the finish of those.

We used to get the bombers a bit near sometimes. We just all felt we wanted to be together and we used to come together in the kitchen, sit down in the lowest part and make a cup of tea and all have it together…German planes kept going round and round and round not dropping anything…that was the most worrying because we were all downstairs and couldn't go to bed. We used to put the children in the cupboard. We had made it safe as far as we could. The shelters were full of water and gnats - not much use taking children there. We thought we'd have to one night - they dropped on the common the bombs that hang in the air - candelabra. The common was just like daylight…

Isa Lavis recalled that, during winter evenings, Church Youth Club meetings were held at the Vicarage.

...Most members were in the choir, including several landgirls. One winter night, as several of us walked up the field toward the church yard, a "doodle-bug" approached from the Harlow direction, the engine cut out and it turned and glided towards Roydon Hamlet and landed at Roydon. Being frightened, we raced for the Vicarage. This was yet another escape for the church.

Doris Cook remembered

two lots of bombs in Nursery Road. Windows were blown out, glass light fittings came down but did not break, as they fell on soft furnishings; photos in glass frames were turned round and two glass flower vases ended up on the floor, unbroken with flowers and water still in them. Two people were injured, Mrs Bidwell and her daughter, Elizabeth Stantiford. The other was at the end of the garden on the aerodrome. There was also one on the corner of Keysers, where a ballast lorry was flattened. One fell on Boxing Day on Perry Hill, could have been a rocket, all the paper chains were up and they were having their dinner; there was dust everywhere and they couldn't find their knives and forks.

Doris and her brother worked at Ediswans in Ponders End right through the war. She recalled the hazards of travel to and from work:

For some of the time we started at 7am and worked until 7pm, but to 5pm on Saturday and Sunday. This meant leaving home at 5.45am to walk to the station. Sometimes there were bombs on the line and one morning we went over one but did not find out until the evening when no trains were running because of it.

When we were on our way to work, if the warning went, we would dive in the ditch and would put our umbrellas up as, for some unknown reason, we thought that would save us. A friend had said 'They'll think we're mushrooms'. One day when the road was machine gunned I got down under the bridge at the entrance to Nursery Road, which was wooden then instead of the concrete it is now, and wobbled as you walked over it. My father wondered where I was as he knew I had got off the bus and the family was in the shelter, a brick shed to which my father had added sandbags.

Les Kimm and his friends

spent many hours hunting around for pieces of shrapnel and selling them at a shilling a time. We had a good business out of that until the Red Cross caught on to what we were doing and [asked] people to give the pieces into them and they were selling them to raise money for the Red Cross.

On one occasion a bomb exploded in Tatsfield Avenue. In the side of the crater there was a big hole, so Les and his friends started digging for pieces of shrapnel and the spade hit something metallic. Ralph Newton told his father, who was the street ARP warden. Charles Newton looked into the crater and

called the bomb disposal people over and it was actually an unexploded

A bomb crater in St. Leonards Road. From the left: ?Bert Brown, Jim Crowe, Sid Myson, unknown, "Dusty" Brace, unknown, unknown, Kath Brett, Wally Byford and John Welch. Robin Pallett is standing in the crater.

bomb buried in the crater of the one that went off...We all had to move out of the area. Royal Engineers came and they pulled it out and took it up on the common somewhere and exploded it. We ran a bit cold when we thought we'd been clanking this thing with a spade!

Les also remembered a Heinkel bomber being chased by two Spitfires and discharging its load on the Common.

Although there must have been many other cases of bombs being dropped on Nazeing randomly or in error, there can be little doubt that the village was targeted deliberately as well. The comments of Col. Andrew and Lord Haw-Haw show that the Germans were attacking Nazeing Common specifically, at least until they realised that the airfield was a dummy. Ted Tulley who owned a nursery in Hoe Lane suggested that likely targets were the glasshouses, the real airfield, and the gravel extraction industry, as well as the Powder Mill nearby at Waltham Abbey.

The V2 rocket tragedy

The war had been going on for five years and amazingly, despite the heavy bombing, nobody in Nazeing had been killed. People must have been optimistic that the village would escape without any fatalities when, at 11.30 on the sunny Sunday morning of 12th November 1944, a V2 rocket fell in St. Leonards Road, killing ten people from seven families,

Destruction caused by the V2 rocket in St. Leonards Road, 12th November 1944.

and injuring many others. Having failed to cause any deaths with targeted bombing, the Germans succeeded with an unmanned missile which could have landed anywhere. Of all the episodes in Nazeing's long history, few can have been more tragic.

The rocket landed in the centre of the road opposite Lynton, a wood and asbestos bungalow owned by the Rumsey family, and produced a crater that "was large enough to take two double-decker buses". It set light to the gas main and burst the water main. John Weare from the Crooked Billet and Basil Rumsey were playing football in the drive of Lynton, and both were killed instantly. Basil's father ran a greengrocery van that was totally wrecked by the rocket; some recall picking up £1 and 10s notes fluttering from the remains of the van. For many years after the war Mr. and Mrs. Rumsey owned the grocer's shop on the corner of Hoe Lane.

Edward Carter, who was Chief Warden for the Waltham Holy Cross ARP Sub-Area, kept a diary which is a remarkable day-by-day record of his experiences. He helped with the rescue work in St. Leonards Road:

113

We drove right round by the [Bumbles Green] school…and on reaching the crossroads were told that we couldn't get down there as the road was blocked…

With all the open fields nearby, the rocket had fallen in the one place where it could do most damage; clean in the middle of the road among the small community of houses there. As we walked to the scene, there was the impression of dirt and devastation, two gaunt chimneybreasts pointed to the sky from the mounds of rubble where N.F.S. [National Fire Service], A.R.P. workers, and civilians worked, anxious to trace casualties. Here and there rose the thin wisps of dirty smelling smoke from small fires caused by burning coals blown by the blast from the cottage fires. The crater yawned right across the road…one side of the crater flamed from the escape of gas from the main which the explosion had shattered, while on the other side of the crater, a severed water main poured its contents into the gutters and the ditch…

…already the number of bodies had increased to six. One of them was a lad of about sixteen, and just as we were about to place him on the stretcher a young fellow of about eighteen arrived. He feared that it was his brother, and pulling back the blanket he took one look, and in rather a dry voice admitted that it was…

…More and more services were arriving, and ambulances filling and departing. Helpful neighbours and A.R.P. workers brought out the walking cases; faces white with shock under the dust of the explosion, thin trickles of blood running from cuts and scratches. Their world, in the midst of their preparations for their Sunday dinner, had suddenly vanished in a confusion of sound, dirt and violence and they seemed rather pathetic and helpless.

A stretcher is carried by, with a tiny child, not occupying one half of its length laid upon it; another is brought to the Ambulance with an elderly woman wrapped in blankets and wearing a large black hat at an awkward angle…

The rocket fell during morning service at All Saints' Church, and Connie Cordell recalled that "the earth shook even in Upper Nazeing, but it was a long time before we knew what had really happened". The vicar, James Sutherland, nevertheless guessed that it might be serious and went to the scene immediately.

On 16th November 1944 all the bereaved families attended a joint funeral service taken by Sutherland, having agreed that the victims should all be buried in a single grave. They were the first to be interred in the new churchyard, for which special permission had to be obtained from the

Bishop, as the graveyard extension had yet to be consecrated. Connie Cordell's daughter Betty Lamb, who was in the choir during the funeral service, said that the poignancy of the rows of coffins in the church was an abiding memory. Funerals are usually sad but the emotion and magnitude of the combined grief on that occasion must have been overwhelming.

In 1947 Sutherland held a meeting with the victims' relatives, who expressed their wish for a memorial in All Saints' Churchyard and agreed on a design. In *Nazeing Church News* for August 1948 the vicar's letter contains an appeal for contributions:

The Rocket Memorial in All Saints' churchyard is honoured every Remembrance Sunday.

> I want every householder in the parish to respond to the appeal and not to leave it to those who always give to good causes. Someone who is not at all well off came to the Vicarage with a donation last week and said: "Will you kindly accept this out of gratitude for our escape. It might easily been one of us lying there." It might have been one of us, yes, quite easily, and we were spared, and one way of showing our gratitude is by helping to erect as worthy a memorial as we can to those who were not spared. I had hoped that the graves of the civilian war dead would be looked after by the Imperial War Graves Commission, just as the service dead are. It was when I was informed that this was not to be the case that I made a first move about a memorial.

The target was £300, which would allow a balance for upkeep, and Cinderella Sainsbury of Brook Cottage, Middle Street, acted as Treasurer.

In 1994, on the fiftieth anniversary, a commemorative service was held beside the memorial and wreaths were laid. Afterwards Fred Sewell wrote to the vicar, Martin Webster. His moving letter was printed in *Nazeing Parish News*:

"Constant worry and anxiety"

Dear Martin

I know that during this year commemorating the D Day landings and next year's V E celebrations there will be many reunions of service men and women, and many will meet up with comrades whom they have not seen for many years. With this thought in mind I thought you might like to hear my story.

On receiving the November Parish Magazine, I noticed the announcement that part of this year's Remembrance Service would be held at the graveside of the V2 rocket casualties. Thinking I might be the only survivor attending this year's service, I decided to lay a wreath to the memory of my friends and neighbours tragically killed 50 years ago. I will mention at this stage I was only 7 years old at the time and lived with my parents and grandmother in the house called "Clovelly" in St. Leonard's Road. My grandmother and myself were dug out from the ruins of that house that Sunday morning in 1944.

As we filed round the grave side yesterday I became aware of a man standing beside me also holding a wreath. You asked this man to lay his wreath first and called him Mr. Lucas. This name immediately registered and I realised he had been my neighbour 50 years previous. After the service we met again in the churchyard and after introductions I invited Mr. Lucas (Jim) and his wife home for a cup of tea; as you can imagine we had much to talk about. Sadly Jim's story is not as happy as mine. He was 17 years old in 1944 and on that Sunday morning was out with his dog. When the bomb fell he returned to find his home flattened and rescue workers looking for his family. His mother Kate, brother George, and sister Ruby were all killed; only his sister Dolly and himself survived, both homeless. Four months later Jim was in the Army.

Over the 50 years since Jim has travelled from his home in Thundersley to Nazeing to lay flowers on the grave. In all those years he never met anyone he knew. That is until yesterday. In our two hour reunion yesterday we both recalled your reading of the account from E.J. Carter's *Diary of an A.R.P. Warden* in your address. I have known for some time that I was the tiny child referred to as not occupying half of the stretcher, and my grandmother was the elderly lady with the black hat. Jim told me he was the boy who identified his dead brother on the stretcher. Jim in recent years has kept contact with his surviving sister Dolly.

We said goodbye to each other at about 7 p.m. last night promising to keep in touch. A happy ending to a Remembrance Sunday which I will never forget.

Fred Sewell, Tatsfield Avenue

Clovelly was severely damaged, and Fred also recalled that, whereas he might normally have been out in the road playing with friends, he happened to be indoors at home with his grandmother. Although knocked unconscious like her, he escaped serious injury for the rather bizarre reason that he was under the kitchen table prodding some bags of chicken feed with a stick, since there had been signs of mice. Fred remembers coming round on a stretcher and seeing the flames of the gas main and water spouting up from the burst water main. Fred's father was at the Chapel and his mother was in the back garden feeding the chickens. Although she was blown the length of the garden by the blast, she escaped serious injury.

Jeannette Wardle, née Nichols, also wrote to Martin Webster:

> …I spent my childhood in Lower Nazeing and my grandmother, Mrs Ada Merrifield was one of the unfortunate victims on that November day…only by good fortune I wasn't with her that day, as I usually joined her for a cuppa but chose to do other things. However, when we heard the explosion and saw the plume of smoke, I cycled towards it, only to be confronted by an enormous hole in the road outside her home and nothing left of her dwelling other than the chimney stack. My grandmother was eventually dug out but died in the ambulance on the way to Hertford. I was asked to identify others but someone had the good sense to stop me, as I was only 16 (very young in those days)…

Seventeen year old Les Kimm, whose family had lived at Lynton until two years before, heard the explosion and saw the smoke from as far away as Wormley. He cycled over with a friend who, like him, was in the Air Training Corps (ATC). He recalled that

> There was lots of activity, people running about, and we immediately started removing rubble to try and get people out until the Special Constables came along. We were in ATC uniform but despite the fact that we were helping and they were all my friends under there, these Specials turfed us out. They said, "It's too dangerous, you can't go in there".

Many others still have haunting memories of this sad event, but none more vivid than some of the survivors who were within a few yards of the spot where the rocket landed. Several were youngsters at the time, including Robin Pallett who was ten. Robin lived with his parents at 4 Tatsfield Cottages, on the corner of Tatsfield Avenue nearer to the crossroads. He was playing in a field on the opposite side of the road with other children, including Don Newton and Cyril Hall, the three of them having climbed a large ash tree. Ironically, Don had been using his penknife to carve a V1 or "doodlebug" in a branch. Robin, Don, and Cyril were all blown out of the tree, Robin landing in some hay. Two of their friends, William and David King, were cutting sticks out of a hedge close to where the rocket landed and were very severely injured, dying later in hospital. In hindsight, Robin reckons the three of them survived only because they were well off the ground when the rocket landed. Instinctively they ran away from the scene, at first towards the crossroads, only to find their way blocked by the barn of Mulberries, which was on fire. They doubled back past the huge rocket crater and crossed St. Leonards Road to take refuge in Don Newton's home, Hillview, on the corner of Tatsfield Avenue further from the crossroads. The house was relatively unscathed, although they heard later that Don's father, Charles, had been outside and had been killed.

Robin, Don, and Cyril, who were all injured, were first taken to a temporary first aid post at The Rookery, and thence by ambulance to Hertford Hospital. Cyril, having had many tree splinters removed (the scars of which can still be seen), was discharged after about fourteen days, as was Don. As Robin's wounded neck had healed up, he

anticipated leaving hospital at the same time. At the last moment, however, an X-ray showed up a black shadow of something metallic in his neck, so he had to remain another two weeks for the object to be removed. Astonishingly it turned out to be a shattered half-inch nut, presumably from the rocket itself, which Robin still carries as a talisman on his key-ring. He, Cyril Hall, and

The nut that was embedded in Robin Pallett's neck. He still keeps it on his key-ring.

perhaps others suffered ear damage from the blast.

Hector Hall, Cyril's brother, was thrown some distance and found unconscious by his sister Rosemarie. He was severely injured, with a fractured skull, burns to this stomach, and many shrapnel wounds. He was taken to Hertford Hospital, remaining unconscious for a week. His parents, fearing that he would not survive, arranged for his Christening in hospital. He gradually recovered, however, and still remembers feigning sleep on Christmas Eve, as a nurse left presents at the bottom of his bed. Some of the shrapnel fragments are still in his chest and show up in X-rays.

The terrace of Nos. 1 to 4 Tatsfield Cottages was demolished except for the odd chimneystack. Robin's mother in No. 4 had been buried in the rubble, but was dug out virtually unscathed. When the rocket landed, Robin's father was about to cycle home from work at the Co-op nursery in Hoe Lane and would almost certainly have been killed or injured had the rocket landed five or ten minutes later.

These are those who died, whose names are inscribed on the Rocket Memorial:

Amelia Helen Green	35	3 Tatsfield Cottages
William George King	12	} Franwell, Tatsfield Avenue, bombed-
David Henry King	7	} out evacuees from East London
Kate Lucas	44	2 Tatsfield Cottages
George William Lucas	20	ditto
Ruby Gladys Lucas	12	ditto
Ada Rachel Merrifield	71	1 Tatsfield Cottages
Charles James Newton	42	Hill View, St. Leonards Road
Basil Rumsey	10	Lynton, St. Leonard's Road
John Henry Weare	9	Crooked Billet, Middle Street

Victory and after

On 8th May 1945 the war in Europe ended and soon parties were being held in streets and halls. Irene Rosendale, née Johnson, attended the one at Allmains Close (see picture overleaf):

I joined in the street party to have a bit of fun with my friends. I mean they were giving away free food and drink, so we all thought we would join in with that. I was 18 at the time and this was supposed to be a children's party [for five to 15 year olds], but I don't suppose they minded, it was just a bit of fun.

The party must have been on a weekend, as there was so many people there that would have been at work had it been held on a weekday. All the mothers baked cakes for the party, and it was a really good day as it was so hot and sunny. I remember there was a table in the middle of the road with all the food on it. I don't know how cars were supposed to get past with that table in the way, but then again, not many people had cars in Nazeing at that time.

Service personnel were being demobilised and there was a new Government but, although some wartime restrictions were being relaxed, in some ways life became even harder. In 1946, for example, the parish received a gift of food from Australia. The District Food Office at Epping wrote urging the necessity for economy in the use of bread and

Two VE Parties in 1945. Above at the Home Guard hut near Whitehall Farm in North Street. Below at Allmains Close.

the avoidance of waste but the parish council decided that "the situation was well appreciated in Nazeing". In 1950 parish councillors read in the local press that the Nazeing Food Sub-Office would be closed for reasons of national economy, shortage of staff, and low use, with only twelve callers per week in the previous three months. They protested, but to no avail.

As late as 1951 the Reverend Harold Hawkins suggested that rationing and shortages were forcing his parishioners to fast quite enough without the Church's telling them to. Soon afterwards all rationing and Food Offices were abolished in the "bonfire of controls" that followed the return of a Conservative Government.

Civil defence in peacetime

Although one war had ended, a new and greater conflict soon threatened. In 1946 Winston Churchill spoke of an "iron curtain" between East and West and by 1950 there were fears of nuclear war. The Government, with assistance from county and district councils, attempted to revitalise Civil Defence, so nine members of the Nazeing Women's Voluntary Service began to be trained. In 1952 a revival of the Home Guard produced only six volunteers in Nazeing. The detachment was in the 10th battalion and Kenneth May was the local commander. By 1956 there were still only 56 men and 5 five women enrolled in west Essex, so the battalion was reorganised on a reserve basis.

This lack of response was widespread, so the Home Office and county and district councils took responsibility for emergency planning and worked on the assumption that a war would be nuclear. Parish councils were not to be involved.

North of the road leading to Lodge Farm are the remains of a Royal Observer Corps post, constructed in the 1950s to be used to measure radiation and fall-out in the event of nuclear attack. The information would have been transmitted to the regional headquarters at Kelvedon, which was not decommissioned until 1994, when it became a tourist attraction. The Royal Observer Corps was disbanded later and the bunker by the road to Lodge Farm was filled in and covered over because it was flooded and the depth of water was considered hazardous.

The village would be informed immediately in the event of a nuclear attack. Controls for the air raid attack warning siren, housed behind the Bumbles Green school, were linked to the main area control at

Fylingdales in Yorkshire as part of the four-minute early warning system. Russell and Barbara Haynes, who lived at Old School House, were "caretakers" of the electrically operated siren and controls from 1962 until their decommissioning in 1993. Russell said:

> As ex-war service people we always thought this the right thing to do. During the cold war period the air attack warning system formed a vital part of the civil defence arrangements and in rural areas relied heavily on the spirit of community and responsibility of individuals.

When their duties ended, they received tributes, including one from the Home Secretary. In the 1990s, with the end of the cold war, contingency planning was limited to civil emergencies and Parish Council Emergency Response teams were created.

Service personnel and war memorials

In the First World War a total of 5.1 million British men enlisted, of whom 744,000 were killed. From Nazeing 153 men went and 33 did not return. Of those, four came from one family, which gives some idea of the great sacrifice made.

There was throughout the nation a profound desire to commemorate those who sacrificed their lives for the common good. Less than three weeks after the war ended, a special Parish Meeting resolved to erect a memorial which should "take the form of some work of public utility of advantage to the Parish" and a Memorial Committee was formed. There was from the outset a regrettable lack of unity over the matter, for the vicar proposed an amendment, seconded by the father of one of the fallen and only narrowly defeated, that a second memorial be placed in All Saints' and subscribers decide which their gifts should support.

The preference was for a scheme to prevent the flooding of the brook on the road between Greenleaves and Marshgate, with a memorial bridge at Dean's Brook. The Memorial Committee commissioned a survey, generously carried out free of charge by the district council's surveyor, estimating the total cost at £2500 to £2800. The committee thought this "in excess of what we might reasonably expect to raise" and made no recommendation, so a second special meeting voted for a more modest scheme costing £850. Walter Hargreaves told the Annual Parish Meeting in March 1919 that "the matter was in abeyance for a while in order to obtain the relatives' consent to the placing of fallen men's names on the Memorial Bridge", but no more was heard of the scheme.

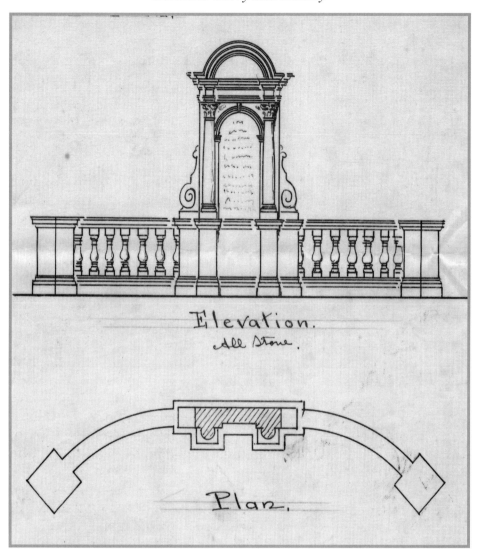

In 1919, plans for a war memorial at Dean's Brook bridge. It was never built.

In October 1919 the Chapel decided to act independently and so set up a Memorial Fund that was well supported by people throughout the village. A tablet was erected outside the chapel, at a cost of £75 5s 6d, and every parishioner was invited to a ceremony on 8th May 1920, when the memorial was unveiled by Alfred T. Davies, MP for Lincoln. The unveiling was quite a grand affair, with a big report in the local paper, and the large congregation included most of the leading figures in Nazeing.

Three cheers! Welcome home celebration outside the Chapel, 1919. The woman is probably Sophie Pegrum.

In 1924 the Parochial Church Council of All Saints' Church decided rather belatedly to erect its own war memorial. It would take the form of a lychgate to replace the worn out gateway at the entrance to the churchyard and would be inscribed with the names of the dead. The cost would be defrayed by public subscription and a letter of appeal would be sent to every householder, followed by a visit from a member of the PCC, which itself would contribute £20 towards the cost. The architect advised that the names should be recorded on a tablet in the church, so the lychgate was simply inscribed "Erected to the memory of those of this Parish who gave their lives in the Great War". The unveiling by Brigadier-General R.B. Colvin took place on 30th June 1925, with the Bishop of Barking, the Right Reverend James Inskip, conducting the service. Leaflets were sent to every household in Nazeing, seating was kept for the relatives of those who had died, and special tickets ensured that those who had lost friends in the war could find room. The PCC approved the accounts for the construction: "Expenditure on lychgate £460/5/5d. Receipts from subscriptions £460/5/5d." That seems very neat but begs one major question, to which no answer has yet been found: since that sum could have bought one of the small terraced houses then being built in the village, why did the work cost so much?

Although as many men and far more women went into the forces in the Second World War, far fewer were killed than in the First. It is difficult to be sure exactly how many Nazeing people fought in 1939-45, as there is no definitive list of service personnel. The British Legion Roll of Honour and other sources suggest that the total was about 260 men and women, some 13 per cent of the village population, of whom fourteen died on active service. These numbers reflect the national pattern where 4.7 million enlisted out of a population of 48 million and 398,000 were killed in action. Those from Nazeing who died in the 1939-45 war were commemorated in 1948 with a second board in All Saints', and in 1997 with a plaque next to the original one at the Congregational Church.

In 1995 the Nazeing Branch of the Royal British Legion marked the 50th anniversary of the end of the Second World War in two ways. With the support of the PCC, it placed next to the lychgate of All Saints' a Yorkstone memorial plaque which the vicar, Martin Webster, dedicated as part of the Remembrance Day service on Sunday 12th November 1995. In the same month the Legion planted a commemorative tree at Aerodrome Corner near one planted by the Nazeing branch of the Royal Air Force Association.

The new war memorial next to the lychgate of All Saints', 1995.

Although by 1996 the official list of war dead could be seen in three places, it was not complete. A man's name could be included only with

125

his family's consent and, by the time the memorial was erected, they too might have died or moved away. Further research has already revealed the additional names of C. Biggs, N. Bugg, J. Flack, W. Norton and H. Rose for the First World War, and more may be discovered.

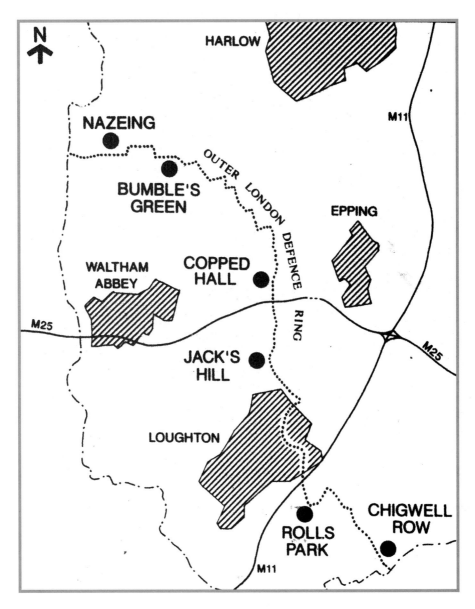

The path of the Second World War, Outer London Defence Ring that ran through Nazeing.

126

CHAPTER 4

"BUILDING SPECULATORS AND PRIVATE INDIVIDUALS"

The development of the village

In 1960, at the end of a decade in which 560 new dwellings were built in the village, the Nazeing Conservative Association told the parish council: "This Association...views with apprehension the continual applications by Building Speculators, Private Individuals and Commercial Firms to build within the Green Belt and in particular within the Parish of Nazeing." This unholy trinity, somehow rendered more sinister by the Use of Capital Letters, was responsible for most of Nazeing's development in the twentieth century, during which the number of dwellings increased from 173 to about 1,800. In order to understand why and how the village grew so rapidly, we must first look briefly at the broader national and local picture.

Planning policy

During the nineteenth century governments began to recognise the importance of planning in restraining the excesses of unbridled development, but their efforts were directed initially at the towns. Agricultural labourers were so poorly paid that it was uneconomic to build new houses for renting to them, and many rural cottages were, by contrast with our cosy chocolate-box image, squalid and insanitary. Early in the twentieth century middle-class conservation groups began to campaign on rural issues and the Liberal Government levied a tax on the improvement value of land. The tax proved both cumbersome and ineffective but, in attempting to implement it, the government carried out an extraordinarily detailed valuation survey. Popularly known as the New Domesday, it has proved an invaluable source of information about the countryside at the time.

The survey for Nazeing was carried out in 1912. It revealed that most dwellings, owned by conscientious landlords such as Ralph Palmer and Ralph Bury, were in good or fair condition. A substantial minority, however, were poor and described as "much out of repair" where they were damp or the walls had bulged out and needed tying in. Influential though the old gentry families were, they lacked the wealth and

127

**Aerial view of Bumbles Green, which could have been built up if Epping Rural
District Council's original ideas had come to fruition. The prominent
greenhouses were there for a short while in the early 1960s.**

inclination to put money into new or improved housing that would have
enabled the village to grow.

The greatest catalyst for national change was the First World War and
its immediate aftermath. Crippling estate and death duties meant that
between 1918 and 1922 a quarter of the agricultural land in England was
sold, mostly to those who farmed it. Much of it became available for
building, including land at Nazeingbury owned by the Wakes and the
Palmers.

In the 1918 election campaign, Prime Minister Lloyd George pledged
to build "Homes fit for heroes". During the short post-war boom, when
economic reality briefly matched social idealism, a start was made on
fulfilling his promise. The 1919 Addison Housing Act laid a duty on
local authorities to produce Town Planning Schemes (a phrase which
covered rural areas also), showing how they would meet the demand for
housing in their districts. The Act provided cash to support both public
and private housing projects, so Epping Rural District Council took up
this offer and built 28 council houses at Bumbles Green. The council

school, the King Harold's Head, and several shops were nearby so the council may have intended to develop the area further but, if that were the case, it altered its policy.

There was soon a deep slump and it became obvious that the provisions of the 1919 act were far too ambitious. In 1922 the Minister of Health introduced an interim order which allowed local councils that had not produced their schemes to permit reasonable development. Epping used this provision to initiate a form of zoning, under which it authorised housing development at Nazeingbury, with housing and light industry at Riverside. In 1927 the council resolved to produce a comprehensive Town Planning Scheme covering the whole district and the Town Planning Officer explained the objects of the scheme to Nazeing Parish Council, which considered it "advantageous to the interests of this Parish". The district council then had to wait over seven years for the Ministry of Health to produce "model clauses", without which it could not submit its scheme to the Ministry. For council officers it was difficult to set up a satisfactory system of control before an approved Town Planning Scheme was in place, while for intending developers it must at times have been like trying to play a game without being told the rules. Recognising the rapid growth of Nazeing and Roydon, the district council issued detailed byelaws with respect to the construction of new streets and buildings in the two villages.

In 1932 the first Town and Country Planning Act of any substance gave councils additional powers, which were intended to prevent piecemeal development, but its effect was weakened by their having to pay compensation "where injurious loss has been suffered by a building owner" through refusal of planning permission. The Act authorised councils to work together in planning matters and eleven west Essex authorities chose to do so, commissioning a wide-ranging report from Stanley Adshead, Professor of Town Planning at London University. The Adshead report provides a vivid portrait of west Essex in the 1930s; many of its ideas were to be adopted by county and district councils in the following years. They included proposals for a Green Belt in west Essex and for a major road interchange at Stoneshot Common.

In 1935 Epping published the first draft of its Town Planning Scheme but Essex County Council asked for modifications to meet the requirements of the 1932 Act. It made an offer, which the district council accepted, to revise and complete the scheme. Early in 1939 Essex published the Epping Rural District Planning Scheme, which owed much to the Adshead report and laid the foundations for planning policy still in force today. Brian Hills and others were still using the accompanying multicoloured map in the 1970s. The twelve categories of land use fell into three broad groups - residential, industrial, and rural. The plan abandoned any intention of developing Bumbles Green for housing and opted for Keysers and Nazeingbury, which had already seen some growth. Those areas therefore changed out of all recognition, while other parts of the village remained relatively unaffected. The Nazeing New Road area was earmarked for industrial development because it was close to the railway and the floodplain of the Lea.

During the 1930s increasing car ownership and new underground lines meant that London was sprawling outwards rapidly, so the London County Council (LCC) and town planners such as Patrick Abercrombie advocated the establishment of a Green Belt to put a limit on its expansion. In 1938 their proposals were enshrined in the first Green Belt Act, which authorised the LCC to assist the surrounding counties in buying up land to prevent unsuitable development - a surprisingly effective measure that pointed the way to policy introduced much later. The LCC and Essex tried to buy land at Denver Lodge Farm and Colemans Lane for £50 per acre but nothing came of it. After the war councils relied on stronger legislation to enforce Green Belt controls on private owners.

The Second World War meant that the 1939 plan and others like it had to be put on hold. As the war came to an end, however, the idealistic determination to build a better world was, if anything, even greater than before. In 1947 the Labour Government passed a much stronger Town and Country Planning Act which gave local authorities sweeping powers to buy up land and develop it for housing. An Agriculture Act in the same year envisaged a partnership between planners and farmers that would manage the countryside on behalf of the wider community.

The Town and Country Planning Act obliged county councils to produce development plans that would state whether individual settlements would be selected for growth or allowed to decline. In 1952 Essex was one of the first to publish its plan, which showed "the proposed ultimate development of Nazeing". Some residents may have deplored the growth of the village but the experience of other remote villages suggests that the alternative might have been worse. The population

An aerial view of Nazeingbury in 1960 when development was almost complete. The Nazeingbury crossroads is close to the left edge, slightly below the centre. Middle Street runs from there to the centre of the picture then turns towards the bottom right. Shooters Drive and Palmers Grove are at the top.

would almost certainly have declined and amenities such as Nazeingbury Parade and St. Giles' would not have been built. The new school at Hyde Mead would not have been built and the old one at Bumbles Green might still have been closed. Rapid housing development throughout the south-east meant that the 1952 Plan was out of date even before the Ministry of Housing and Local Government approved it in 1957; a Review Plan begun in 1955 was not approved until 1964.

The election of a Conservative government in 1951 resulted in the restoration of a predominantly free market policy for housing development. The powers of local authorities were weakened and they became dependent for the execution of their plans on landowners and builders, who had the incentive of being allowed to make and keep substantial capital gains. Private developers carried out most of the housing development in Nazeing after 1951. In 1956 the Nazeing Liberal Association complained about "the uneven density of house planning in Nazeing", to which the parish council chairman, Frank Radford, replied that "the building now being carried out was planned in 1938-9 and could not be altered." The uneven density was no accident but a deliberate policy limiting growth to specified areas, known in planners' jargon as the "village envelope".

In 1955 the previously somewhat *ad hoc* Green Belt arrangements were adopted as government policy. The parish council declared that it "appreciated the advantages of being located within the Green Belt" and would "use its influence to ensure that any development outside the residential boundaries but within the parish boundary" should be consistent with Green Belt policy. For developments in Nazeingbury and Riverside councillors contented themselves with commenting on comparatively minor matters such as footpath diversions. They raised no objections to appropriate small scale building elsewhere; their comment on an application to redevelop two derelict cottages in Back Lane was that "one good dwelling is better than two untidy below standard dwellings". They did however, oppose successfully, proposals for developments in the Green Belt, such as applications in the 1950s and 1960s to build houses on the field between Darmers and Newlands in Middle Street.

In his plan for the post-war Greater London region, Abercrombie proposed eight new towns beyond the Green Belt to absorb the overspill population from the capital. The New Towns Act was passed in 1946, with Harlow as one of the proposed sites. Nazeing Parish Council objected immediately and representatives attended a public inquiry at Harlow, where they learnt to their relief that the designated site for the New Town constituted the parishes of Harlow, Netteswell, and Great and Little Parndon, together with the eastern end of Roydon. Under a local government reorganisation begun in 1949 and completed in 1955, the rural district councils of Epping and Ongar merged to form Epping and Ongar Rural District Council, while Harlow became a separate urban district.

Even then Harlow had no covetous intentions towards Nazeing. Yet, when the preliminary findings of the 1961 census were published, they showed that a quiet social revolution had taken place. The children of the first generation of Harlow settlers were now setting up their own homes, thereby almost doubling the number of households. The government mooted the possibility of enlarging the new towns and Harlow Development Corporation saw the opportunity of expanding into surrounding villages. The story of west Essex over the next twenty years consists above all of the largely successful fight against that expansion, ending only when the Corporation was wound up in 1980.

In 1970 Nazeing and Roydon had been identified as being in a "mature commuter area" where house prices were being forced up more rapidly than anywhere else in west Essex. In the 1960s an average of 100 dwellings per year had been built in the two villages but the only scope for expansion in the 1970s was for 150 houses in Nazeing. They were built at Barnard Acres and various smaller developments.

By the 1970s the climate of opinion in the countryside had changed greatly from that of 1947. Planning policies were considered too inflexible, while increasingly intensive farming methods were seen as spoiling rather than protecting the land. The countryside nevertheless became increasingly a place to escape to rather than from, and many Londoners "leapt across the Green Belt" to settle in the surrounding counties. They brought to their adopted villages effective campaigning skills, but also they attracted accusations of self-interest, so that a new word entered the language: a nimby (not in my back yard) was someone who opposed development close to their home. Interviewed in the early 1980s, the chairmen of 38 planning committees in the south-east complained that preservation societies almost invariably argued against change, regardless of the local situation or the wider context. Yet without such organisations the countryside would have been despoiled even more than it has. Often, as in the case of the Nazeing Conservation Society and the Roydon Society which fiercely opposed the expansion of Harlow, official opinion has eventually come round to the side of the village organisations.

In 1974 another local government reorganisation sought to unite urban and rural districts in new larger authorities. Epping and Ongar Rural District Council (less five parishes that went to Brentwood) was merged with the Urban District Councils of Epping, Waltham Holy Cross, and Chigwell to form Epping Forest District Council. This delayed further the submission of a new Essex County Structure Plan, which was approved at last in March 1982.

By then the 1979 Conservative government had declared that planning policy would be more responsive if carried out closer to the grass roots. So in 1983 Epping Forest District Council produced a detailed draft local plan for Roydon, Waltham Abbey, and Nazeing. It emphasised the huge economic influence of London, where almost half of the local working population was employed. Some did little more than sleep in the village without becoming involved in the community, thus arousing the resentment of locals. The influx of senior managers seeking to enjoy the amenities of the countryside pushed up house prices, so that young people were unable to secure housing in their own villages. There was an unbalanced population profile with a disproportionately low number of people in their twenties and a conversely high proportion in their thirties. The council therefore sought sites to provide low-cost housing for young first-time buyers but often met resistance, thus highlighting the conflict between preservation of the Green Belt and provision of new housing that bedevilled planners in the late twentieth century.

Riverside

The first part of Nazeing to be developed in the twentieth century was

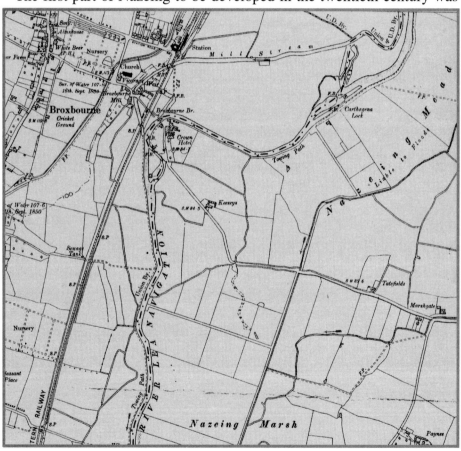

Riverside in 1898, as shown on the Ordnance Survey ...

Riverside, the area west of Nursery Road and Paynes Lane. Having always been liable to severe flooding, Riverside was unsuitable for large-scale building until the late nineteenth century, when the Lee Conservancy began to deepen the channel of the river and raise the level of the adjoining ground. At that time the area was home to some eighty people living in fourteen households. A century later there were 392 households and about a thousand people, making twenty-five times as many households and thirteen times as many people.

Riverside was always part of Essex and of Nazeing but the Post Office never recognised such administrative boundaries, resulting in the odd quirk that properties there still have Hertfordshire postal addresses and Hoddesdon telephone numbers. Some new Riverside residents therefore only realise that they are living in Essex when their first council tax demand drops through the letter-box.

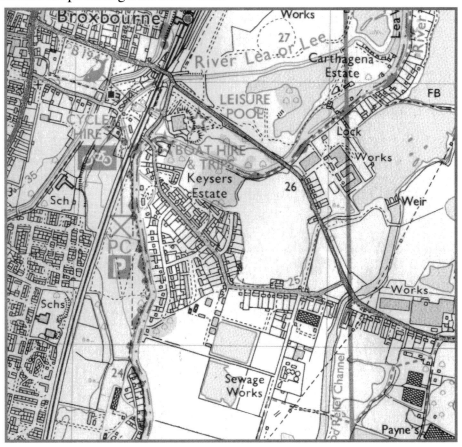

... and the same area a century later.

Development began in 1908, when Nazeing New Road was constructed and land around Keysers Farm was sold for development. A "Plan of Freehold Land" published in that year shows proposed roads, houses, shops, and a hotel, not all of which materialised. Seven bungalows and five houses were soon completed but the First World War halted progress. But for this early residential development, the Lea in Nazeing and Broxbourne could well have looked utterly different because inter-war planning policies at national, regional, and local level all envisaged that such floodplain areas would be zoned for industry. Nazeing Parish Council was successful in opposing proposals in the 1939 Hoddesdon Town Plan to build factories on the Hertfordshire side of the river because they would be situated opposite residential property.

As Keysers developed, there was on both sides a sense that it was separate from the rest of Nazeing. When the new estate had problems with sewage disposal, Epping Rural District Council recommended that a field should be rented "where the tenants might dispose of the contents of their cesspools". The parish council was most unsympathetic, arguing that "all lands in Nazeing that are suitable for housing [had] manure pumps, which can be obtained from Agricultural Engineers and used by householders to the advantage of their gardens". Keysers, by contrast, was not suitable for dwelling houses; "being water logged in winter, and

Old Nazeing Road on the Keysers Estate in 1960.

136

without any natural drainage fall ... a state of affairs that must have been obvious to the builders or purchasers of houses ... We are unable to recommend that the occupiers of houses at Keysers should be relieved of their responsibilities..."

In 1922, residents complained about the lack of publicity for elections to the parish council, which insisted that notices had been properly posted but conceded that, "in view of the large numbers of residents in the outlying districts known as Keysers Estate", an additional notice would be placed at the Crown. At first this made little difference, for in the 1925 elections four Keysers men stood but none was elected. When in 1926 Keysers residents suggested to Essex County Council that the area might be formed into a new parish, Nazeing Parish Council commented that it "had no desire to oppose the scheme in any way", but nothing came of the proposal.

By 1934 relations had improved. The district council's Town Planning Scheme had designated the Riverside area for industry, and Keysers people began a campaign to have their part of the area "de-zoned" for residential use. The council refused to reconsider its decision and advised them to "ventilate their troubles" at a meeting that the Ministry of Health would organise when the scheme was published. Having satisfied itself

Keysers farmhouse, which stood at 104 Old Nazeing Road, was demolished in 1971 as part of the North Barn development.

that Keysers residents were united on the matter, Nazeing Parish Council advised them to ignore Epping and go straight to the Ministry. At Archdale Palmer's suggestion they approached Winston Churchill their MP, who tried immediately to meet with the Minister. As this was not the most influential period of Churchill's political career, the Minister "did not feel inclined to carry out the proposal". Therefore the campaigners changed tack and decided to await the promised public meeting. This was not needed in the end for, when Essex County Council published the scheme in 1939, Keysers was zoned as residential.

The bulk of the original Keysers estate was built between the wars at Riverside Avenue, Old Nazeing Road, Buttondene Crescent, and Green Lane. After the Second World War more houses were erected in those roads and Keysers Road was laid out. Between 1969 and 1974, with the building of Crownfield, Great Meadow, and North Barn, the development of Riverside was more or less complete.

From annotations on the 1908 Plan and the deeds of a house in Riverside Avenue, we can trace a typical development. Plots 50, 51, and

St. Raphael, Riverside Avenue.

52 had a combined river frontage of 270 feet, while a stream snaked across no. 51 to the Lea. The plots passed through various hands until, in 1935, Frederick Wrighton of the furniture manufacturing family purchased all three for £1,900. On Plot 52 he built a bungalow named St. Raphael, as a one-room weekend retreat, and added to it over the years. He laid out tennis courts on Plot 51, which remained intact for nearly thirty years. In 1965 a large part of the site was sold off for the building of four houses and a culvert was constructed for the stream to flow under them. In the late 1990s three of the owners purchased land from the Broxbourne Rowing Club for river frontage.

Part of the splendid interior of St. Raphael, Frederick Wrighton's new riverside bungalow, would not have been out of place in one of Nazeing's many historic buildings.

The development of the Riverside area was not without its problems. In 1937 the "simply appalling...dangerous and unsightly" road surface of Riverside Avenue was blamed on neglect by the frontagers, who were told that, if they did not maintain the road, Essex County Council would make it up and bill them. In 1957 concrete posts were installed at Keysers Road, then an unmade roadway intended for pedestrians only, to prevent a builder's lorries from using it as a short cut to the new bungalows he was building in Riverside Avenue. In 1968 "the disgusting state of land owned by the Essex Construction Company at Old Nazeing Road, where weeds were four feet high and the footpath was impassable", led Councillor Laird to complain "in the bitterest possible terms about the deplorable state of verges, footpaths, and hedges in Riverside" and to allege that "County Highways did not want to know". Soon afterwards the blocking of watercourses, due to pumping out of water in preparation for the building of Great Meadow, caused flooding and subsidence in Riverside Avenue.

A view of Keysers Estate and the River Lea with Broxbourne Lido top left.

A group of small developments in Nazeing Road, including Tatsford Villas, was known between the wars as the Brooklands Estate. There was good money to be made from them, though not necessarily by the builders: one terraced house completed in 1924 was bought by an estate agent for £400 and sold later the same year for £600. By 1939 Kingsmead and Black Adder Cottages also had been built.

Plotlanders

Between the wars many people living in big cities bought plots of land in the countryside, in many cases for £5 or even less. These pioneers had various names but in London they were called plotlanders. Land was cheap in the agriculturally depressed areas of south and west Essex so

A typical plotlander cabin in 1931. Lynton was destroyed by the V2 rocket that fell on St. Leonards Road in 1944. (see page 112)

Nazeing, being close to the railway and the river, was a prime candidate for this type of development. The plotlanders were concentrated in Riverside at Carthagena, Old Nazeing Road, and Nursery Road, and there were some at St. Leonards Road. Planning regulations were still fairly relaxed and the new arrivals were able to put up dwellings which varied considerably in quality, from converted railway carriages used mostly for weekend breaks to well-built permanent houses.

The late Roy Leach's grandparents built a bungalow in Nursery Road:

It was named after Lord Northcliffe, who gave employees a bonus, and it was bought and built with that money. My grandmother had a large picture of Lord Northcliffe hanging in her bedroom. Bill Porter is Doris Cook's nephew and the people who lived in Wilbank were also her relatives, bungalow named after William (Windy) Banks. Arnold, Charlie, and Lewsey [other

141

Nursery Road residents] were in the trenches together in the First World War - Arnold had severe scars from mustard gas and all their lungs were affected by it. They all came to buy plots of field 320, which was being sold off by the man who owned Nazeingbury and was going bust.

I was born in January 1934 in a hospital in London, as Nursery Road was not suitable for babies - they had no water or electricity, just gas. Then I was brought to Nursery Road later, where my parents had lived since 1928. My father and grandfather worked in Fleet Street and they would come to Nursery Road after a good day's work except in the bad weather, as they had property in London. They could only travel by train so they stayed in London in winter. In the summer my dad, grandfather, and two uncles worked on Northcliffe, the only one they owned. Others were acquired as owners sold up...

Doris Cook also remembered those pioneering days:

I was born in 1923 and lived in Nursery Road with father Mr Dale who bought land from Benjafield which had a field by the side; more people bought plots and gradually filled the field...Aunt and Uncle bought next plot, so Dad and Uncle used to go down on Friday nights, with food, and Mum would take children down on Saturday or Sunday, walking from the station along what is now the Old Nazeing Road. There were gravel workings and Great Meadow etc. were fields. There were plans to build houses but, as ground was too marshy, bungalows were built instead - my brother-in-law had put a deposit on one but ended up buying a house in Western Road, which I remember as fields.

Shamara, built by Arthur Harknett along the Lea near Dobbs Weir Lock. On the left is the house under construction and on the right it is nearly complete.

They lived further along from the Leaches in what is now Plowmans, which has brick on the outside of their wooden house - shiplap, tarred and creosoted every year. The roof was a combination of flat and gables - two rooms as you went in through porch - living room and bedroom with bunk beds, two more bedrooms added - parents and brother, then two more rooms added - a bedroom, and a room you walked through to get to it, as an antique room with black beams on white walls and antiques, not necessarily valuable. I take after my father as regards a love of antiques, being one myself...

Paddy Hutchings recalled that her father, Arthur Harknett, built three bungalows, the first of them near the Fish and Eels. The second, at the Meadgate end of Nursery Road, was slightly larger; when he had completed it he moved into it and sold the first. The third was larger still; again he moved into it and sold the old one. The first two were comparatively flimsy and did not survive, but the third, Naivete (now Naivette) in Nursery Road, was rebuilt and extended in 1993-4.

The 1932 Town and Country Planning Act was intended to prevent piecemeal developments of this sort and may have impeded them in Nazeing. In 1945 the district council formulated a scheme intended to "prevent the erection of unsightly Shacks" at Riverside; the stronger 1947 Act, which enforced tighter regulation of rural areas, brought plotland building to an end.

Nazeing Glass and The Meads

At the time of the New Domesday survey in 1912 the area where the Nazeing Glass industrial estate and 1-12 The Meads now stand was occupied by one substantial farmhouse and a few outbuildings. The house was called Goats and had been owned since 1899 by Herbert Edward Hughes. It boasted some twenty rooms, and verandahs with fine views over the river. The outbuildings included an electricity generator, greenhouses, stables, pigsties, and a purpose-built brick shed that housed fifty goats of the then famous Broxbourne breed, which gave the farm its name.

In 1865, under the Nazeing Enclosure Award, the Palmer family had acquired the adjoining piece of grassland; in 1908 Ralph Palmer allowed Nazeing New Road to be built through the middle of it. In 1924 Archdale Palmer offered it at auction as two lots, one either side of the main road. The following year he sold the lot south-west of the road for £1,200 to the Enfield Highway Cooperative Society, which incorporated the land into its Rusheymead Nursery and in 1933 built a house for its manager.

143

This view of Goats Farm from across the river shows just how impressive a building it was. Carthagena Island is in the foreground.

In 1928 Palmer sold two acres of the lot north-east of the road to Hughes and soon afterwards the bungalows at 1-4 The Meads were built there. The local builders Charles Judd and Edward Coleman had offered £1,050 for the whole of this lot but complained that "the land in question was entirely covered with water and therefore unsuitable for building development". Palmer's solicitor replied with some justice that "since Mr Judd lives in the locality he must have known that the land is liable to be flooded at uncertain periods".

Both sides, however, had something to gain and 1931 Palmer accepted Judd & Coleman's offer of £800 for the remaining land. The agreement was for them to start with the plot nearest to the river and build pairs of houses in order but, after they had completed 5-8 The Meads, they had a specific request for a house to be built at the other end of the row which, with the agreement of Palmer, they did. This left the third plot undeveloped. Presumably Judd & Coleman could not raise the money to do it, for it was not until the 1990s that the gap was plugged. Their concerns about the Riverside area's suitability for housing were not entirely unfounded, because there has been subsidence at The Meads and on Keysers Estate.

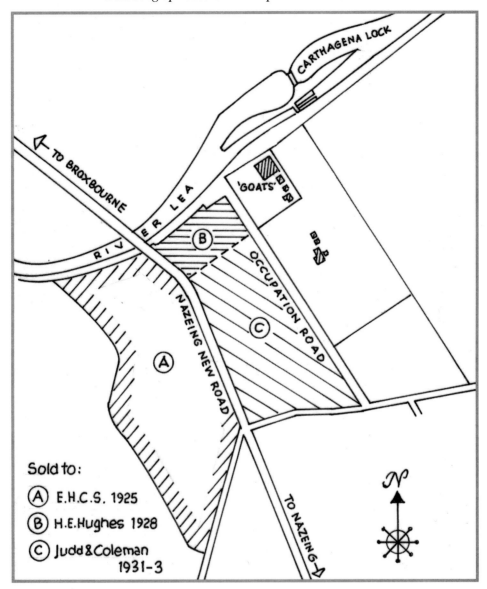

Between 1925 and 1933, Archdale Palmer sold his land either side of Nazeing Road. The Nazeing Glassworks estate and The Meads were developed on the north-east side of the road.

In 1928 Hughes sold Goats and four acres of land to Richard Kempton and two of his brothers, the owners of the Albert Glass Works at Vauxhall. The company was founded in the seventeenth century, when the famous diarists Samuel Pepys and John Evelyn visited it. By the 1920s it was one of many firms looking to take advantage of better road

145

An early view of Nazeing Glassworks, probably taken in the 1930s.

communication and move away from cramped London premises to more spacious countryside locations capable of expansion. Goats Farm was ideal. It was close to the railway and, more important for the transportation of relatively small scale fragile goods, the recently improved A10 arterial road. It was already "town planned for factories and warehouses" and mains electricity was in the course of being laid. The Kemptons demonstrated their commitment to their new site by renaming their firm the Nazeing Glassworks and adopting the Broxbourne Goat as the company emblem. Initially they set up their works in the old goat shed but they expanded gradually, acquiring more land and erecting a purpose-built factory. The company's motto of "Glassmakers to the World" is well justified, for it exports a wide range of practical and ornamental glass products to Europe, the Commonwealth, and elsewhere.

There were other light industrial enterprises in the area. James Jones and Harold Higgins were employees of a wallpaper company in Islington. In 1933 they started their own firm, Muraltones, at Hoddesdon. Four years later they erected a new factory, the Bridge Works at Nazeing New Road, where they had some ten employees. Their products developed a high reputation. When war broke out, wallpaper was classified as a luxury item and the government took over the factory for fertiliser

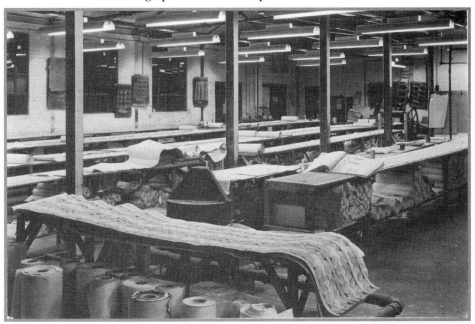

Interior of the Muraltones wallpaper factory in the 1930s.

production. Later it was used to repair training aircraft at the aerodrome, where Jones and his employees worked for the rest of the war. Afterwards the factory was returned to Muraltones and the directors restarted the business with such paper as was available, but decorative fashions had changed and it never regained its previous popularity. The factory was still producing papers as late as 1956 but after Jones died in 1957 it was sold to Nazeing Glass.

Council housing

In 1919 Epping Rural District Council announced its plans for council house building but the parish council "saw no need for twenty agricultural labourers' cottages in Nazeing". Ralph Palmer told Epping that it was "not incumbent upon my committee...to incur outlay on building...in order to meet the convenience or the natural desire of persons employed elsewhere than in Nazeing". He added that "repairs or rebuilding of existing cottages will be carried out as soon as the prices of building materials & of labour permit". Nevertheless, the houses were erected at Long Green and a further eight were built across the road at Allmains Close. Strongly influenced by the garden city movement, the government had set standards for high-quality, low-density working-class housing and the spacious houses with their good-sized gardens demonstrate clearly the

**The dignitaries on the platform probably contributed towards this 1919
Welcome Home meat tea at the Chapel Hall, but refused to help with housing
and other longer-term needs of returning soldiers.**

latest architectural thinking of the time. Despite, or perhaps because, of
the parish council's concerns, all or most were tenanted by Nazeing
people who were moved out of substandard housing elsewhere in the
village. Eventually the parish council did have to pay £50 towards
sewerage for the new houses but it seems to have accepted the charge
without demur.

In 1924 Epping introduced a scheme for "working class persons in the
Parish who required housing accommodation and would be prepared to
build for themselves provided they were granted the subsidy of £75 by the
Rural District Council". Nazeing Parish Council posted notices
advertising the scheme but no responses were recorded - perhaps not
surprisingly, given that a house would have cost several times that to
build. The parish council reported also that it knew of no cases of
overcrowding, although this may have been a rather optimistic view of
the housing situation in the village.

When the economic situation improved in the late 1930s, the

Professors Adshead's 1933 report declared that "labourers' cottages are best erected in groups on the roadside and houses best congregated round existing villages". The council houses at Nazeing Long Green around that time.

government announced a new council house programme. In 1938 the district council announced plans to build a further eighteen houses on land at Allmains Close which it had bought in 1935. This was on the initiative of George Chapman of Langridge, the leading Nazeing nurseryman. He told fellow parish councillors that "there were 600 Nursery Hands working in Nazeing of whom 95 per cent resided outside the Parish - many having to journey 8 miles daily". Councillors recognised an "undoubted shortage" of housing accommodation in the village and "cordially welcomed" the proposal, provided the houses were let at reasonable rents, which should be no more than 10s per week including rates. The houses, completed in 1939, were designed less ambitiously than the original twenty-eight. The parish council considered that eighteen would not be nearly enough and requested more. Epping agreed to build a further twenty-four but war broke out before a start could be made.

Immediately after the war, in line with government guidelines, the district council began to prepare a council housing scheme. The parish council had a long discussion on "the means that could be adopted to expedite the building of new houses and repair of damage", and asked the district council to "take any action which may hasten the erection of Council Houses in the Parish". The district council identified suitable sites at Barnfield and St. Leonards Road but was unable to reach voluntary agreement with the owners and so acquired them by compulsory purchase. By October 1946 Epping had obtained authority to build thirty council houses in Nazeing. The Barnfield houses were of the standard, pre-cast reinforced concrete, Airey type, but they had generously sized gardens, reminiscent of those provided at Bumbles Green in 1921. A further eight council houses were erected at 14 to 28 Pecks Hill by a local builder. Modern, well-equipped council houses were much sought after and, as they went up, speculation was rife as to who the tenants would be.

Connie Reynolds was deeply involved with the development of council housing in Nazeing. She met Leah Manning at the House of Commons and enlisted her support. She placed her usual wallpaper and paint notices in the shops, inviting all women wanting a council house to attend a meeting at her home, Trevone. She proposed a resolution, accepted by her parish council colleagues, that Epping should be urged to implement a points system for the allocation of new and requisitioned houses. By 1947 there had been 87 applicants for council houses of whom 45 had four children. As the houses were intended mainly for agricultural workers, the district council refused to adopt a points system, which would have taken family needs into consideration. District Councillor Alfred Barratt sought to explain the workings of the housing list but Connie Reynolds and George Chapman did not accept his arguments. She wanted the parish council to ask Epping "why certain persons had not been allocated council houses" but no action was taken.

The difficulties were eased with the building of some fifty dwellings on land east of St. Leonards Road, completed in 1948. Houses in St. Leonards Road and Hyde Mead were built in a style reminiscent of the inter-war ones at Bumbles Green, whereas those in Pound Close were Airey ones. Already land was at a premium and the plots were considerably smaller, so tenants began to enquire about the availability of allotments. Evidently they were not all agricultural workers, who would have been used to the more robust aspects of country life, for in 1953 some of them complained about the smell from the pigs at the neighbouring Mulberries Farm.

Despite its Conservative majority, the parish council was very positive for two and a half years about the provision of council housing in Nazeing. Then in October 1948 the council held a public meeting, where the consensus was that there should be no further development unless the people of the village were informed. Apparently the force of the attack took councillors by surprise and, with parish council elections only six months away, they went along with the feeling expressed at the meeting.

Remarkably, given that Alfred Barratt had been a district and parish councillor when the 1939 Town Planning Scheme was published, the parish council claimed not to know of any such scheme and formally asked for a sight of it. The general question of the village's development became mixed up with the specific issue of providing council houses, perhaps because under the Labour government they were almost synonymous. The council sent a resolution to the district council on the provision of council housing and deplored Epping's refusal to accept it.

In 1949 rumours began to circulate that the district council was acquiring more land in Hoe Lane for council housing. Epping confirmed that it had bought ten acres but had not yet decided how many houses were to be built. The newly-elected parish council objected to the lack of consultation as "an affront to its members and parishioners alike", opposing the development not just for its impact on the overall planning of the village but also because it was council housing. It was surprised at the failure of Nazeing's three district councillors to vote on the issue, a complaint that has not been unknown since. It gave various reasons

An early picture of Unity type council houses at Palmers Grove shortly after their completion in 1951-2.

including difficulties in transporting children to school, decline in property values, heavy traffic associated with the Hoe Lane greenhouse industry, and - rather contradicting their previous point - "the iniquitous destruction of the rural amenities associated with this lane". A public inquiry was held and the development was completed in 1951-2 at Hoe Lane and Palmers Grove, which was named after the recently deceased Archdale Palmer. A commemorative plaque was placed there but, sadly, disappeared soon afterwards.

In 1950 the district council proposed to develop the field opposite the Bumbles Green school but in 1952 it dropped the idea in favour of plans to build fifty additional council houses at Hyde Mead. This too never happened, although the council did compulsorily purchase the field, where in 1959 it built 17 to 55 Hyde Mead, opposite the new Nazeing County Primary School. Conservative governments between 1951 and 1964 preferred private housing schemes but made no attempt to reverse what had been done already. By 1976, however, Nazeing council houses were being sold to tenants and in the 1980s the Thatcher Government's "Right To Buy" policy accelerated this process. Epping Forest Council's already limited ability to place Nazeing people in Nazeing houses was further restricted. "For Sale" signs were increasingly in evidence and home improvements such as double glazing and new front doors proliferated. The uniformity that had, for better or worse, been a feature of the original council house estates began to disappear and with it, some felt, the sense of community enjoyed by the tenants.

In 1987 the district council discovered faults in hundreds of Airey and Unity houses, including those at Barnfield Close, Pound Close, and Palmers Grove. Barnfield was one of five sites to be investigated under the heading "Defective Dwellings - Potential for Redevelopment". The council emphasised that no decision would be taken until there had been full consultation with the residents but decided nevertheless to demolish Barnfield Close. Some of the occupiers had spent much time and money on their homes and gardens, so there was considerable sympathy for their plight and 276 people signed a petition from Nazeingbury Residents' Association opposing the demolition. The district council's housing committee noted, however, that only two of the affected properties were represented on the petition and proceeded anyway, because the larger gardens meant that the site had greater redevelopment value. The days of large-scale council estates were long since past, so in 1993 the district council reached an agreement with the North Housing Association for the building on the site of 22 homes for rent. The houses at Pound Close and Palmers Grove had smaller gardens and therefore were not demolished but refurbished, most of them being refaced with attractive brickwork.

Nazeingbury

The break-up of the Wake and Palmer estates released land for building and Epping Rural District Council designated the area around Nazeingbury crossroads for development. Between 1920 and 1980 it was transformed.

The largest single piece of land sold off was the 331-acre Nazeing Bury Farm. In 1919 it was bought for £10,000 by Joseph Pegrum, the sitting tenant, who had lived and farmed there since the late 1870s. Three years later he sold some 300 acres to Walter Benjafield for £11,000. Unfortunately for Benjafield, he chose to buy just as a deep agricultural slump was beginning and soon he was, in Roy Leach's words, "going bust". The selling of sites at Nursery Road and St. Leonards Road to the plotlanders was an attempt to recover something on his investment.

Meanwhile Joseph Pegrum had retained Langfield, two large grass fields of approximately 28 acres north of Middle Street and east of North Street. In 1925 he conveyed this land, valued at £3,000, to his son David, who in the previous year had paid Archdale Palmer £1,775 for Whitehall

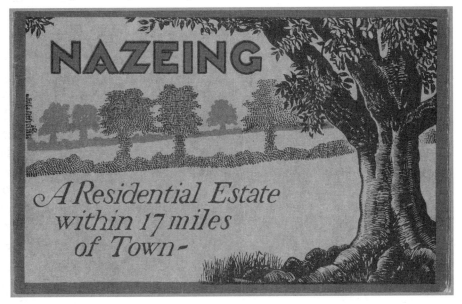

The Nazeing Estates Ltd. prospectus, published in 1927.

153

Farm, which lay immediately north of Langfield. Thus by 1926 David Pegrum owned over a hundred acres and was listed in *Kelly's Directory*, along with Archdale Palmer and Ralph Bury, as one of the three chief landowners in Nazeing. He conveyed the fields to a company called Nazeing Estates Ltd. which, over the next few years, built a group of luxury houses including 4, 8, and 12 North Street, St. Helens, Mickleton, Oak Porch Cottage, Four Ways, and 15 Western Road. From the design of the houses the area acquired the name of the Tudor Village, which was shown in bus timetables of the late 1920s and was still being used in 1947.

In 1927 Nazeing Estates Ltd. issued a prospectus entitled *Nazeing: a Residential Estate within 17 miles of Town*. The intended market was shown not only by the title but also by the offer of a motor car lift from Broxbourne Station and a summary of "What Nazeing offers you". Prospective purchasers were offered the option of buying an existing house or having one built to their own design. Some were ready built, while others were under construction, and all would cost about £1,000. The North Metropolitan Electricity Supply Company would lay mains in the near future and every house had been wired for electric light in readiness. Standard plots were 60 by 120 feet but larger plots were available, as land was plentiful. David Pegrum was the managing director

The view south towards Mayflower and the Crooked Billet in Middle Street ....

154

and the prospectus was issued by Arthur E. May.

For David Pegrum the venture was not a success. As a farmer he had been exempted from service in the First World War. As farmers prospered during the war, he was able to make enough money to buy Greenleaves and Darmers, where the Pegrum family had been tenant-farmers for over a hundred years. David's distant cousin, Bernard Pegrum, regarded his apparent prosperity as a mixed blessing:

> Alas! The 1914-1918 war both 'made' David and ruined him...he gave up farming and went into speculative building. He built Langholm in North Street for himself...but he had got mixed up with some doubtful characters in a business he knew nothing about and it is my opinion they only wanted his money...I have been told that every house he sold, he sold at a loss. At last he saw the red light and he cleared out. Rumours concerning him and his whereabouts were rampant at the time, but they lacked foundation...

Even in 1920, before he became involved with property speculation, David Pegrum had resigned suddenly as a deacon and a member of the Chapel. All of this must have been a bitter pill for his father; it is said that but for old Joe's standing in the village and the respect in which he was held, things would have gone much worse for David.

Arthur May was possibly one of the "doubtful characters" referred to by Bernard Pegrum. He was not a native of Nazeing and was apparently

... shortly after the development of the Langfield estate began.

155

The Langfield Estate under development. The photograph was probably taken from 12 North Street, showing the junction of Highland Road and Shooters Drive.

no relation to Col. Kenneth F. May. He lived on the corner of Highland Road and Shooters Drive in a large five-bedroom house called Langfield Hill, built for him by David Pegrum in 1926. Precise details of the business relationship between the two men are not known. Yet somehow Arthur May escaped the financial disaster that overtook David. It appears that in 1929 a separate firm called Tudor Homes was set up as the selling arm of the business. At different times May described himself as a journalist, an estate agent, and an advertising agent, which is presumably why he became the director of Tudor Homes. He may well have engineered the division between the two companies, leaving Pegrum with the chancy business of building the houses while he pouched the money from selling them. It seems a classic tale of the green country boy being swindled by the sophisticated interloper.

Before he came to Nazeing May was a county councillor, which may be how he learnt of David Pegrum's move into speculative building; later he was elected an alderman. In the 1930s, while Pegrum had to leave the village of his forebears in disgrace, May became a leading figure in

Nazeing. He was chairman of the Nazeing Conservative Party and a supporter of Ralph Bury at the time of his conflict with Churchill. A parish councillor from 1931 and trustee of Nazeing Wood or Park after the death of F.W. Green, he organised village events such as the 1937 Coronation celebrations. His colleagues expressed their appreciation of "invaluable services unstintingly rendered" but, when bombing made Nazeing a hazardous place to live, he moved away, the only village leader to do so.

By 1939 May owned land in Highland Road, Shooters Drive, Western Road and Crooked Way, all of which he had begun to develop. He retained it until after the war and in 1946 claimed £325 for repairs to war damage at 42 North Street. He then sold the land off to builders such as William Daniels, who was obliged to provide "full rights of way thereover for everybody who uses the passage on the north side of the land", a reference to the path between 36 and 38 North Street and 45 and 47 Highland Road, which existed already and remains in use. Langfield Hill was demolished in 1963 and the land, together with the grounds of Clovelly (50 North Street), was used for new dwellings in Shooters Drive, Highland Road, and Whitehall Close.

One small portion of Archdale Palmer's Whitehall Farm property was bought not by David Pegrum but by the sitting tenant, Langham King. Now known as 60 North Street, its present industrial use seems out of keeping with the surrounding residential development, but the firm was there first. It was one of Nazeing's ancient common right cottages and had been occupied by the King family for many years. By 1912 there were on the site, as well as the cottage, a timber and corrugated iron workshop, a paintshop, and a range of old timber and tiled outbuildings. When there was a misunderstanding about property names and Archdale Palmer had to correct one of the solicitors, he did so in his typically courteous way: "You speak of 'Whitehall <u>Cottage</u>'. This should, I think, be 'Whitehall <u>Farm</u>' as I rather think that Mr L. King has purchased the property known as Whitehall Cottage." Palmer was correct in this assertion because King had paid £300 for the property in 1924. He was a versatile tradesman who described himself on his letter-head as "Builder, Plumber, Painter, Glazier, Paper-Hanger, House Decorator etc", adding "Special attention given to well-boring".

Between the wars there were various abortive plans to develop Middle Street. In 1925 Margaret Meller obtained permission to build houses on

157

North Street, 1930s. On the left can be seen the gable of a house which was Pearce's dairy, later Squires' general store and now a private house. Just behind it is Fowler's shop which replaced Squires soon after the war.

land next to her home, Old House Farm, but took the matter no further. In 1928 Arthur May, David Pegrum, and Joseph Pegrum embarked upon an ambitious project to build select estates on 22 acres at Mansion House Farm and 15 acres on the land opposite, known as Oaklands. These plans were a casualty of their financial difficulties and they sold out in the mid-30s. Plots at Oaklands were bought by individuals such as Arch Coleman, father of Maurice, who had Howards built on the field of that name by Judd & Coleman.

In 1935 the leading estate agents, A. Savill & Sons, obtained planning permission on behalf of Ralph Bury to erect houses on land west of Mansion House Farm. Nothing was built then, although Mollie Wood recalled some sort of road layout before the war and commented that springs there may have made building difficult. In 1938 Savill's and Bury applied unsuccessfully to develop Charpickles, the land either side of the brook between Nazeingbury crossroads and the Crooked Billet. By 1939 the only new houses south of Middle Street were Tudor Lodge, Littlebourne, and Crowlands, built in Crooked Way by Tudor Homes. Charpickles was only developed in the 1960s but, although Epping Rural District Council compulsorily purchased the land west of Mansion House Farm in 1953, it was not until 1979 that Barnard Acres and Tovey Close were built there.

In 1933 Adshead had advocated the building of "a satellite town on rising ground above Pecks Hill where development has already taken place", adding the rider that it "was not likely to materialise unless an organisation of importance were to decide upon purchasing a large area of land and with ample finance develop it on a large scale". If that had happened, doubtless the residents of plucky little Harlow would have campaigned against the predatory Nazeing New Town. No such organisation and finance materialised, however, and there were only a few small-scale developments, mostly in North Street. The 1939 Planning Scheme provision for "a considerable number of houses" at Nazeingbury thus formalised guidelines already in place. Essex County Council opposed an application to build houses behind Curringtons because the land was designated for agriculture, but plans for further development at Langfield fitted in with the scheme and were agreed.

Then the Second World War intervened and it was only during the 1950s that most of the fifty acres purchased by David Pegrum were developed. In a few cases the standard 60 x 120 feet plots that had been offered in 1928 were bought by individuals, as were some of the detached bungalows in Shooters Drive, where the jagged field-boundary between the old Wake and Palmer properties can still be discerned in the gardens backing on to Whitehall Close. Mostly, however, it was "Building Speculators" rather than "Private Individuals" who were responsible for the development.

In 1948 there began a complicated and ill-tempered series of negotiations about the site of the old Nazeingbury pound at the corner of Middle Street and St. Leonards Road. The details are unimportant but the upshot was that the parish council would provide the concrete base for a new layout at the site. In 1952 it placed a newspaper advertisement inviting tenders. After hawking the work round all the Nazeing builders, the council gave it to an outside contractor whose bid of £15 was more than £5 below the lowest local one. This apparently minor decision was in the long term far more significant than the shenanigans that preceded it, for the name of the contractor was George Compton, who was to play a major role in the development of the village over the next quarter of a century.

For a builder it was a good time to become involved with Nazeing. The new Conservative government had already switched the emphasis from public to private housing and the 1939 scheme had made provision for new houses which had not been built yet. Within a year Compton had bought the field where St. Giles' Church now stands and made it available for village events such as the Coronation celebrations. He had the reputation of being able to get planning permissions, when others had failed, and tended to buy up individual plots or rebuild decaying properties, including several in North Street, Middle Street, and Old Nazeing Road. Around 1956 Compton bought Whitehall Farm, 36 North Street, which he refurbished, extended and sold on. He retained the yard and outbuildings, erecting at 34 North Street a shop and office that were used later by J.W. Fencing, who subsequently took over the Ballards Nursery site at Pecks Hill. He lived at Rose Cottage, an old common right property, which he pulled down in 1976 in order to build his biggest development, Elizabeth Close.

The parish council minutes give the impression that in the 1950s parts of Nazeing were little more than a glorified building site. There were complaints that "Maplecroft Lane had been left in a bad state by the developers of the recently constructed housing estate nearby", and that builders' debris from Western Road had been dumped opposite 23 North Street. The highway in parts of Highland Road, Shooters Drive, and Western Road had still not been made up and those parts that had been made up were not being cleaned properly.

Footpath diversions were sometimes contentious. The path from Western Road to Middle Street originally emerged near Wheelers and in 1956 a builder, George P. Walker of Enfield, moved it forty yards west to its present line. The parish council was "not aware that a diversion had been agreed" and complained that a building was in construction "squarely across the Langfield footpath". The chairman and clerk interviewed Walker who claimed to have applied to Essex County Council eighteen months previously and "received verbal permission to proceed". He paid £900 for construction of the new path. Eventually the parish council received a copy of the order, so they took no further action.

In 1958 C. Paine and Sons applied for planning permission to develop the land between Shooters Drive and Maplecroft Lane. Perhaps surprisingly, since it fell within the village envelope, Essex County Council opposed the application but the builders made a successful appeal. Again there was concern about footpaths and the parish council received many letters on the matter but an amicable settlement was reached in the end: the developers provided access to Maplecroft Cottage, and the parish council supported a diverted route connecting Maplecroft Lane to the Western Road footpath as an "added amenity". The new development, Banes Down, was completed in 1961.

It was the duty of builders to make up the roads serving their new houses, but in 1967 the developers of Highland Road and Whitehall Close "could not be traced and were believed to be in liquidation". Therefore they "could not be called upon to fulfil their obligations" and the road remained unmade. The residents were understandably dissatisfied with this state of affairs but were told that "No county or district department could intervene". In 1978 they learnt that Essex County Council had not followed the later practice of obtaining from the builder a bond ensuring against such an eventuality, so "the cost of bringing that part of the highway to adoption standards would fall upon the frontagers concerned". In the 1990s the local residents revived the issue, claiming that their stretch of road was used by through traffic which, ironically, included Epping Forest District Council lorries coming to repair other roads. Parts of the road were sometimes exposed right down to the steel reinforcement. Despite approaches to various organisations and individuals, it proved impossible yet again to pin down responsibility for the unfortunate situation, which seemed insoluble.

The development of the Nazeingbury area was completed in the 1970s, when six dwellings were replaced by over fifty: Sunnyside and Green Gables became Sunnyside; Oak Tree (Arthur Harknett's bungalow) and Cedar Lodge (the former Women's Land Army Hostel) became John Eliot Close; Treona, built in 1946-7 for his retirement by P.H. Panter, the Waltham Abbey baker who delivered bread in Nazeing, became Mayflower Close; Rose Cottage became Elizabeth Close. Other older dwellings had infill housing built in their generously-sized gardens.

In 1977 Epping Forest District Council went into partnership with Fairview Homes to provide seventy low-cost dwellings for people who might otherwise have had to wait for a council house. The parish council objected on the grounds of overdevelopment but the partnership was in line with government policy and the high-density layout was modelled on the recently adopted *Essex Design Guide for Residential Areas*, so Barnard Acres and Tovey Close were completed in 1979. By then land prices had soared and the newer properties were on much smaller plots. Unless some future plan makes radical new proposals, the development of Nazeing had become substantially complete.

Gravel extraction has changed much of the River Lea flood plain from
farmland to lakes. Above: Langridge Farmhouse with Neil Chapman, c1940,
was built in middle of the land farmed from it. Below: today, the farmhouse
stands on the edge of a large lake similar to this one near Meadgate Lane.

CHAPTER 5

"VOCIFEROUS OPPOSITION"

Campaigns

In 1983 Epping Forest District Council's draft local plan commented somewhat ruefully: "Several attempts have been made...to expand Harlow westwards into Roydon and Nazeing in order to expand the population of the town. All these attempts have failed because of...the vociferous opposition put up by the local communities in the area." Vociferous opposition was nothing new in Nazeing. Threats came from Harlow, from other local authorities, from public utilities, and from private companies. Beginning with the victory over the mighty Metropolitan Water Board described in *Five miles from everywhere* (p.171), the campaigning of Nazeing people to preserve the village they loved was a theme that recurred throughout the twentieth century.

Staying rural

Few topics would seem less likely to provoke passionate debate than the apparently dry matter of local government boundaries. Yet the administrative unit of which a community is part says something about its relationship with the outside world, particularly when, as in the case of Nazeing, it is situated "five miles from everywhere". On several occasions the village had to fight hard to remain part of a rural district.

Following the 1929 Local Government Act, Waltham Holy Cross Urban District Council applied to Essex County Council for an extension of its boundaries to include Nazeing and Roydon. Nazeing Parish Council, "being unable to discover any advantage, financial or otherwise from the proposed fusion", recorded its "most emphatic and unanimous protest against the proposals". In 1935, somewhat ironically given later developments, the parish council was successful in opposing a transfer from the then rural Electoral Division of Harlow into Waltham Abbey.

The coming of Harlow New Town meant that the 1949 Boundary Commission would have to recommend changes in west Essex. Hoddesdon and Cheshunt Urban District Councils (UDCs) both wanted to take over Nazeing and the parish council complained that it "had been kept in the dark" as to what Epping Rural District Council (RDC) had said or done about this unwelcome suggestion, which would have made the village part of Hertfordshire. The chairman and clerk of Epping attended a parish council meeting and answered questions from the public about the proposals, which eventually came to nothing.

When in 1953 it was proposed that the Epping RDC and Ongar RDC should amalgamate, Waltham Holy Cross UDC suggested a merger of itself, Roydon, and Nazeing to fight Harlow expansion. Nazeing Parish Council and the Epping & Harlow branch of the National Farmers' Union saw this as an equally undesirable threat and opposed what they saw as the "urbanisation of Nazeing", reflected in the very descriptions of the district councils as urban or rural. The parish council's preference to "stay rural" as a separate parish within a merged Epping and Ongar RDC was approved at a public meeting attended by representatives of the various councils and some 170 Nazeing residents. Nevertheless the matter went to a public inquiry. Two rival petitions were sent round and the parish council emerged the winner, gaining 690 signatures in favour of a link with Epping and Ongar RDC, whereas the Nazeing Labour Party obtained only 300 for a link with Waltham Holy Cross UDC. Cannily the parish council postponed the purchase of a typewriter for its clerk until the result of the public inquiry revealed whether Nazeing would remain a separate entity that even needed a clerk, much less a typewriter. Graeme Finlay MP conveyed to the Parliamentary Secretary, William Deedes, Nazeing's "strong objection to absorption by Waltham Holy Cross UDC". Not until November 1954 was it announced that Nazeing would be part of Epping and Ongar RDC. The parish council deemed the £59 9s spent on briefing a junior barrister at the boundary inquiry "reasonable".

Residents' Associations

Nazeing is "a vast and scattered parish" which only briefly had a single Ratepayers' Association. Instead, local associations have usually campaigned on specific issues related to their immediate area. In the 1920s, for example, there was an active Keysers Ratepayers' Association, probably formed because people there saw themselves as being neglected by the parish council and the older parts of Nazeing. In the late 1930s two Keysers residents were elected to the parish council and apparently the association developed into a Nazeing Ratepayers' Association, covering the whole village. It was active in opposing "grossly excessive rates" in the years before the Second World War; although it was still in existence in 1946, it faded soon afterwards.

The Nazeingbury Residents' Association was founded in 1962 in order to ginger up a parish council which some residents saw as unnecessarily stuffy. The campaign was successful in at least one important respect, for founder member Jeff Franklin was elected to Nazeing Parish Council and then became its chairman. In that role he introduced the open session which has given villagers the opportunity to bring matters of concern to the attention of the parish council and thence often to politicians, to district and county councils, and to other organisations. All residents of Nazeingbury Ward were automatically members of the association, which later took on a broader campaigning role. It pressed the district council to impose strict conditions on the gravel companies; later it played an important part in the opposition to Harlow expansion and major developments within the village.

By the late 1980s the Nazeingbury Residents' Association had several major achievements. A well-attended barn dance at Harold's Park Farm raised £500 for association funds. After an eight year struggle, which included the organising of a traffic census at Nazeingbury crossroads, the association obtained lorry bans on Nazeing Road and Dobbs Weir Road. In the first four months of the bans the police issued 120 tickets to offending drivers. A £30,000 revamping of Nazeingbury Parade, first suggested by the association twenty years earlier, provided more parking spaces and made it safer. As a highways engineer met local people at the parade to examine the association's proposals, a car reversed out and collided with another that was coming along Nazeing Road, providing a graphic illustration of the safety issue.

During the 1990s the association continued to campaign on major issues and a popular series of village walks regularly attracted over fifty people. Gradually, however, support dwindled. Fewer people offered themselves as committee members, so fundraising activities were less successful. The association finally folded in 1998 and its remaining funds were divided between the All Saints' Church Pilgrim Room appeal and the Nazeing History Workshop.

There were at various times other residents' associations for Riverside, Crownfield, Green Lane, and Bumbles Green. They tended to be inactive until their immediate area was directly affected by some major issue when, like a desert flower after rain, they blossomed briefly into vigorous life before returning to their dormant state to await the next crisis. This intermittent activity is very effective, for it husbands scarce resources of

165

time, money, and energy, while ensuring that there is an organisational mechanism in place when needed.

"Unnecessarily extravagant and costly": the 1935 sewerage scheme

As the village grew, matters which had previously been arranged privately became issues of public concern. In 1921 Keysers residents enquired about a sewerage system for their area and David Pegrum told the 1926 Annual Parish Meeting that such a scheme would soon be necessary, "particularly in view of the increase in house building that has taken place in the last two years". When, in 1927, Nazeing Estates and the Keysers Ratepayers Association both asked Epping Rural District Council to investigate the possibility of installing a system in the village, they were told that the heavy expenditure would not be justified. Four years later Arthur May, by then director of Tudor Homes and a parish councillor, raised the question again and Epping proposed a limited scheme costing only £2,000. This was rejected by the Ministry of Health as inadequate, so the council proposed to make Nazeing a Special Drainage Area, which meant that the village would have to pay the entire cost, estimated at £21,900.

The 1935 Annual Parish Meeting passed a unanimous resolution recording its "emphatic protest against any Scheme which would...necessitate a Rate that is beyond the power of the Rate-payers to pay". On 23rd April 1935 the parish council forwarded the motion to the district, which announced the next day that there would be a public inquiry. Ralph Bury, then in the midst of his conflict with Churchill and at his most belligerent, wrote to the parish council condemning the scheme as "unnecessarily extravagant and costly". At his suggestion, the council approached Major A.J.S. Waters VC, an independent sanitary engineer who could provide an assessment of Epping's two schemes. The parish council had intended to argue for the original £2,000 scheme but Waters agreed with the Ministry of Health that it was inadequate.

Therefore at the public inquiry, eventually held by the Ministry on 6th May 1936, the parish council took a different line. The case for Nazeing was put by Archdale Palmer, who argued that the £21,900 scheme covered only a limited portion of the parish and would involve a rate increase of 50 per cent from 2s 10d in the pound to 4s 3d. He appealed to the Ministry to make a contribution itself and to call upon Epping to spread the expense across the whole district. The Ministry was almost as dilatory in reaching a decision as it had been in issuing its model planning clauses (see page 129); for nearly three years no further references to the scheme are to be found, other than three minor problems with its implementation.

Then the Annual Parish Meeting of 29th March 1939, held at the Chapel Hall and attended by 120 people, passed a motion proposed by the Nazeing Ratepayers' Association. It requested a joint deputation of the association and the parish council to the Ministry of Health, to "ascertain whether any relief could be obtained in respect of the special Sewerage Rate". A further resolution expressed the opinion that the county and other rates were, "having regard to the amenities available...grossly excessive and causing grave hardship in the district". Then Alderman Arthur May mounted a "spirited defence of the county council and its methods", arguing that the council had many statutory duties and gave good value for money, so a third motion, expressing "complete lack of confidence in the County Council", was defeated. The stance of the Ratepayers' Association offered a classic example of nimbyism forty years before the word was invented. The parish council, acutely aware of the dangers of excessive parochialism, argued that "the Deputation should not stress the interests of Nazeing more than those of the other Parishes which are similarly situated". Evidently the deputation achieved its objectives, for in July the parish council learnt that the cost of the scheme was to be shared out more equitably.

After the Second World War a sewerage system with several pumping stations was installed but houses in some parts of the village have never been attached to it and continue to have their own cesspools or septic tanks.

"Spoliation of Nazeing amenities": gravel extraction

Gravel is a coarse sediment of pebbles and small rocks, often found mixed with sand and clay, that makes an ideal building material. In the Lea Valley, deposits averaged twenty feet in depth, from which some 25,000 cubic yards could be extracted in a year. It was long known that gravel was there, and some was taken from pits at Nazeing Bury Farm, but regular flooding deposited rich sedimentary soil on riverside land and made it more valuable for agriculture. No systematic attempt was made to exploit gravel before the twentieth century, when London's rapid growth increased demand and road improvements meant that it was more easily transported there. Gravel became more profitable than farming and owners sold out to extraction companies.

By 1933 Broxbourne Sand & Ballast Pits Ltd was established at Old Nazeing Road and the St. Albans Sand & Gravel Company (SASGC) at Nazeing Meads. In 1937 the district council turned down a request from the SASGC for a footpath diversion at Nazeing Meads so the matter went to a public inquiry, where the Ministry of Health granted the company's application provided it left a 50 foot wide strip for the path. The ministry favoured the "winning of materials from surface workings" and opposed excavation within 200 feet of housing. Wartime necessitated a relaxation of this policy, so that in 1941 there were complaints about noise from the SASGC excavations, which were also causing gardens at Carthagena to be drained.

John King recalled that during the war huge amounts of gravel were extracted for the construction of runways at several RAF airfields in Essex, including the very long one at Stansted, used for American bombers. During the extraction continual pumping out of water in the pits lowered the water table along the Nazeing Road but it caused no structural damage to properties there because the loam above the gravel did not shrink. By contrast, in the area of North Street where the rising ground has a substantial stratum of clay, there were serious difficulties. One of King's North Street neighbours used hose-pipes to create a continuous flow of water around his house in order to keep the foundations moist. German prisoners of war laid land drains, possibly of straw, in what is now Shooters Drive and part of Highland Road; this may account for many of the structural problems in that area.

After the war the rebuilding of bomb-damaged London and the development of Harlow New Town increased yet further the demand for gravel. In 1947 the SASGC was granted a licence for excavations at Carthagena so residents there, led by Commander H. Burt and supported by Nazeing Parish Council, complained that excavations were causing subsidence and "endangering the population". A gravel pit at the end of Sedge Green Lane was "very dangerous in dark and foggy weather", so the parish council asked Epping to fence it off. Following complaints that the SASGC was pumping water into the Lea and the Nazeing Brook, there was a public inquiry in 1949 where all parties employed barristers. The SASGC obtained a licence for further excavations, despite strong opposition and a finding that "the abstraction of gravel was proceeding at an enormous rate and lowering the water table". The company "contravened" the footpath from the river to Pecks Hill by laying a light railway across it, and was ordered to install a bridge instead. Meadgate Road was in a "deplorable state" and SASGC agreed to "put it into repair".

In 1952, responding to proposals for extraction of sand and gravel from the aerodrome site, residents presented a petition to the parish council, which met officers from the county and district councils. Parish councillors felt that they had achieved all they could but the petitioners disagreed and called for a special Parish Meeting, at which they described the problems being caused and left no doubt about the strength of feeling about them. Residents were "increasingly concerned by the drastic and unrestricted way in which gravel pits were being opened", and the "spoliation of Nazeing amenities". Some had encroached to within a few yards of back gardens at Carthagena and others had left houses surrounded by water and/or excavations on three sides, with consequent safety implications. The SASGC was pumping out water even in summer so that the water table was being lowered, resulting in damage to property from subsidence and possibly disastrous effects on the glasshouse industry. Backfilling was very slow and might take ninety years to complete. Further excavation at the aerodrome site would aggravate the problems but, if the authorities did allow it, they should at least ensure that any conditions were strictly enforced. It seemed that planning decisions were being made in secret because the SASGC would not have bought the aerodrome site unless it had been assured of being able to work it. For Nazeing the only redeeming features of gravel working were that water extraction made farming on the Meads easier and relieved the danger of flooding. The petition obtained little support and was dropped, although a government directive that gravel was essential for new building would probably have meant its rejection anyway.

In 1954, in spite of objection by Nazeing Parish Council, Epping and Ongar Rural District Council approved an SASGC application to abstract underground water at Carthagena, although it did impose the condition that the company must backfill the excavated land. The parish council opposed gravel working at Meadgate Road because houses there would be cut off on three sides, and protested to the Ministry of Transport which asked the council to withdraw its objections. The council refused, and disputed the company's claims as to the progress it was making with backfilling. The Ministry of Housing and Local Government (MHLG) held an enquiry about further extraction at Nursery Road but failed to notify the parish council, which therefore was unable to lodge an objection. The council was then told that if it continued to oppose the activities of the SASGC at Meadgate, the Ministry of Transport might call an enquiry where it would have to brief counsel. So threatened, the council agreed to withdraw its objection, provided that the backfilling was accelerated and Meadgate Road was reinstated within five years rather than ten.

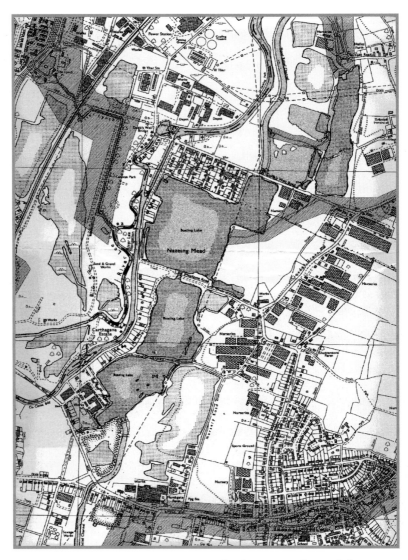

Lakes formed by gravel extraction have transformed the riverside landscape.

The MHLG stated that lagoons created by gravel excavation would be "an attractive feature if properly treated with planting of trees and shrubs", but the parish council regarded this as an excuse to delay the backfilling which it wanted the ministry to enforce. Councillors had every right to be concerned that they were being fobbed off but the landscaping was done well on the whole and, more recently, the Lee Valley Regional Park has developed Nazcing Meads as a pleasant area for informal recreation (see page 333).

During the early 1960s gravel was extracted progressively southwards from the nurseries in Nursery Road, Blacklands, Hainault, Leabury, Winhope, and Westmead. By 1966 St. Albans Sand & Gravel Company had been taken over by Redland-Inns, who applied to work the remaining 48½ acres of Westfield and Bridgewater Nurseries, on the Nazeing Road frontage between Langley Green and Nursery Road. There was strong opposition and the matter went to a public inquiry. In May 1967 the MHLG approved the workings, which proceeded quickly, so that the land was soon restored to agriculture. The backfilling, however, was done mainly with household rubbish containing a large amount of impermeable material such as plastic, and natural streams that used to drain into the lagoon behind the Glassworks were not reinstated. Storm water from the

The archaeological dig of 1975-6 with gravel andspoil heaped in the background.

171

top of Pecks Hill and North Street therefore cannot drain away, so the houses in Nursery Road are flooded frequently.

One unexpected bonus for the village was that gravel extraction revealed the existence of a previously unknown Saxon nunnery at Blacklands, described in *Five miles from everywhere,* pp 17-19. Skeletons had been discovered nearby in 1934 but the major archaeological dig that took place in 1975-6 revealed far more about the area and was in itself an important part of Nazeing's history.

As soon as the companies moved in, there were objections not only to the extraction itself but also to the nuisance caused by lorries transporting the gravel. A complaint in 1937 that an SASGC lorry had broken private water pipes was the first of many; others were about gravel lorries which shed their loads or which damaged road surfaces. In the 1950s lorries at Aerodrome Corner caused "obstruction and inconvenience" and "most unsightly" rubbish from backfilling fell on to the roads. Despite further complaints about mud on the roads caused by gravel lorries, the relationship between the companies and the village became rather less acrimonious, until in 2000 and 2001 it took a vigorous local campaign to defeat the Lafarge Company's plan to install concrete-crushing machinery at Green Lane.

These problems were, however, as nothing compared with those that would have arisen if any of the drastic schemes for building major roads through Nazeing had ever been implemented.

Motorways

As the inter-war period saw a rapid growth in road traffic for which the existing network was inadequate, in 1933 the Adshead report proposed two major new arterial roads. A North Orbital Road would come from the Thames via Ongar to Hoddesdon, mostly by improving existing roads but also by building new sections, including one through the more sparsely populated northerly parts of Nazeing from Broadley Common and Stoneshot Common to the Lea. This would have met a 60 foot wide Norwich Radial or Lea Valley Road, which would have run from the London Docks to Waltham Abbey, swept round east of Langridge and parallel with North Street, cut through Sedge Green, and ended where it met the North Orbital Road at Dobbs Weir. This, it was claimed, "would improve, connect together, and greatly assist the development of lands not only in the Valley itself but also in the border lands about."

Essex County Council adopted these proposals, variations of which were to form part of its plans for the next forty years. In 1938 it bought from Walter Benjafield part of Nazeing Bury Farm to use for the Lea Valley Road. Any proposals for development along the published route were firmly resisted, although permissions for glasshouses were given for temporary periods to expire by the projected construction date of 1971. The plans were suspended during the war but revived soon afterwards, so that in 1949 Nazeing Parish Council "urged the Ministry of Transport to definitely decide on the siting of the new arterial road". When the County Development Plan was published in 1952, Essex was required by a Ministry of Transport directive to include the scheme, although the planned route for the Lea Valley Road had been moved eastwards. The parish council and the Conservative Association objected to the North Orbital Road, although it too was not due to be constructed until 1971.

In 1964 Essex County Council's revised development plan put forward a scheme that revived the 1933 proposals, and added a second outer ring road that was eventually implemented as the M25. The proposed North Orbital Road had become a six-lane east-west motorway, which met the

Artist's impression of the Lea Valley arterial road that could have passed through Nazeing to a major intersection at Stoneshot Common, bottom right. Broxbourne station is at the top left, and the smaller intersection, bottom left, is where the arterial road would have crossed Nazeing Road near Nursery Road.

173

north-south Norwich Radial Road with a mammoth junction at Stoneshot Common. It would have consisted of four separate interchanges covering an area about three quarters of a mile square, probably much like that between the M11 and the M25 at Theydon Garnon. Another road proposed by the county council in 1967 would have followed the line of the ancient track from Waltham Abbey via Harold's Park Farm and Nazeing Common to Broadley Common, but that was abandoned in the face of determined opposition by Nazeing Parish Council and others.

As the proposed Stoneshot junction would have destroyed Nazeing as we know it, it was fortunate that the government abandoned both roads in favour of the M11 and M25, routed well outside the boundaries of the parish. Probably influenced by the huge costs involved in traversing the densely built-up portion of the Lea Valley and its low-lying marshland, which is subject to frequent flooding, the government suddenly published proposals for an alternative motorway to go through the much more open Roding Valley, then east of Harlow, and on to Cambridge.

Another reason for the change of direction may well have been that it was intended to serve the proposed Stansted Airport. Several Nazeing people were active in the Lea Valley Opposition to Stansted Organisation, which appeared to have achieved its aims when in 1971 the Roskill Commission proposed that the third London airport should be located at Cublington in Buckinghamshire. The Government rejected that proposal and opted for Foulness (Maplin), only to abandon that choice in 1974. After the publication of a White Paper and further lengthy reviews Stansted was chosen after all. By the time that the new terminal building was opened in 1985 the M11 was in place to serve it.

The construction of the M11 during the 1970s removed the threat of a north/south radial route that had hung over Nazeing for nearly forty years. By ensuring that Harlow would develop on the east where there were links with the new motorway, it influenced the government's later rejection of plans to expand the town westwards into Nazeing and Roydon. When firm plans for the M25 were published, the parish council engaged legal representation for the public inquiry in order to oppose a suggestion for an alternative route through Nazeing. In 1975 the report on the motorway found against the proposed Nazeing route because the costs were even higher and the objections even stronger than for the one eventually chosen.

The pylons campaign

Although most campaigns saw Nazeing people united against a threat from outside, in one important case they were deeply divided amongst themselves.

In the 1960s electricity was supplied to the Epping and Ongar area by a substation at Epping, which failed to meet demand every winter from 1962-3 onwards. The Eastern Electricity Board (EEB) and the Central Electricity Generating Board agreed that the necessary reinforcement should be provided by a 132 Kv line from Rye House, where there was spare capacity. The EEB could not get voluntary agreement for five of the necessary wayleave (a right of way over another's property, e.g. with electricity pylons, usually under a statute) consents and so sought to have them imposed compulsorily. The Minister of Power's inspector granted one of the wayleaves but required the EEB to investigate an alternative route proposed by a major objector, the Central Board of Finance of the Church of England, which owned Harold's Park Farm. In May 1967 the minister put forward a route that would have taken the pylons straight across the centre of Nazeing Common, so on 4th July the trustees organised a Special Meeting of freeholders, which was open to all local people. On a beautiful summer's evening ten days later, there was a major protest meeting in the new pound on the common. The parish council circularised every house in the village about a further meeting, which was held on 4th September. It was attended by about a hundred people, who passed unanimously a resolution approving a compromise route proposed by the parish council.

The minister and the EEB had given serious consideration to putting the cables underground or bypassing Nazeing altogether, but despite vigorous lobbying by Nazeing people these possibilities were eventually rejected on financial and technical grounds. It was then a question of where in the village the overhead lines would go. There were three proposed routes, which became known by the colours assigned to them on the documentation prepared for the public inquiry. The original EEB proposal was black, the Church of England alternative was red, and the parish council compromise was yellow. The red route would have gone directly across the common so, in November 1967, at yet another public meeting, local organisations and individuals expressed strong objections to it.

The EEB therefore went back to the minister and sought permission for

Pylon protest meeting on Nazeing Common in July 1967. Copy Wood is in the background.

the black route but he, noting that the parish council's compromise proposal had won unanimous support at the public meeting, asked the EEB to investigate the black and yellow routes. The main differences were that the black route passed through Bumbles Green, whereas the yellow one crossed the tail of the Common. A letter from Stan Newens MP to the parish council indicated that Essex County Council supported the black route and "had no intention of listening to public and local requirements". The campaign went on, however, and in June 1968 the EEB announced in the *West Essex Gazette* that it intended to adopt the yellow route and that objections should be lodged by 1st July, which they duly were.

The choice was particularly hard for those Bumbles Green residents who also held Common rights. Although the black route avoided the Common, it went close to seventeen common right houses whereas the yellow one went close to only five. Private meetings of rightholders in September 1967 and May 1968 were divided on the issue, but on both occasions voted by a majority of seven that the trustees should not oppose the yellow route, which was "the lesser of two evils". The trustees apparently ignored this mandate, for at the public inquiry they favoured the black route and their land agent declared that "those who supported the yellow route were simply trying to protect their own little interests at the expense of the Common".

The public inquiry was held on 3rd and 4th December 1968 at St. John's Hall, Epping, where the inspector heard evidence from many organisations and individuals. The county council summarised the arguments, which remained delicately balanced:

> ...The black route would have a damaging effect on Bumbles Green, whereas the yellow route would not affect the residents in the same way. The yellow route was however in the main higher than the black route and would accordingly be rather more conspicuous and detrimental to the amenities of the area generally...The conflict was between the local people who preferred the yellow route and the general public who preferred the black route...

In his report the inspector immediately rejected on technical and amenity grounds the two proposals that would have bypassed Nazeing. He also ruled out the red route because of the strong opposition expressed at the public meeting in September 1967. Therefore he had to adjudicate between the black and yellow routes, which was not an easy task because opinion among the interested parties was evenly divided. Support for the black route from Essex County Council, the trustees of Nazeing Wood or Park, and the Council for the Preservation of Rural England was balanced by support for the yellow route from Epping and Ongar Rural District Council, Nazeing Parish Council, and the Central Board of Finance of the Church of England. Objectors on both sides refused wayleaves where the pylons would be situated on their land.

Following an inspection of the proposed routes, the Ministry of Housing and Local Government's amenity assessor commented:

> The crucial point is (a) should the black line affect for every day of the year the lives and proper enjoyment of the villagers...or (b) should a line cross a 'Common' which when seen is not a common in a true sense and is virtually land only farmed by arable methods with restrictions of public access...The black line...would have a severe impact on the inhabitants as on two instances, the conductors would only be 50 ft and 60 ft away from dwellings...

The inspector was strongly influenced by this argument and found in favour of the yellow route, adding that

> The main objection to the yellow route was the effect it would have on the views to and from Nazeingwood Common, but from inspection it was clear

that there was little to choose between this route and the black on this point; indeed the yellow route would be sited along generally lower land.

He was, however, concerned that 66 trees would require felling and lopping, as opposed to 48 on the black route. He therefore proposed a slight deviation that would reduce this number and "be an improvement to the amenity of the area generally". In conclusion, he recommended that consent for the black route be refused, and that the EEB be invited to realign the yellow route according to his suggestion and to obtain new wayleaves as required.

After some negotiation, the EEB reported that they had managed to "obtain voluntary wayleaves for a minor variation of the yellow route from all the parties except the trustees of Nazeing Wood or Park and one of their tenants". Though still unwilling to grant a voluntary wayleave, the trustees recognised that the variation would reduce the tree felling and were therefore prepared to leave the matter to the minister. In January 1970 he granted compulsory wayleaves for the variation and the pylons were erected soon afterwards, none of them actually on the Common although the wires pass above it.

Harlow

Uncertainty about the precise locations of new motorways and the third London airport meant that in the 1960s plans for the expansion of Harlow remained somewhat nebulous. The greatest threat to Nazeing came in the early 1970s. A Royal Commission on Local Government recommended enhanced powers for parish councils, which Nazeing Parish Council welcomed, and a reorganisation of higher-level councils, of which it was suspicious. It opposed a suggested transfer of Nazeing into East Herts, of which no more was heard. Soon afterwards, however, the spectre of Harlow loomed over the village. The parish council expressed its "apprehension and disapproval" of proposals to extend the boundary of Harlow to Jacks Hatch and Harknett's Gate, but worse was to follow. Representatives of Nazeing, Roydon, Sheering, Matching, and North Weald met to co-ordinate their response to proposals to incorporate them all into an enlarged Harlow District Council. The parish council minutes recorded doggedly:

> No stone will be unturned in fighting the approaches made by the Harlow Urban District Council. All the alleged benefits would be provided in any case. This council has already lodged the strongest of complaints with the

Department of the Environment against the suggested expansion.

There was at the time a property boom and the Conservative government was determined to increase the number of houses being built. In 1973, on the insistence of the government, the Harlow Development Corporation (HDC) published a plan so far-reaching in its assault on the Green Belt that Sir Frederick Gibberd, architect-planner of Harlow from its inception, almost resigned in protest. It engulfed Roydon and Jacks Hatch, even creeping over the Nazeing parish boundary to embrace the cricket ground on the Common, although compulsory purchase of land protected by the 1947 Nazeing Wood or Park Act would have been very difficult. Andrew Bardsley had just been appointed General Manager of the HDC, following the retirement of Ben Hyde Harvey; he must have wondered what he had let himself in for. In his words, residents of the villages around Harlow "rose as one", making their views abundantly clear in stormy public meetings. The first stage of the fight was won when, in the nation-wide local government reorganisation of 1974, Nazeing and the other villages found themselves part of Epping Forest District Council. Yet much remained to be done.

The property boom proved shortlived and, chastened by their experiences, HDC officers were relieved when in 1974 the incoming Labour government approved a new plan that had a less devastating effect on Nazeing and Roydon. Gibberd was now happy but the villages were less easily mollified, so he and Bardsley visited the newly-formed Epping Forest District Council and the battle-hardened Nazeing Parish Council to "explain the merits of the plan", which the councils continued to oppose. Bardsley wrote later:

> Alas, their minds were closed even before we crossed the threshold...The Nazeing meeting was a much more informal and pleasurable affair [than the Epping Forest one]. The village community wanted to know how the plan would affect Nazeing Common, the cricket ground and the already inadequate road to Waltham Cross. Still, we left knowing that we had not made the slightest impression on them.

A hard-fought public inquiry lasted through the hot July of 1976. The eminent QC Sir Frank Layfield represented the district council, with John Drinkwater QC appearing for Nazeing, Roydon, and seven other parishes. Layfield hammered away at the theme of threat to the Green Belt, and convinced the inspector that Harlow should expand by building on agricultural land within its own boundaries.

179

The decision was announced in April 1977 by Peter Shore, Secretary of State for the Environment and a former Harlow resident, as part of a general statement curtailing the expansion of new towns. The thinking was that their continuing to swallow up the open countryside around them would defeat the object for which they were established in the first place. This was a change of heart that owes much to the "vociferous opposition" of Nazeing and many similar communities throughout the country. Shore's statement also provided for the abolition of New Town Corporations and the transfer of their powers to the appropriate district council, which in the case of Harlow happened in 1980.

Harlow District Council turned its attentions eastwards to develop the open agricultural areas of land now known as Church Langley. Although the 1998 Essex County Structure Plan saw Nazeing as a Green Belt buffer between Harlow and East Herts, many local people did not dismiss the possibility that plans might be changed because of the high demand for housing throughout the south-east. One Nazeing resident expressed the feelings of many in the village: "With such an avaricious neighbour the small Essex parishes of Nazeing and Roydon have had to be on their guard continually...One gets the feeling that there is a smoking time bomb just over the boundary waiting to explode".

Nazeing Conservation Society

In May 1973 over one hundred people attended a meeting at St. Giles' Hall, hastily convened by the parish council to protest against the most radical of the Harlow expansion proposals. At Nazeing County Primary School in July, 130 people attended a second meeting and the Nazeing Conservation Society came into being, pledged to do everything possible to resist Harlow expansion. The founding of the society was principally led by John Mackie, Chris Robinson, and Ron Warren, who became respectively President, Secretary, and Chairman, with David Stevens as Treasurer. Collectively the officers and committee were a cross section of villagers who had individual expertise in various fields, including experience, in Nazeing or elsewhere, of public campaigning.

John Mackie was the Labour MP for Enfield East from 1959 to 1974. Born in 1909 into a prosperous Scottish farming family, he joined the Labour Party because he believed a planned economy was the only way to ensure the adequate redistribution of wealth and social provision. Influenced hugely by the poverty he saw within agriculture, he was incensed to see potatoes and milk being dumped in the north of Scotland because the price had collapsed, while people in Glasgow were suffering

increasingly from rickets and many of them were living in abject poverty. Later he was unsuccessful in arguing within the Labour Party for the nationalisation of land.

He was a successful farmer but always pursued other interests. He was particularly keen on advancing technology and improving nutrition, and he was at the forefront of improving housing stock within the agricultural community.

Having fought Scottish constituencies twice but without success, John Mackie won Enfield East in 1959. He bought Harold's Park Farm in 1955 against advice from friends who thought it too run down but, having benefited from prosperous years in farming, he was enthused at the

John Mackie was a leading figure in the Conservation Society and its first President.

prospect of revitalising the farm, and making it into a comfortable home from where he could commute to the Commons. In the 1960s he sold Harold's Park to the Central Board of Finance of the Church of England and became a tenant farmer.

He was parliamentary secretary in the Ministry of Agriculture in the 1964-70 Wilson government. The controversy over the M25 route gave him divided loyalties:

> When the M25 was being planned my constituents in Freezywater
> understandably did not want it through their way. They came to me with an
> alternative route but I had to tell them that they could not rely on my
> unqualified support - it went straight through Harold's Park.

He did not seek re-selection in 1974 because he believed his pro-

European views were at odds with the Labour Party in his constituency.

From 1976 to 1979 John Mackie was chairman of the Forestry Commission, a rewarding job that gave him the opportunity to implement the old Aberdeenshire proverb, "Aye be sticking in a tree". In 1981 he went into the House of Lords to be Labour's agriculture and forestry spokesman. Somewhat reluctantly he took a life peerage, changing his name by deed poll to be known as Lord John-Mackie. He recalled that when he suggested incorporating the name of Bumbles Green into the title "the gentleman who deals with titles advised me against it". He had the unusual distinction of serving both in the Commons and in the Lords with his brother George, a Liberal politician.

When John Mackie died in 1994, his coffin was made by joiners on the farm from wood grown at Harold's Park. On the day of his funeral his son, George, drove a tractor to take him for a last tour of the farm steadings on a trailer that John himself had built in the 1930s, before driving him to All Saints' where he was buried in the churchyard.

The new Nazeing Conservation Society committee had three initial tasks, local awareness, membership, and money. The society launched a huge campaign to promote awareness of the Harlow proposals, publishing a sensational leaflet showed Broxbourne station with its car park extended to cope with 4,000 cars. It may have seemed alarmist considering the small number of cars parked then but in the light of later parking problems it seems remarkably prescient. Vigorous press publicity led to a membership campaign which in a short time recruited over a thousand people, each having a distinctive long yellow membership card. This huge membership gave the society considerable credibility.

The officers and committee knew, however, that they might have to brief lawyers to represent the society at any public inquiry. The financial target had to be in thousands of pounds, which was way beyond the money raised from membership subscriptions. To help raise such a sum three hugely successful Highland Games were run at Nazeing Park in 1975, 1976, and 1978. Though held in an Essex village, they were the genuine article. They were the inspiration of John Mackie, who fed and watered at Harold's Park Farm a group of top Highland Games athletes flown down especially on each occasion. At one games the raffle prizes were presented by the footballer Alan Ball, who lived in Middle Street for a few years and was a World Cup medal winner.

The probable attendance at the third and last games was over six thousand people, at least twice the then adult population of the village. It was an immense logistical exercise, involving hundreds of local and outside people, which included the distribution of 30,000 handbills throughout west Essex and east Hertfordshire, liaison with over twenty outside organisations, and compiling a parking roster with sixty people. Suitably Scottish music and dancing, and games such as throwing the haggis made it a day out for all the family. One thing did not quite go according to plan: there was a sheep dog demonstration during which the dogs found the haggis an easier target than the sheep.

The three Highland Games raised almost £6,000 but in the end little of the money was used. At the public inquiry in 1979 the parish council took the responsibility of putting

Nazeing Conservation Society

Highland Games

NAZEING
ESSEX

Opposite Nazeing Common
between Epping, Harlow and
Waltham Abbey
Enquiries Nazeing 2172

**SUNDAY
10th SEPT.**

10.30 a.m. - 6.00 p.m.

A SPECTACULAR DAY FOR THE WHOLE FAMILY

TOP ATHLETES

Sheep Dog Demonstration ✦ Pipe Band ✦ Solo Piping Contest
Tossing the Caber ✦ Highland Dancing Contest ✦ Shot Put ✦
Hammer ✦ Weight Events ✦ Trade Exhibitors ✦ Roundabouts
Inter-Pub Tug-o'-War ✦ Fun Fair & Side Shows ✦ Refreshments
Scottish Country Dancing ✦ Tossing the Sheaf
Pillow Fighting ✦ LICENSED BAR ✦ Children's Races

Adults £1. Children, OAP's 50p. FREE PARKING
Children under 5 FREE

Printed by : Precinct Press, 59 High Road, Broxbourne, Herts.

The three Highland Games, held at Nazeing Park in 1975, 1976 and 1978, raised almost £6,000 for the Conservation Society's fight against Harlow expansion.

forward Nazeing's case against Harlow expansion. Duplication by the society was considered unnecessary, although it did contribute around £1,500 towards the costs. In any case the inspector, rather to the surprise of many, found in favour of Nazeing Parish Council, which was awarded costs. In 1984 there was a Countryside Day at Harold's Park Farm, with stalls, tractor rides, and other entertainment but since then there have been no large-scale fund-raising events. The society has, however, sold an attractive range of goods inspired by Nazeing locations, thereby augmenting its healthy financial reserves, which passed the £10,000 mark in 1996.

Nazeing's heritage buildings

In 1975 the Nazeing Conservation Society turned its attention to a major conservation issue within the village, the preservation of ancient buildings. During the twentieth century a dozen or more were destroyed and no record of them survives even in the form of photographs, although the New Domesday does give detailed descriptions of their state in 1912. Ham Farm, an old timber and thatched house near the site of present-day Nazeing County Primary School, was already "in ruins". Among the agricultural cottages later demolished and never replaced were two near Nazeing Park and one in Cemetery Lane, described as "in poor condition". Two old timber and slated cottages at Clappers Weir, then "in fair condition and repair", were replaced in 1957 by Little Dormers.

Nazeing Chapel, from Clapper's Weir   D. BELL

Clappers Weir, Middle Street c1900 with the chapel roof showing over the trees. In the centre, the weather boarded cottages were replaced in 1919 by Newlands and Trevone. The road-side building in front of the cottages is Jenny Judd's village shop.

Snows was "a small freehold country residence in excellent condition...brick and timber built and slated...with 3 recreation rooms, 4 bedrooms, dressing room, bathroom...old conservatory at side in very decayed condition"; unfortunately it was burnt down around 1928. The replacement house, not built until forty years later, was named Marhaba and later Laun House, thus obliterating all record of its historic status.

Sometimes the development of agricultural land rendered the house from which it had been farmed redundant. Between the wars 40 and 42 North Street replaced The Old Cottage, next door to Whitehall Farm which survived, albeit extensively altered. When in 1957 Curringtons made way for 2-12 Pecks Hill and 1-15 Maplecroft Lane, the parish council complained about the mess left by the developers. Councillor Douglas Ragg expressed his concern about preservation of old buildings, in particular an old barn at the Rookery in St. Leonards Road; his colleagues recorded their view that old houses with historic associations should be preserved. They were clearly encouraged that "a good number had already been put into a good state of repair for resale and were now occupied by good class tenants", but they seem to have overlooked the irony of discussing the recently demolished Curringtons at the very same meeting. Douglas Ragg died in 1959 and when, three years later, five new bungalows replaced the Rookery and its barn, nobody continued his campaign. All of these buildings were described in 1912 as being in good or fair condition and, while they may have deteriorated, it seems more likely that their only fault was to be in the way of "speculative builders".

None of these losses was regarded with any great concern but the same cannot be said of Mansion House, architecturally one of the most notable houses in the village. The New Domesday described the house as "Brick & timber & tiled - 4 Bedrooms, 2 Living Rooms, Scullery & Dairy - Old but in very fair condition". In 1881 Harry Bugg had taken on the tenancy and in 1906 it passed to Harry's son George Sinclair; both were parish councillors and school governors for some years and George was a churchwarden from 1923 to 1934. George's brothers, a schoolmaster and a commercial clerk, had by 1891 changed their surname to Sinclair, perhaps because they found it embarrassing in their professions. George's great-grand-daughter Joy Tizard said that George followed suit because his prospective wife refused to become Mrs Bugg. Family tradition does not reveal why the brothers chose the name Sinclair, which was not, as often in such cases, the maiden name of a female relative.

**Mansion House Farm in the 1920s. Its demolition in 1975 led within ten years
to the listing of 45 historic Nazeing buildings.**

In 1924 George Sinclair bought Mansion House Farm and the
adjoining Brook House from Archdale Palmer for £1,550. Soon
afterwards he moved to Brook House and sold Mansion House
farmhouse, buildings, orchard, and about three acres to David Pegrum and
the rest of the land to Arthur May. It is possible that Pegrum and May
lent him the money so that he, as sitting tenant, could buy it at a
favourable price. Their plans to develop the property failed and the
ownership of the farmhouse and the buildings was split. In 1951 Norman
Robson purchased the house and part of the orchard, with the remaining
land and the outbuildings being bought by Harry Hutchings, who had
rented them since 1929.

In the 1940s and 1950s thousands of historic buildings throughout the
country were destroyed with scarcely a murmur but the wanton
destruction of the Euston Arch in 1962 was the catalyst for a radical
change of attitude. When, therefore, over one weekend in April 1975
Mansion House Farm was demolished by its new owners, many in the
village were shocked, as they might not have been fifteen years earlier. It
emerged that the house was not officially listed so no misdemeanour had
been committed. The Conservation Society was concerned, however, that
other old houses might go the same way.

Mansion House Barn before and after conversion into a private dwelling.

Epping Forest Council lacked the resources to carry out a survey of buildings thought worth considering for listed status, so the society undertook the task and produced a preliminary report. Cecil Hewett was a senior officer in the Historic Buildings and Conservation Section of Essex County Council, and the author of *The Development of Carpentry 1200-1700: an Essex Study*. He visited the village to appraise local buildings for possible listing and was shown around by members of the society. Their enthusiasm persuaded him to bring forward the review of Nazeing's historic buildings before those of equally deserving Essex villages, so that 45 buildings were listed in a schedule published in 1984.

One of them was the barn at Mansion House Farm, a timber-framed structure of Baltic pine that was built around 1700. By the late 1980s it was deteriorating and was redundant as a farm building, being isolated in the middle of a residential area. The Hutchings family obtained permission for an attractive and imaginative conversion that shows how new uses can be found for old buildings.

The Conservation Society publicised the significance of Nazeing's historic buildings in three main ways. First, it commissioned wall plaques to be offered at a small charge to residents of heritage buildings. Secondly, it devoted its March 1985 meeting to a talk entitled *Dating Your House in Nazeing* given by Adrian Gibson, an enthusiast for vernacular architecture, who later visited some of the properties to identify interesting features which were often unknown to their occupiers. Finally, it published *Nazeing's Heritage Buildings*, which has become known as the Black Book. Compiled by Colin Gibbons with photographs by Russell Robertson, the book covered not only the 45 listed buildings but also all the properties (and buildings on the sites of properties) recorded in the Tithe Award of 1847. In the preface Adrian Gibson wrote that "Nazeing is a small area of Essex that has miraculously survived the expansion of London and is an example of rural life lasting right up to modern times". The Nazeing Conservation Society was itself one of the agents of Nazeing's miraculous survival.

The apparent abandonment of plans to expand Harlow westwards and the listing of 45 historic buildings meant that two of the initial reasons for the Conservation Society's existence had tended to fade but, as other important planning issues arose in the 1990s, the society continued to be a strong voice for conserving Nazeing's unique position in the Green Belt as a buffer between Broxbourne, Waltham Abbey, and Harlow.

Dutch Elm Disease

In Nazeing, as in much of Essex, the elm was the dominant hedgerow and parkland tree for centuries and several Essex village names point to the significance of this majestic tree. There were thousands of fine specimens on the boulder and London clays of middle and upper Nazeing, with English, Smooth-leafed, and Wych Elm flanking the fields where houses stand now. Yet urbanisation and modern

Above: the elm avenue at Harold's Park, c 1880 and below, after Dutch Elm disease.

agricultural practices played a comparatively minor role in the tree's downfall when compared with the scourge of Dutch Elm Disease. The disease is a fungus which is carried by a beetle from tree to tree, where it grows in the new ring of wood, just inside the bark, on which the tree relies almost totally for its flow of sap. When the fungus blocks the sap vessels the tree dies from the top downwards.

One of the most impressive elm avenues in the whole Epping district was the one that ran from Bumbles Green to Harold's Park Farm. The Town Planning Scheme of 1938-9 contained intricate detail about policy but mentioned only two specific places, North Weald Aerodrome for its expected part in the war which by then seemed inevitable and, remarkably, the Harold's Park avenue. The trees could not be cut down without the district council's permission but, unfortunately, in the period between the preparation and publication of the scheme, the disease had already accounted for the Harold's Park elms and many others in Nazeing. The outbreak abated leaving survivors throughout the parish, although in 1954 some diseased elms at St. Leonards Farm were cut down. Nazeing was said then to be "considerably over-treed", so that owners could, with permission, "take a tree crop".

Then in 1971 a particularly potent strain of the disease entered England in unbarked tree trunks, spreading it seemed from the ports of Southampton and Tilbury. The parish council requested the co-operation of larger landowners in preventing its spread and the Nazeing Horticultural Society offered to help in any way it could. The Conservation Society produced a series of widely distributed newsletters which urged owners of dead and dying elms to fell and dispose of the wood, to preserve other deciduous trees such as oak, ash, lime, and field maple, and to plant replacement trees, for which there were grants available through Essex County Council.

The loss of elm continued unabated until by 1980 scarcely a mature tree remained. At Nazeing Park and elsewhere in the village trees had been lost despite efforts to protect them by injecting fungicide. The following extract from a Conservation Society Newsletter dated July 1979 makes grim reading:

A panoramic photograph of Nazeing taken from the top of Perry Hill in the high summer of 1970 showed a landscape of a leafy village with almost every horizon lined with a row of English elms. Lower down, the urbanised areas of the village were softened and shielded by specimen elms, small groups of trees and high elm hedges.

All this has gone. In 1971 a close-up lens fitted to the same camera would have shown the tell tale symptoms of yellowing leaves in the topmost crown of some trees. By early autumn many of those trees had shed their leaves prematurely and for the last time. Dutch Elm Disease had arrived and the village's landscape and environment was about to undergo a violent change which would leave its scars for half a century.

In the following years the disease spread at an alarming rate throughout eastern and southern England. Locally some fine elm specimens were lost, such as those dotted along the length of Middle Street, several flanking St. Leonards Road, those at Langley Green, the row adjoining King Harold's Head…the list of losses is a lengthy one running into more than a thousand trees.

Dutch Elm Disease still infects young hedgerow trees when they reach 15 to 20 feet in height, so the reference in the newsletter to "half a century" may well be an understatement.

Fortunately the elm was not the only species of tree in Nazeing. With the co-operation of Epping Forest Council, the Conservation Society obtained Tree Preservation Orders on many trees, both singly and in groups. A row of limes at Highland Road was described as "the most magnificent grove of lime trees in the County of Essex". Willow and alder were the dominant trees on the lower ground towards the Lea, where gravel extraction resulted in losses but left lakes whose margins provide ideal sites for such trees to re-colonise. Managed woodlands of trees such as oak and beech are no longer to be found on any significant scale but a satisfying number of hedgerows, some of considerable antiquity, has survived, in spite of the post-war housing development, increased farm mechanisation, and the construction of an extensive golf course.

Epping Forest District Council

It is ironical that in the last quarter of the twentieth century some of the greatest threats to Nazeing appeared to come not from Harlow but from the district council Nazeing fought so hard to join.

Epping Forest's 1983 Local Plan, which mentioned the "vociferous opposition" to Harlow development, was itself a source of further controversy. One of the sites identified for the possible provision of low-cost housing was Fernbank Nursery, sixteen acres north of Nazeing Road and east of Nursery Road. The plan suggested that 200 houses could be erected there, even though one of its major aims was to prevent consolidation of Nazeingbury and Riverside into "a single large sprawl of housing and industry". The site was in the Green Belt and the district council sought "the permanent establishment of Green Belt 'wedges'" by means of tree planting and "voluntary legal restrictions on the use of these extensive areas for other purposes".

Brian Hills had, as a planning officer, fought for thirty years to maintain the Green Belt, especially in his home village of Nazeing. He was horrified by the proposal and, as a member of the Working Group with the council's Planning Department, opposed it strongly. He was told that the Draft Plan was a consultation exercise, in which "negative" proposals such as Green Belt presumption against development needed to be balanced with "positive" proposals such as Green Belt land for housing. The rather cynical view was that some proposals would be rejected and others accepted, while public consultation would be just a smoke-screen.

Nazeing Parish Council responded quickly, congratulating the district council on its wide-ranging plan but going on to direct attention to "those inadequacies and contentious parts which affect Nazeing in particular". The parish cited the Essex Structure Plan, which imposed a presumption against any Green Belt development in Nazeing and envisaged within the built-up area a hundred extra houses, many of which had already been built at Barnard Acres. The parish council quoted the district's own warning against "forming a continuous sprawl very nearly two miles long", commenting that "it could not have put the case against the proposed development more cogently itself". It argued that voluntary conservation measures were by definition unenforceable and found the concept of protecting the Green Belt by building on it "definitely self-contradictory", adding that

> It is not everyone's desire to live in a village with little night life and poor communication with the City, but for those who do, it would be unreasonable to deny them the chance by spoliation of the village by over-development.

The parish council pointed out that the inadequate load-bearing properties of the backfilled soil at Fernbank would require heavy expenditure to reach the gravel base needed for the foundations. This would have priced the houses beyond the reach of the very people for whom they were intended, an outcome which the district council could have done nothing to prevent. It concluded by arguing that 200 new dwellings would increase the population of Nazeingbury by one-fifth, thus causing traffic problems and extra pressure on the school and other services.

The guest speaker for the 1984 mid-term meeting of Nazeing Conservation Society at St. Giles' Hall was the district council's chief planning officer. There was standing room only and some could not get into the hall at all, so when the meeting was thrown open for questions feelings became heated. Many people had moved to Nazeing for its rural setting and feared a substantial urban estate no different from many in north London. Society president Lord John-Mackie warned that such a development would affect the quality of life in the village but urged those who enjoyed the privilege of living in Nazeing's pleasant surroundings to be aware of the housing needs of others. Thus, in one short speech, he summarised the tension between growth and conservation that has characterised twentieth-century Nazeing, and indeed much of the country.

Nazeing Parish Council, the Nazeing Conservation Society, and the Nazeingbury Residents' Association formed a Joint Action Committee to oppose the Fernbank Nursery estate plan, which in 1987 went to appeal. Brian Hills handled the case for the district council. He was able to declare that the parish council and the local groups had considered the proposals positively and had positively rejected them; the county and district councils took their views into account and concluded that the land should remain as undeveloped Green Belt. Not surprisingly, the Inspector agreed.

The district council turned down plans for smaller-scale developments on Green Belt land at Carlton Farm in Middle Street and Brook Farm in Hoe Lane. The period of major housing development in Nazeing seemed complete but there were still other campaigns to be fought. All produced packed public meetings and all were largely successful.

The Draft Local Plan had revealed also that Essex County Council proposed a partial revival of its 1967 plans for a new road from Waltham Abbey to Harlow, although it would have stopped short at St. Leonards Road. The parish council's commendably quick response to this proposal was little short of poetic:

> ...lorries continue to thunder along the Crooked Mile, vibrate through Bumbles Green at all hours … not only interfering with the amenities of the residents of this ancient hamlet but also detracting from the scenic beauty of Nazeing Common as these juggernauts toil laboriously on their way.

There was an exhibition at St. Giles' Hall and, in June 1986, county and district highway engineers attended a meeting of the parish council which did a good job of publicising the visit, so that 105 members of the public squashed into the Bumbles Green Leisure Centre - about a hundred more than usual. The parish council, the Conservation Society, and the Nazeingbury Residents' Association carried out a survey. It established that nine out of ten villagers shared the strength of feeling expressed at the meeting, because the road would have encouraged even more traffic on to the already heavily used Harlow to Waltham Abbey route. All three organisations were represented at the public inquiry in November 1986. The inspector complimented former planner Ray Stevens on the quality of the evidence he presented on behalf of the Residents' Association, but found in favour of the county council. The village and in particular the association had the last laugh, however, as one of their main arguments had been that the scheme would cost at least two million pounds. When the estimated cost had almost doubled to £3½ million, Essex County Council formally abandoned the scheme.

In 1990 Blue Circle Industries closed the Wrightons kitchen furniture factory on the former aerodrome site, with the loss of 160 jobs, so that the land became available for development. Although it was in an area zoned for industrial use, BCI's subsidiary Saxon Developments proposed a scheme for 120 new houses and, once again, St. Giles' Hall was packed for a public meeting. The majority opposed the scheme because additional housing would have put great pressure on village services, although there was a substantial minority in favour. A compromise scheme that would have seen a mixture of housing and industry was put forward but eventually it was agreed that continuing industrial use could provide much-needed jobs. No single buyer could be found and so the Hillgrove Industrial Estate was established with separate business units.

Then, in 1994, following the government putting forward proposals for relaxation of Green Belt policy, the district council suggested a drastic reduction in the size of the Nazeing and South Roydon Conservation Area, which had been established in 1979. Planning controls in such areas are particularly strict and their relaxation could have led to a rash of small-scale industrial developments inappropriate to an area designated for the attractive quality of its landscape. Appropriately, the Nazeing Conservation Society joined with the Roydon Society and the two parish councils to organise a meeting at St. Giles' Hall which was, as always on such occasions, packed. Within a few weeks the district council had withdrawn the proposals, claiming somewhat disingenuously that they were "purely a consultation exercise". The government, too, beat a rapid retreat.

In 2001 Nazeing people had other successes, opposing the siting of a telecommunications mast at St. Leonards Road, the installation of gravel-crushing machinery at Green Lane, and the withdrawal of their bus service. They were still fighting campaigns over flooding and medical services. This is a book of history, not prophecy, but if there is one forecast that can be made with some degree of safety it is that the twenty-first century will see many more such battles. That the campaigners will have a village worth fighting for owes everything to the dedicated and stubborn resistance of their predecessors in the twentieth century.

John Argent Nicholls in front of one of a pair of cottages in Middle Street, 1929. These were pulled down in 1957 and replaced by Little Dormers. The New Domesday (see page 184) described them in 1912 as being "in fair condition and repair".

Ralph Frederic Bury in the uniform of a Deputy Lieutenant. He was the last member of his family to live at St. Leonards House and to take a leading role in the village's affairs. From portrait dated 1937 by Philip Naviasky.

**Above: a portrait of Walter Hargreaves by J. Riviere, presented to him by
Lloyds underwriters in 1919. Below: the energetic Sir Hereward Wake in the
churchyard beside Courteenhall in 1998. Courteenhall is just visible through
the mist in the centre of the picture.**

Above: the ruined gatehouse and garden wall at Netherhall. It was part of Nazeing until 1946 but is now in the parish of Roydon. Below: Netherhall as it used to be, from an engraving, 1784.

Above: the Hutchings family, c1914. The family had moved to Nazeing in the 1860s and have lived there continuously up to the time of writing. Below: on the River Lea to the south of the Rowing Club, probably 1930s. The club house is visible just to the left of the boat.

Colour illustrations

**Nazeing Park c2000 following the extensive restoration carried out by
Jim and Jayne Egan. Below is the magnificent dining room.**

Above: The buildings at Mansion House farm in 1970. On the left is the farmhouse that was demolished without warning in April 1975. On the right, the rearmost barn was converted into a house about 1990. Below: Darmers in the snow. Today these older houses are centrally heated but they must have been comparatively cold in the first part of the twentieth century.

The 1995 All Saints' Flower Festival had the theme *Songs of Faith*. The flower adorned screen depicted "The Church's one foundation is Jesus Christ her Lord".

**Despite being just *Seventeen miles from Town* Nazeing is still a country village.
Above: A view across Nazeingwood Common towards Copy Wood and
Harold's Park Farm. Below: a view from Galley Hill towards Bumbles Green,
centre left. The white building is Nazeing Park.**

**Above: the storm in October 1987 disrupted transport severely and caused
considerable damage to trees and property. This tree fell across Western Road.
Below: The boardwalk is part of the improvement made to the Triangle,
Nazeing Upper Town by Epping Forest Countrycare in the 1990s.**

CHAPTER 6

"IMPROVEMENTS FOR THE SOLITARY PARISH OF NAZEING"

Transport, utilities, and services

In 1908, when the new road from Broxbourne Station to Nazeing had been completed, the former Nazeing Parish Council chairman Ernest Jerrard Wills told a newspaper that the road was "an improvement for the solitary parish of Nazeing" (*Five miles from everywhere*, pp171-3). It was the first of many such twentieth century improvements, without which the events recounted in the previous two chapters could not have happened.

Transport

Before the middle of the nineteenth century movement from a rural community like Nazeing was, for all but the richest, undertaken only for economic reasons such as the occasional fair or market. The railway and later the bicycle made a difference but in 1914 Nazeing was still "five miles from everywhere", an isolation that ended only when tarmac roads paved the way for motor traffic.

The railway

The railway reached Broxbourne in 1840 but it was to be many years before it had a major influence on the everyday lives of Nazeing folk. In the early 1930s more Nazeing residents worked in the local horticultural industry than in London but in that decade the steady development of private housing brought about a shift in the balance. The important Annual Parish Meeting of March 1939, which discussed the sewerage scheme, was postponed from 6.45 to 7.30 at the request of the Nazeing Ratepayers Association, "many of whom were engaged in London and would find it difficult to be present at the earlier hour".

In 1937 came the first of many complaints about lack of co-ordination between commuter trains and bus services to Nazeing. Evening buses were timetabled to leave Broxbourne station just before the train arrived, a less than helpful practice which, at the request of Nazeing Parish Council, the London Passenger Transport Board (LPTB) soon changed. Frequent train delays meant that commuters "invariably missed the bus service to

Broxbourne Station. G. E. R.

Broxbourne Station c1905 before the building of Nazeing New Road.

Nazeing in the evening", so in 1946 the LPTB promised to instruct drivers to "wait for passengers when a train was in sight".

Although the railways of Britain were nationalised on 1st January 1948, passengers saw little change. They still travelled in the same pre-war carriages, hauled by ever ageing steam engines. In 1955, however, a report entitled *The Modernisation and Re-equipment of British Railways* promised to sweep all that away. The lines from Liverpool Street to Hertford and Bishop's Stortford were among those to be electrified; modernisation work started in 1957. Professor Adshead and many others had advocated electrification, but after the war economic considerations had prevailed; any available money had gone to schemes such as the electrification for the London Underground's extension of the Central Line from Liverpool Street to Epping.

On Monday, 21st November 1960, the long awaited first public electric train pulled out of Broxbourne. Exhaustive testing had taken place but the switch did not go smoothly: during the winter of 1960-61 nearly all the new electric multiple units were withdrawn for repair. A motley collection of older electric units from other parts of the country, diesel multiple units, and even a few steam hauled trains were brought in to maintain the service. Only late in 1961 were steam hauled passenger trains finally removed from the line; the full electric service did not start until 18th June 1962.

The new rolling stock was not a great improvement over the previous steam hauled coaches, as the design reflected the thinking of the time. It still had slam doors and high backed seats filled with horsehair. Over half of the coaches had compartments, the one next to the guard's area being for women only.

The economic considerations which had prevented earlier electrification still influenced the 1960 scheme. In order to save money, the Lea Valley route via Tottenham Hale was omitted at first. Before electrification, services from Broxbourne had used the Lea Valley route, calling at all stations and taking 50 minutes for the journey to Liverpool Street; a few Cambridge expresses also called at Broxbourne, with a journey time of around 35 minutes. The electric service along the newly reopened route from Cheshunt via Lower Edmonton took 34 minutes to reach London, but very few Cambridge trains called at Broxbourne and most Lea Valley trains started at Cheshunt, so that passengers had to change.

Life for the commuter then stabilised. On 1st September 1968 the first section of the Victoria line opened from Walthamstow to Seven Sisters, but it was not until the new line was extended through central London on 7th March 1969 that it was much use to travellers. Two months later electrification of the Lea Valley line was completed and trains from Broxbourne started to use both routes. At the same time, some trains became second class only. A reconstruction of Liverpool Street Station, which had been advocated by Adshead as far back as 1933, took place at last in 1991. It eliminated the bottleneck on the approach to the station which had been one cause of delays, and won the prestigious Watson Steele award for its architects.

In the 1980s travel brightened up literally, when all the coaches underwent an "interim refurbishment". Compartments were replaced by open saloons and lighting by fluorescent tubes was introduced. Sliding door trains were first used in 1984, and slam door stock was withdrawn finally in 1992. Commuters could no longer throw open the doors as the train entered the platform and leap off as close to the stairs as possible, a habit that caused many accidents. One man who thought he had arrived at Broxbourne station jumped out, only to find himself in the river. Fortunately, he sustained no permanent damage. Doug Ball remembered a less dangerous habit: "Nazeing commuters often travelled together and it was not unknown for one who had had an exceptionally hard day to be unkindly awakened with the cry 'Stortford', as the train drew into Broxbourne". Privatisation in the late 1990s brought new colour schemes but the trains were still twenty years old and for passengers there was no obvious improvement in service.

On 3rd November 1960 an official party had visited Broxbourne to open the new station, slightly to the east of the original building, which was demolished in the redevelopment. At the same time a larger car park was provided. When the Lido was opened about twenty years later, many commuters avoided paying the station's parking charges by using its car park, so that the closure of that car park in the 1990s hit them hard. At about the same time additional parking space was provided at the station from areas in the goods yard previously used for traffic to the coal depot. In the 1990s English Heritage placed Broxbourne Station and its signal box on a provisional list of railway structures worthy of preservation but it was Harlow Town that received a Grade II listing.

Roads and traffic

In 1900 the Nazeing road network had changed little for centuries; even a hundred years later Nazeing New Road remained the only major addition to it. Peter Brent recalled that one of the few ways of getting out of the village was the horse and trap: "A few people had a bicycle but you were always getting punctures as the roads were made up with gravel. In the summer months they were very dusty and during the winter they were very muddy and had potholes six inches deep." Villagers often shovelled up the manure to use on their gardens, where they grew their own vegetables and fruit.

Soon after the First World War Epping Rural District Council began to surface the principal roads with tarmac. In 1921 the parish council requested "the extension of the graniting of the road leading from the Lower School to the Parish Chapel", so evidently part of Middle Street had already been completed. Most of the roads were improved in the 1920s; by 1929 only Waltham Road remained to be done, although some of the old roads such as Cemetery Lane and Tinkers Lane were never upgraded and remained as bridleways, often impassably muddy. The method used is indicated by an episode in 1934 when it was done poorly and Archdale Palmer complained to the Road Surveyor about the "unduly large pebbles recently laid upon the Parish Roads, and especially the wholly inadequate manner in which the Steam Roller had...carried out the rolling". The steamroller came once a year and was kept overnight in a council depot, used mainly for storage of shingle, where Nazeingbury Parade now stands.

Throughout the 1920s there were constant complaints about the quality of the roads and their increasing use by motor traffic, so discussion of "danger spots" became a regular agenda item at parish council meetings. Councillors suggested that "the use of Char-a-bancs" should be banned on narrow and dangerous roads, and that the hedge at "Pegrum's Orchard" (the corner of North Street and Middle Street) should be replaced by "a wooden fence which could be seen through". Motorists unfamiliar with Nazeing sometimes tried to avoid the gates and the toll road over the Common by going down the cul-de-sac at Belchers Lane, so the district council installed a new road sign.

Deep hollows in Middle Street meant that often the children could not get to the council school and that when they did their feet were wet, so the headmaster complained and the district council filled the holes with gravel. The sharp bend at Bentons was a constant problem. White timber fencing, installed in 1923 to increase awareness of the danger, was evidently ineffective, for two years later the situation was even worse and Walter Hargreaves branded Middle Street a disgrace because of the "grave danger from its surface and narrowness for motor traffic". In 1955 parish council chairman Frank Radford was called away from the meeting at the council school to answer a telephone call from a driver whose car had stalled in rainwater there; it is unclear what she expected him to do about it, other than come out and give her a push, but the parish council referred her to the Essex County Council Highways Department. In the rest of the century there were many more accidents at this corner.

In the 1930s the burden of complaints shifted from the quality of the roads to the quality of the driving on them and to the nuisance caused by lorries. In 1932 the parish council asked the Automobile Association to erect a "Danger Post" in North Street where there were frequent instances of speeding, particularly by lorries. At Aerodrome Corner lorries often damaged the pavement and one smashed a seat. Councillor Emily Drane reported that lorries were driven past the council school in a dangerous manner, so a warning sign was erected in Middle Street. In 1935 a national speed limit of 30 mph was introduced for built-up areas but

Nazeing, being without street lighting, did not qualify. The parish council decided not to apply to the county council for a speed limit but pressed

The rise of the motor car presented Nazeing people with new opportunities, and the Welch brothers opened their garage in a converted wheelwright's shop at Bumbles Green. Above: (left to right) Andrew Welch, Bob Johnson, Stan Welch and Stan Traveller in 1935. Below: the garage in the 1970s.

for better supervision by the police of "the present reckless driving". Immediately they brought a successful prosecution against a dangerous driver.

The parish council's complaint in 1954 that "despite much correspondence no appreciable improvement in Nazeing roads has been observed" was a regular theme for many years after the war. Overgrown bushes at road junctions and overhanging trees on main roads were a constant hazard. In 1948 the "reckless driving of POW lorries", probably carrying prisoners of war to work in Nazeing nurseries, was referred to police. In 1949 the secretary of the Nazeing Road Safety Committee arranged for the showing of a film at the Parish Hall in Betts Lane and at the school. In 1954 the Transport and General Workers Union considered the Nazeing roads too dangerous for the use of double-decker buses. In 1957 councillors asked for a white line to be painted at the junction of Hoe Lane and Middle Street; when after several months nothing had happened they grumbled that it was "by no means the first time discourtesy had been extended to the Parish Council by the County Authorities".

A dangerously steep camber to the road outside Nazeing Glassworks was first reported in 1953. A bus "leaned over so alarmingly that women and children passengers panicked", so the parish council wrote to the county council warning that there would be an accident. Essex promised to improve the camber, provided that it could purchase land to widen the road, but this proved a major obstacle. In July 1958 there were two lorry accidents. Its patience exhausted, the parish council sent a complaint and copies of its correspondence over the previous five years to Graeme Finlay MP, who reported that the Ministry of Transport had granted the county council the money for the job but acquisition of the land was still proving difficult. Finally, in April 1959, the land was bought and soon afterwards the work was done.

As a result of complaints about lorries causing "obstruction and inconvenience" at Monty's Café on Nazeing New Road, the Ministry of Transport approved "No Waiting" regulations in 1955. When a resident suggested to the Annual Parish Meeting that this was "somewhat harsh because it affected the livelihood of a nearby café owner", the chairman pointed out that the order had been introduced as a result of strong local pressure. The café closed soon afterwards.

The use of cars grew rapidly during the 1950s. It seems that when

Pound Close was laid out in 1948 there had been no expectation that council tenants might aspire to car ownership and so garages were not provided. Yet within two years there were complaints about "parking without lights and noise from starting of cars". Palmers Grove was already being planned but the lesson was not learned and by 1960 street parking there was a serious problem. A traffic census carried out in 1956 showed that a total of 7,350 vehicles passed along Middle Street in one week, so the parish council asked for it to be designated a B road but, to the council's great dissatisfaction, the Ministry of Transport declared it unsuitable for upgrading.

Alan Pond (left) at the opening of his garage in 1962. It was the second self-service garage in the country and the first in the south-east.

In 1961 there was an application for a new petrol station at Nazeingbury and the parish council voted 8 to 3 that it "would not be a desirable amenity". Councillor Bert Brown was not convinced that this represented the views of the electors and requested a public meeting, which voted in favour of the proposal. The parish council was nevertheless evenly split on the issue, and decided on the chairman's

212

casting vote to continue its opposition, which proved unavailing. Soon there were complaints about an illuminated sign that was thought to be out of keeping in a country village, and about the use of loudspeakers to assist those unfamiliar with self-service.

As traffic increased in volume and speed, sharp bends became accident blackspots. In 1969 the parish council noted that at St. Leonards Road in the previous three years there had been two fatalities and 51 other accidents. These were attributed to "the dangerous double bend opposite the farm and house". Soon afterwards a start was made on widening the road and bypassing St Leonards House.

The Cross Roads, Nazeing.

FRITH
NZG 14.

Nazeingbury crossroads before it was re-aligned in the 1950s.

Nazeingbury crossroads had become a major hazard even before the Second World War, when the parish council complained to Essex County Council about "the especial danger at the Pound, through Motorists' not being notified which of the Cross Roads was a Major and which a Minor Road". After the war, St Leonards Road and Nazeing Road were designated as part of the B194, and therefore the major roads. In 1950, after the fourth accident in four years, the parish council asked for HALT rather than SLOW signs at North Street and Middle Street. In a typical bureaucratic compromise Essex replaced the North Street sign but not the Middle Street one. By 1975 the road markings were totally inadequate and when pressure for the installation of traffic lights failed to get action from higher authorities, the possibility of militant action was discussed. Finally, in 1979, the Parish Meeting was told that traffic lights were to be installed soon, but meanwhile the road markings at St. Leonards Road and North Street were lost and the position was even worse. The lights that were eventually installed were second-hand and in 1993 a long campaign for more modern ones was successful.

Buses

Before 1914, motorbus routes in rural areas were a rarity; in Nazeing there were no tarmac roads that could have taken them anyway. After the First World War the demobilisation of troops and the availability of cheap lorry chassis provided the means for a rapid increase in public transport by road. Initially Nazeing was missed out but in 1926 the National Company's Watton-at-Stone to Broxbourne service was extended to Nazeing Gate where the crews often needed to top up their buses' radiators with water. This was obtained from behind Brent's Stores, while Ivy Brent made a cup of tea for them.

In 1928 Walter L. Thurgood founded the People's Motor Services which challenged National with a new route from Hertford to Wormley, some journeys being diverted away from the main road to serve the Fish & Eels, Tudor Village, and Keysers Estate. National's attempts to buy out the People's were thwarted; then the passing of the London Passenger Transport Act meant that all services within the area were taken over by the new London Passenger Transport Board (LPTB). The LPTB adopted a new system of numbering for all their routes, and from 3rd October 1934 Nazeing's main service was the 327 Rye House to Nazeing Gate.

Another bus company had Nazeing connections although it never operated in the village. In the early 1930s various firms took advantage of rapidly improving roads and vehicles to offer a service of fast coaches between London and various key towns. One such was the highly regarded Acme Pullman Company which, from 1929 until its transfer to the LPTB in 1934, operated between London and Bishop's Stortford, with some services extended to Newmarket. Its chairman was Frederick George Smith and the company secretary Constance Beatrice Smith, both of Nether Kidders Farm in Laundry Lane, who between them owned two-thirds of the company.

After 1934 the services stabilised until the start of the Second World

War, when the 327 was extended to Hertford. Bomb damage to vehicles and increased demand for bus travel meant that the LPTB had to hire buses during the war. Thus, between October 1940 and August 1941, passengers in Nazeing found themselves travelling not on the familiar green buses but on red and white vehicles belonging to United Automobile Services Ltd, of Darlington. An extraordinarily complicated series of instructions given in 1943 as to how buses should be reversed at Nazeing Gate was a typical example of the detailed record-keeping that was a feature of wartime life. Throughout the war many small timetable changes were made to save fuel or to meet the requirements of local employment such as "the works at Broxbourne Aerodrome". Late in 1944 double-deckers began to operate on the Nazeing route.

Double-decker number 327 bus negotiating floods in Nazeing New Road, 1947.

The bus service still terminated at Nazeing Gate but as soon as the war ended residents began a campaign to have it extended to the top of the Common and beyond. The LPTB replied that "potential and existing traffic did not justify the extensions asked for". James Sutherland told the 1946 Parish Meeting that the LPTB had "only given feeble reasons for failure to comply with the request", and suggested taking it up again

215

because Nazeing residents visiting the Food Office at Epping had to catch the bus from Hertford at Broadley Common. After three years of prevarication the parish council wrote to Leah Manning MP, to whom the LPTB had promised such a service, to the Minister of Transport, and to Sir Cyril Harcomb, rather mysteriously described as "the official head of the whole of the transport of England". It was not until 1949 that Nazeing gained its first bus link to the east and the recently designated Harlow New Town, when the 393 Hoddesdon to Harlow route was introduced, running via North Street and Hamlet Hill. In 1951 the 327 was extended over the Common and turned at Betts Lane.

The early 1950s perhaps marked the highpoint of bus services in Nazeing, when there was a seven days a week service to most areas of the village. The service was so well used that there were complaints about the last Saturday night bus from Hoddesdon, which was often so full that people could not get on and were stranded. Soon, however, came the first signs of decline.

In 1949, after three years' preparatory work, over 400 people from Waltham Abbey, Roydon, and Nazeing had signed a petition for a route linking the three places. Despite the support of Leah Manning and the Transport Users' Consultative Committee, and a succession of meetings at venues that included the House of Commons, the LPTB was unconvinced and asked for further evidence. Finally in 1952 Biss Brothers obtained a licence from the LPTB to run a private service from the Black Swan, which is just in Roydon, via Nazeing to Waltham Abbey. They promised that "if necessary, relief buses would be run to deal with an excess of passengers", but unfortunately this provision was superfluous. The service made a loss and, despite "an agitation set up by Nazeing residents", was reduced to Fridays only in July 1953 and was withdrawn in February 1954.

Perhaps this failure justified the obduracy of the LPTB in refusing to provide the service; more probably, however, it was an early example of the threat to rural bus services brought about by the growth of private car use. As early as 1952 the cancellation of the 10.00am bus meant that there was no service to the doctors at Hoddesdon during surgery hours. In 1956 petrol rationing during the Suez crisis gave bus operators a temporary boost in traffic but it did not last. Despite protests the 327 was steadily curtailed, although in 1964 it was extended along Betts Lane to Triangle. In 1961 there were complaints that the service was inadequate, especially on Sunday afternoons, but at the end of 1969 Sunday services were dropped altogether, with no recorded protest.

On 1st January 1970 London Transport ceased to be responsible for bus services in the area and the green country buses were taken over by an operating company called London Country Bus Services (LCBS), a wholly owned subsidiary of the National Bus Company. The change did not improve matters, for in the 1970s there were constant complaints about unreliable service. Then in 1986 LCBS abruptly withdrew from operating the 392 and 393 routes. For six years services were provided by Golden Boy Coaches, based at Sedge Green, who enjoyed a high reputation for timekeeping and courtesy. In 1992 Golden Boy reverted to being solely a coach operator and sold all their bus operations to TownLink/County Bus, the privatised successor to LCBS.

Three new services were introduced between 1988 and 1997. The 1985 Transport Act had enabled county councils to designate unprofitable routes as "contracted services", which could also cover roads not previously served. In 1988 Essex County Council introduced an hourly service via the Common and Bumbles Green to Waltham Abbey. In 1997 the county council started "Service 2000", which ran from Waltham Abbey to Harlow with vehicles adapted to take wheelchairs, a service that would deviate up to half a mile from its set route to pick up pre-booked passengers. To serve the various attractions in the area, the Lee Valley Park introduced the summer only Lee Valley Leisure Bus.

These gains were more than offset when in 1997 the 392 and 393 routes were taken over by Arriva. Soon afterwards they withdrew the 393 and made other cuts, but their service continued to be unreliable and therefore ran at a loss. On 21st December 2001 the company pulled out completely and the next day Firstbus took over the service on a temporary contract.

Emergencies and services

As Nazeing grew, it became less self-sufficient, so that outside bodies increasingly took responsibility for emergency and other services which had been organised in the village previously.

Firefighting

Except during wartime, the village has never had its own fire station.

Above, the thatched cottage at Jacks Hatch in the 1920s, with the
"Faux Bros Haulage Contractors" Cadillac. Below, the fire that
destroyed the cottage in 1939.

The 999 system was introduced to Nazeing only after the Second World War. Until 1938 it had to make its own provision for fire precautions, which it did by negotiating arrangements with local district councils. The earliest mention of such negotiations was in 1915 when Epping Rural District Council asked the parish council to contribute towards the purchase of a motor fire engine. Initially Nazeing declined because of the considerable distance and preferred to co-operate with Hoddesdon Urban District Council which was much nearer. It seems that in the end it had no choice.

In 1922 Parish Councillor Arthur Lipson offered to make available his firm's fire extinguishing apparatus, adding that during the working day some of his employees would be available to man the appliance. Draft notices regarding the use of the pump and instructions for its handling in case of fire were read and approved. Lipson & Co. provided also a new carriage on which the engine was set, and the parish council resolved to defray the cost, amounting to £2 7s 6d. Then in 1924 Lipson resigned from the council, as he was retiring from business and leaving the district. When the property of Lipson, King & Coleman was put up for sale, the fire pump was included. Since the carriage was the property of the parish council for which the sum of £2 7s 6d had been paid, the auctioneer was asked to separate it from the pump itself. The carriage sold as a separate item for 22s 6d - a net loss to the parish council of £1 5s.

A proposal that fire hydrants should be installed at Keysers was implemented in 1927. At that time the parish council seems to have objected on principle to the provision of anything at Keysers; it argued that hydrants were unnecessary as plenty of water could always be obtained from the nearby river. This was not always as straightforward as it sounds, for in 1929 the Epping Fire Brigade hose became choked with mud. In the same year a Keysers resident telephoned Hoddesdon because its fire appliance was closer than the one at Epping. They attended and extinguished the fire but the parish council refused to pay Hoddesdon's charges, arguing that the house owner should pay the bill because he had summoned the appliance without prior permission and the expenditure had not been approved. Evidently he should have given due notice that he was going to have a fire.

In 1934 Nazeing Parish Council arranged to pay Hoddesdon Fire Brigade an annual retainer of £2 for it to attend all fires in the village. The council installed six new fire hydrants, sensibly checking first that their outlets fitted the hoses of the Hoddesdon Brigade. Evidently notices about the new arrangements were not entirely effective because, following a fire at Goodalls, telephone staff followed the old procedure and contacted Epping, prompting a major investigation. In August 1935 the Herts & Essex Water Company's supply broke down and parish councillors were dissatisfied with the company's response, so they asked the Hoddesdon Fire Brigade to make unannounced checks on the hydrants to ensure that water pressure was adequate. In 1938 a new Fire Brigades Act gave responsibility for fire precautions to district councils and during the war the Nazeing Fire Brigade, like all others, was part of the nationally-organised National Fire Service (see page 104).

Early in 1947 a serious fire showed that arrangements for telephoning the Fire Brigade were less than satisfactory. Cover from Hoddesdon was normally good but the nearest full-time stations were at Hertford and Brentwood. If Epping was unstaffed the police re-routed calls to Waltham Abbey, a pointless and dangerous exercise since it was in the Metropolitan area and therefore "not supposed to enter" Nazeing. Surprisingly, it was nobody's responsibility to test water-hydrants and outside brigades did not even know where they were. The summer of 1947 was hot and dry and so water pressure fell and there was real concern that there might be another major incident. Fortunately nothing serious happened. The parish council supported a successful application

A barn fire at Harold's Park Farm in the early 1970s.

by Hoddesdon for upgrading to a full-time station with additional appliances, and shortly afterwards the centralised 999 system was introduced. Latterly Waltham Abbey and Harlow stations have served Nazeing, although in 1990 a crew from Waltham Abbey seemed unfamiliar with the geography of the village.

In 1977 Nazeing yet again had its own fire brigade, but this time its professionalism was in serious doubt. The Fire Brigade Union went on strike and Maurice Coleman, then parish clerk, was worried that it would take a long time for one of the drafted Army units to arrive at the scene of a fire. He asked parish council chairman Jeff Franklin if some of the men in the village would be prepared to volunteer for a small mobile unit that could give some help until the Army arrived. Russell Martin, who as the organiser of a Motor Race Rescue Unit had some experience in fire fighting, agreed to set up a portable unit. Mounted on a trailer that could be towed behind a Land Rover, it was fitted with a 65-gallon galvanised water tank. A portable generator provided electric power for floodlights and a water pump that could deliver some 1,500 gallons per hour. The volunteers borrowed many lengths of large diameter hose from local nurseries and bought a standpipe to connect their pump into the fire hydrants provided by the local water authority, which in normal circumstances would have been illegal. In addition to the pump the trailer carried a range of small hand held water, chemical, and gas extinguishers to deal with many different types of fires. The volunteers' fire fighting abilities were never tested on a house but they did extinguish a fire resulting from a three-car accident at the crossroads. Using the Rescue Unit's sophisticated equipment, they were successful in releasing two persons trapped in one of the cars; unfortunately the driver of the other car was certified dead on arrival at Princess Alexandra Hospital.

In sickness and in health

Before 1914 there were no medical facilities in Nazeing and the nearest doctors lived in Hoddesdon. Dr John Wells, who was born in 1871, moved there in 1896 and joined a partnership at 49 High Street. Two other single-handed doctors practised from 56 High Street and Myddelton House. Patients would have had to travel there on foot or by horse, although there were some home visits. All services were funded privately or by various insurance schemes.

Bernard Pegrum can have been no more than seven years old when he

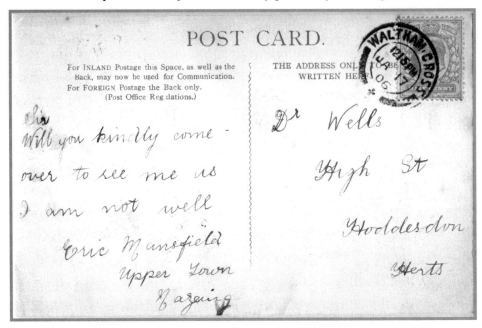

POST CARD.

For INLAND Postage this Space, as well as the
Back, may now be used for Communication.
For FOREIGN Postage the Back only.
(Post Office Regulations.)

THE ADDRESS ONLY TO BE
WRITTEN HERE

Sir
Will you kindly come -
over to see me as
I am not well
Eric Mansfield
Upper Town
Nazeing

Dr Wells
High St
Hoddesdon
Herts

**Postcard asking Dr Wells to call, in 1906. A century later the Post Office could
not have offered such a rapid service, and perhaps a doctor could not either.**

fell down a high step between the living room and the kitchen at White
House Farm and gashed his head open. He recalled the dramatic dash in a
horse-drawn dog-cart to the doctor at Hoddesdon:

> I well remember going down back lane [*sic*] on that journey, round through
> Keyser's Estate – the New Road was not made then – over the Level
> Crossing, past the Mill and the Church at Broxbourne and so to old Dr.
> Hoskin's surgery...I remember the stitches with which he closed the wound
> while my mother held me; also I recall the sweets which he gave me
> afterwards...Strange to say, I have not the slightest recollection of the
> return journey. A veil of oblivion seemed to descend upon me from the
> moment that I popped those "Almond Cushions" in my mouth. Probably I
> slept: perhaps the sweets were "doped".

After the First World War two Hoddesdon surgeries provided general
practitioner services to the residents of Nazeing. In 1920 John Wells
moved to Tylers Cross Farm at Broadley Common, so the range of his
travel increased; by then he was covering Roydon as well. In the
following year he retired to enjoy farming and his family but in 1932, at
the age of 60, he rejoined his old practice, finally retiring in 1947. He
never learnt to drive and for many years did his rounds on horseback or
bicycle. In 1936 he began to use a car that was driven by a chauffeur or,

at night, by a member of his family. He ran a branch surgery in a barn at Tylers Cross Farm.

Nazeing had also a well-loved resident nurse, appointed by Walter Hargreaves. Ruth Thrupp was born at Wheelers on 6th October 1885, one of eleven children of the Judd family, and lived in Nazeing almost all her life. Eileen Bailes recalled that Mrs Thrupp patched her up after she had upset a pan of sausages over her knee in her excitement about a Punch and Judy show. Nurse Thrupp also helped Peter Brent after a mishap at his uncle Nash Hitchin's Leadale Kennels, now in Nazeing Road but then situated behind Brent's shop at Bumbles Green:

> One day, when I went round to the kennels, I put my finger through the wire to stroke a Scottie dog, which promptly bit my finger, piercing the nail. As I withdrew my finger the nail was partially torn off. I ran back to the shop and my dad said: "To the nurse, you!" I ran down Belchers Lane to the nurse, who was at home. She took me inside and I begged her not to put iodine on my finger, which was bleeding badly. She said that she would not use iodine and I was relieved, but only for a couple of minutes because she applied the caustic pencil instead, which was far more painful.

A prosecution brought by the Essex Education Committee in 1923 illustrates the hard choices faced by poorer people. John Brace of Belchers Lane was summonsed for causing his six year old daughter unnecessary suffering, by failing to obtain an operation to remove her badly infected tonsils. The health visitor stated that he could have the operation done at Waltham Hospital for a reduced fee, but he refused because he had six children and could not afford the 30s it would cost, which for him was probably a week's wages. The chairman told him that he was very foolish not to send the child to hospital, to which Brace replied: "I love my child, and do not wish to lose her". "You are more likely to lose her by not sending her," the chairman replied. The newspaper report of the case does not state the outcome.

The Princess Louise Convalescent Home, which had been sponsored by Walter Hargreaves, took convalescent soldiers during the First World War before returning to civilian use. Adelaide Starling recalled that she and other local girls went to a fête attended by Princess Louise in 1919 and were deeply disappointed to find that she was a little old lady in a black dress, rather than the romantic figure they had imagined from fairy tales. Women came from the Prince of Wales Hospital in Tottenham to recover from operations. On arrival they were able to move only with difficulty but gradually they increased their range until, at the end of their fortnight's stay, many were able to walk to Bumbles Green. They went in extended Indian file, with the fittest in the lead, a distinctive formation which the donkeys at Goodalls in the 1970s came to recognise. They would rush to the road gate and lean piteously over it as the women passed, so bringing custom for carrots to Midge Johnson, who used to ask Prudence Dauris with irony: "How are your poor, starving donkeys today?"

With the reorganisation of NHS in the mid 70s the home ceased to be an annexe for Tottenham and was incorporated with local hospitals. This change brought about an increase in staff and the imposition of rules which, for instance, prevented Fred Tenner, the gardener/handyman, from replacing fuses because that was "electricians' work". Not surprisingly the home was soon deemed uneconomic and so was closed. The staff were moved to other hospitals but, when their union found that they had not received the requisite notice, they were sent back, the home was reopened for the six months necessary, and then it was closed again. In about 1980, to the anger of some older Nazeing people, who had helped to raise large amounts of money for it, the building became a private dwelling. Around 1990 the actress Gillian Taylforth lived there for a while.

The Nazeing Parish Council minutes show that before the creation of the National Health Service (NHS) in 1948 much was done on a voluntary basis. During the war the Women's Voluntary Service ran a Hospital Car Service; this was taken over by the Red Cross in 1946. It was operated from Broxbourne and organised by Captain Codrington Crawshay, son-in-law of Ralph Bury, who for a while had difficulty in recruiting Nazeing drivers. Nazeing's awkward position, administratively part of Essex but relying principally on medical services based in Hertfordshire, caused problems. Shortly before the introduction of the NHS, the parish council wrote to Dr Franks of Epping Rural District Council enquiring whether Nazeing would still be able to call on the Hoddesdon ambulance; it considered a reply "purporting to explain the Ambulance situation" to be so ambiguous that the chairman wrote to ask for a further explanation. A medical loan depot started in 1947 was still going strong eight years later. This is the only reference to medical matters in the parish council minutes after 1949, which suggests that the takeover by the NHS was rapid and complete.

When children visited the dental clinic at Waltham Abbey, the pain was as much psychological as physical. In 1949 Connie Reynolds complained that there was only a screen separating those who had been seen from those who had not. A new hut was erected where children could wait, so that "there would be no possibility of hearing what was going on in the clinic".

After the Second World War, with the rapid population increase and the coming of the NHS, Nazeing was for a while served by four medical practices. Then a tacit understanding developed that Nazeing would be shared by the practices of Doctors Freddie Beilby and Leslie Roe at Hoddesdon and Dr Dimmock, generally known as Dim, at Broxbourne. By 1960 both had established branch surgeries in the village. Dr Bobby Sutherland joined the Dimmock practice and set up a surgery, at first beside the newly erected Nazeingbury Parade and soon afterwards in premises above it. When Dr John Gervis joined Doctors Beilby and Roe in 1959, they operated from 56 Hoddesdon High Street, an attractive Queen Anne building. A condition of his appointment was that he should live in Nazeing, so he spent a year at a newly-built house in Middle Street with the dining room doubling up as a consulting room. Then he was able to buy Nazeing Bury, where the old dairy was converted into a surgery and waiting room. In 1965 Bobby Sutherland and John Gervis set up an informal young doctors' group, which met monthly to discuss matters of medical interest,

Dr Bobby Sutherland.

aided by a little beer. Later they became the senior partners in their respective practices. After Bobby's death in 1992 the young doctors' group was renamed the Sutherland Society in his memory.

For most of this period Nazeing continued to have resident district

225

nurse/midwives who were able to offer a similar personal service and assist in home births, which were still the norm. When Nurse Thrupp retired in 1944, she was succeeded by Joan Butcher, who stayed for five years and returned in 1968, as Joan Mansfield. In the intervening period Nazeing was served by Nurse Wagland until 1957, and then by Mrs Thurlow, who was known by some people as the Admiral, because she wore a tricorn hat. She lived at 106 Western Road, designated until 1978 as the District Nurse's home. After she departed in 1961 there came Miss Arundel, Maureen Winch-Furness, Miss Knight, and Carol Andrew.

Health visitors were a useful link for patients, particularly those about to have and having had babies. In 1960 there had been a welfare clinic at the Chapel Hall for some time. A fortnightly clinic for babies and toddlers, perhaps transferred from the Chapel Hall, was started soon after St. Giles' Hall was built and continues to be held there. It was for many years run by health visitor Roz Jones, with a doctor in attendance. At the other end of the age spectrum, Hyde Mead House provided warden-assisted residential care for elderly people not quite able to manage on their own. Opened in 1969, it served in addition as a centre for various social activities such as the Thursday Club.

Looking back after his retirement in 1993, Dr Gervis felt that general practice was more personal in the 1960s. Living "above the shop" gave him a greater sense of togetherness with the patients and home visiting was more common. The arrangements were very informal with no appointment system, but there were consultation facilities, simple diagnostic procedures, and prescriptions as necessary. Both practices ran an on-call system which meant initially a rather exhausting one 24 hour period in three rota, although the doctors knew most of their patients and often were able to dispense advice by phone.

By the 1990s, increasing patient numbers and a more bureaucratic NHS meant that much had changed. Doctors had more paperwork and nurses had to be summoned from further afield. In 2001 the surgery at the Parade was closed and the one at Nazeing Bury opened only two days a week. Often it took a week or more to get an appointment at the main surgeries in Broxbourne and Hoddesdon. People moving into the village were told that the practices were "full to bursting" and unable to take on any more patients. Thus the era of resident GPs and district nurses may come to be seen in retrospect as a golden age for medical provision in Nazeing.

In the first half of the twentieth century the County Hospital at Hertford catered for most of the needs of Nazeing people. Sometimes the partners in the local surgeries worked part-time at the hospital. A surgeon called Donald Bedford, a large bluff man whom some found rather forbidding, was a partner at 56 High Street and an honorary consultant. After NHS reorganisation he became a surgical consultant who carried out a wide variety of operations and invariably telephoned the patient's GP to inform him what he had done. Dr Dimmock combined his GP work at Broxbourne with a part-time paediatric appointment at the County Hospital. Once he came to grief when sawing a branch off a tree while sitting on the wrong end, thereby fracturing both his wrists.

In 1837 the Epping Union workhouse and infirmary was built on Epping Plain. A century later St. Margaret's Hospital was erected alongside these buildings and expanded on being designated as a War Emergency Hospital The wards consisted of huts and were built fanwise. In July 1948, when the NHS was created, St. Margaret's appealed for nurses and Nazeing Parish Council replied that the village could help if Essex County Council provided transport to get them there. A new accident and emergency department and an outpatients department were built in 1969. New theatres and a breast screening unit were added in 1987 and other units have since been established on the site.

With Harlow growing rapidly, a new hospital was authorised in 1957. An outpatients department was opened in 1961 and the Harvey ward received its first patients in 1965. On 27th April 1965 Princess Alexandra opened the hospital that was named after her. Initially equipped with 195 beds, the new hospital was designed to provide for West Essex residents a full range of NHS facilities, including casualty and all medical and surgical needs. The hospital continued to expand. Although there were some 500 beds in 2001, demand for services, including car parking, still exceeded supply. The hospital also provided outpatient cover from a suite at the Hoddesdon Tower Centre. The rise of the Princess Alexandra Hospital meant the closure of all emergency work at St. Margaret's, to the great disappointment of many who enjoyed the friendly working atmosphere.

In 1986 senior radiologist, Dr Ruth Warren, launched an appeal for a scanner at the Princess Alexandra Hospital, so that her patients could be examined in Harlow rather than having to travel to Chelmsford. This eventually exceeded all expectations and raised over £800,000, enabling

Pat Papworth assisted the central Scanner Appeal, decorating eighty new vodka bottles donated by Gilbey's, then in Harlow. Nazeing Glass cut the holes in the sides so that they could take 50p coins, which were too large to go in the top. The bottles were placed in shops, pubs and clubs throughout the appeal area and raised several thousand pounds, including £130 at the Nazeingbury greengrocers.

the Scanner Suite to be furnished. Most of the money was raised by local groups, of which Nazeing's was one of the first. Many local organisations and individuals contributed and the village raised over £6,000. The first two patients were scanned on 20th December 1989 and the next day an infant had a brain scan, thereby avoiding the delay of a trip to Chelmsford.

In 1989, following a Government initiative, a charitable trust was formed to set up a hospice for the districts of Epping Forest, Harlow and Uttlesford, which between them had a population of over 250,000. No fewer than four of the nine trustees came from Nazeing (population 4,500), and they soon became known affectionately as the "Nazeing Mafia". Named after a disciple of St. Francis, whose name was given to a neighbouring hospice, the St. Clare West Essex Hospice Care Trust defined its main object as "The relief of persons who are terminally ill by the provision of a care service to such persons and to carers and the support of such carers in need after bereavement". By the end of 1992 the trustees had established five day-centres, a loan service for equipment such as stair-lifts, a 24-hour helpline, and a friends group to raise funds and provide voluntary help. Large amounts of money were raised by fund-raising efforts such as the shop, while local firms and organisations assisted in cash and kind. The helpline was operated through Epping Forest Council which provided grant-aid also. Harlow Council gave free use of its premises for an office and day centre. The *West Essex Gazette* offered a £50 prize for a new logo and continued to provide extensive publicity.

Having consolidated their activities, the trustees began the search for a permanent headquarters and Stone Barton at Hastingwood was identified as a suitable site. For a while the trust went into debt; if it had failed the trustees would have been personally liable but, by 1997, enough money had been raised to buy the site at a cost of £320,000. Although it was in the Green Belt, Epping Forest Council granted planning permission for development on the grounds of special community needs. New buildings cost £2 million and the annual cost of running the trust was £250,000. The opening of the inpatients unit on 10th January 2000 represented the culmination of a decade of intense hard work and community effort. Local groups were invited to sponsor rooms that would be named after them; one such was the Nazeing Room.

Law and disorder

In 1831 Nazeing was described as "a respectable little place" and the influence of the gentry, the church, and the chapel ensured that the village maintained that reputation well into the twentieth century. Crime went little further than the activities of "the occasional poacher", which seem not to have been regarded very seriously.

When outsiders committed crimes they were sad rather than vicious. In 1921 an 18 year old boy of no fixed abode walked from Bishops Stortford looking for work. Harry Faux of Jacks Hatch gave him supper and allowed him to sleep in a hut, but the next day a watch and 2s were missing from the kitchen. The boy admitted the theft and offered to return the watch but said he had spent the 2s on food. The Bench committed him to the Quarter Sessions for sentence, with a recommendation that he be sent to Borstal.

Various cases that came into court between the wars demonstrate no criminal intent, only that some Nazeing people were slow to come to terms with the rules and regulations being imposed on them by the steadily encroaching outside world. A farmer was fined 10s for failing to register as a cow-keeper and £2 for not cleansing a milk vessel. Epping Rural District Council prosecuted two Carthagena residents for occupying premises without first obtaining a building surveyor's certificate and each was fined £1. A Bench chaired by Ralph Bury fined a shopkeeper 10s for selling imported apples without a label denoting the country of origin, and £5 for selling meat that was stamped with the country of origin but showed no label. When Bury himself sought to eject his former head horseman from a tied cottage, he failed not only to ensure that the man had alternative accommodation but also to obtain the Board of Agriculture's certificate that possession of the cottage was necessary in the interests of food production. Joseph Pegrum was prosecuted because he "could not be bothered" with stamping his employee's National Insurance card every week (see page 73).

The 1930s saw the first complaints about vandalism, a nuisance seldom absent since. Two seats at the Lower Recreation Ground were "continually thrown over and moved around". Archdale Palmer gave instructions that three boys who had maliciously damaged the notice board at the pound should be charged before the Bench at Epping, where each was fined £1 and bound over for six months. Following wilful damage to notice boards at the pound and in Riverside Avenue, the parish council erected new ones "on private land where they might be safe from the attentions of the Wreckers". War brought no end to the nuisance, for in 1940 a notice board at the river was "wilfully damaged by some mischievously inclined person" and an PCC notice board was erected in the garden of 4 North Street by permission of the owner who would "do his best to protect it from damage by boys".

After the war the police were seldom able to prevent frequent cases of wilful damage in the Nazeingbury crossroads area. Targets included garages at Pound Close, litter baskets, phone boxes, the parish council noticeboard, and the notices on it. A favoured occupation was to see whether the bus shelter would float in the brook. After street lamps along Middle Street were vandalised, the parish council suggested that the leader of the Youth Club at Bumbles Green "tell members the danger of tampering with doors to light columns".

In 1935 Archdale Palmer made the first of many complaints about the "Inadequacy of the one Village Policeman". Essex Police could not provide an additional constable but "the possibility of Motor Police Patrols through the Village from time to time was not turned down". The parish council considered the Chief Constable's reply very unsatisfactory, so Palmer complained to the Home Office Inspector of Constabulary about "the inadequate provision of police by Essex in Nazeing". In 1939 there were two cases of shooting in Nazeing, one accidental and one deliberate.

In 1952 the parish council complained about the attitude of the police to "danger on roads" and invited Superintendent Dring to attend one of its meetings. The chairman attributed the "growing menace" of lorry traffic, primarily due to the transporting of gravel from local pits to nearby new towns and of coal from Broxbourne Station to local glasshouses. There were also problems from "heavy farm implements" and weekend campers. The superintendent replied that press criticism of the local constable was unfair since he had to serve a growing population in an area of six square miles. It was agreed that a letter should be sent to the Chief Constable recommending that "the present officer should be made more mobile" and that a second officer should be posted to Nazeing.

The parish council made a point of telling the next Parish Meeting that "PC Leggett had performed his duties in exemplary manner but one constable was insufficient to deal with the vast amount of traffic using the Nazeing roads". Desmond Day recalled that Vic Leggett was

> an excellent policeman who operated from a house in Pecks Hill…and never seemed to have a day off. When I reported a swarm of bees in our garden he turned up with the equipment to capture them. I have seen him perched on his bicycle leading a runaway horse to safety. The village lads held him in awe. There has been no one like him since.

It is unclear whether Leggett acquired his bicycle before or after the parish council's request that he should be made more mobile.

In 1959 the parish council, citing the "vastly increased population of Nazeing during the last few years", requested once more a second policeman for the village. Essex police agreed in principle, but said that no accommodation was available. Later in the year Col. May reported that they were seeking land to build two police houses to be used "when the current manpower shortage is resolved", and soon afterwards the houses were built at 64-6 North Street. Policing remained homely and low-key, for when Doug Ball reported a minor incident the policeman was out and his wife promised to tell him when he came in for his tea.

A succession of policemen came and went without making any great impression on the village. As patterns of home ownership changed, few of them wanted to live in the police houses and so the village seldom had a resident officer. In 1987 several neighbourhood watch schemes were established; more were added later.

Flooding

Flooding is reported to have occurred in Nazeing since the seventeenth century, when farmers were fined for failing to clear blocked ditches. There were, from 1891 or earlier, constant problems near the junction of Hoe Lane and Middle Street. Although the proposal for a flood relief scheme as a memorial to those who fell in the First World War proved prohibitively expensive, the surveyor's analysis gives a valuable insight into the problems. He identified the main cause at the Nazeing Brook, where the proliferation of trees and bushes on its banks meant that when the water rose above a certain level there was nowhere for it to go except to flood. At Greenleaves it spread across Hoe Lane, making the road impassable. The various culverts along the brook were not large enough, particularly near Marshgate, where improvements were essential "so that the water can spread more easily over the marshes which would appear its natural vent in time of flood".

There are constant references in the Nazeing Parish Council minutes to flooding. Often it was a simple failure to clear ditches, as in the testy exchange between two Upper Town farmers where one promised that she would clear her ditch the moment the other had cleared his. Walter Benjafield of Nazeing Bury complained in 1926 that he and other owners had cleared the Nazeing Brook as far as Paynes Lane but it "was obstructed from there onwards, round the property owned by Mr Perkins of Poona Lawn and for some considerable distance in a westerly direction". In 1939 a blocked ditch caused the flooding of houses at Nursery Road and the owners of the aerodrome were asked to install wider pipes.

The main problem continued to be the failure of the relevant authorities to manage the brook, perhaps aggravated by the rapid pace of building that meant there was less natural drainage. In 1925 the occupier of the newly built Cosy Corner, now mercifully renamed Shingles, and his neighbour at 1 Tatsford Villas complained about severe flooding on the Nazeing Road. Archdale Palmer considered that the trouble was because "the pipes intended to convey the storm water from the ground were inadequate, while the ditch itself, to which these pipes lead, was blocked up, and do not allow the water to flow freely away towards the river". In 1937 eleven nurserymen warned that flooding between Hoe Lane and the river was already bad in September, so the parish council successfully urged the Lee Conservancy Catchment Board to take early action before winter weather worsened the problem. In 1943 the Catchment Board and the Essex County Land Agent blamed each other for flooding and in 1946 the Board applied for German POWs to clear the Brook from Hoe Lane to Paynes Lane.

In March 1947, heavy flooding in the Lea Valley severely affected Nazeing. A view looking east from the railway bridge.

Early in 1947 an unusual combination of weather conditions brought exceptionally heavy flooding throughout the Lea Valley. January and February were bitterly cold so that a six-inch blanket of snow remained on the ground in rural areas. Around 12th March rainfall caused a thaw so the snow melted into tributaries of the Lea such as the Nazeing Brook, and thence into the river. The flow of the Lea was twenty times greater than usual and water levels rose unmanageably, returning to normal only

233

a week later. On the night of 15th March 1947, just before becoming a victim of the flood, the Gauging Station at Fieldes Weir was recording a flow of 114 cubic meters per second, or 7 million baths per minute.

The effect on Nazeing was dramatic, with some people being evacuated and others rescued by boat or left stranded for several days. It is said that a lock gate was broken and that it was possible to row a boat along Riverside Avenue. Joan Butcher (Mansfield) spent the first day on a council lorry helping to rescue mothers with babies. The crew had no time to stop to eat until four in the afternoon, when Taffy Jones, a local resident produced a large fruit cake and a bottle of whisky, the latter a comparative luxury at the time and providing a novel experience for a young district nurse. A Flood Relief Fund was established, by which blankets and mattresses distributed to thirty applicants. The Lee Catchment produced a plan intended to prevent future floods, and the parish council urged the need for an improvement at the junction of the brook and the Nazeing Drain, which drained the land near the Glassworks and still runs alongside Green Lane. By the following March the Board had already widened and deepened the drain but Nazeing Glassworks complained that there was a delay on further relief work.

After the 1947 flood a relief channel three metres deep and with an average width of fifteen metres was designed so that in flood conditions it could handle water at a speed of 7 mph. Although the remedial work ensured that flooding was never quite as bad again, it continued to be a serious hazard. Floods in 1949 and 1968 caused vast amounts of damage by the Thames to the area around the Essex Marshes, leading to the decision to construct the Woolwich Barrier which was completed in 1982.

By 1956 two Nazeing flood wardens had been appointed. In 1958 there was another serious flood, which led the parish council to deplore the inefficient reception of flood victims at the Chapel Hall, attributing it to poor liaison between Essex County Council and local people over bedding and other supplies. In 1968 more than ten square miles of land in the Lea Valley was flooded and 700 houses were damaged. Blocking of water courses caused flooding at Keysers and some gardens in Riverside Avenue were inundated by the Lea. Maureen Ball recalled a police car from which was broadcast a warning of flooding with advice to residents to "take precautions"; on being asked what precautions the unfortunate young policeman had no idea.

The problems at the Lea were eased with the construction in 1972 of the Nazeing section of the Flood Relief Channel, which was cut through so that two of the lakes created by gravel extraction could take any surplus water. In 1974, with the agreement of the Thames Water Authority which owned it, the open space to the east of the Flood Relief Channel was laid out by the parish council with planting and seats. The land lies on the Greenwich Meridian.

Aerodrome Corner before 1972, when the Flood Relief Channel was built and the road was realigned, leaving numbers 1 and 3 on the east side separated from the remainder. The signpost says that the road on the left leads to Broxbourne Railway Station although it looks more like Old Nazeing Road, which goes through Keysers.

The construction of the Lea Valley Flood Relief Channel from Ware to Bow Locks was finally completed in 1976 at a cost of 3.5 million. Its very name is open to misinterpretation, however, for the main object of the scheme is not to prevent flooding in the Lea Valley but to prevent London being flooded with water *from* the Lea. In achieving its main aim it stopped flooding at Riverside but seems to have aggravated problems in other parts of the village. St. Giles' flooded only after the channel was constructed and in 1978 the brook undermined the bridge at Langley Green. In 1982 water poured down Bumbles Green Lane while a fountain bubbled up from a nearby drain so that the road was flooded for many feet. In the Great Storm of October 1987 floods washed away some stiles. The Relief Channel was stretched to capacity then and again in October 1993 but since its completion the Lea itself has not flooded, although tributaries like the Nazeing Brook have.

During the winter of 2000/2001 Nazeing suffered its worst flood damage for many years. After a very wet autumn, problems started at about 10.30 pm on Friday 20th October, when houses near the Bumbles Green roundabout were flooded for the third time in six months. By 1.45 on the Saturday morning Middle Street and St. Leonards Road were impassable. Fortunately, however, the rain ceased by 3.30 and the river levels started to recede almost immediately.

On Sunday 29th October things became far worse and by 10.30 pm Bumbles Green was flooded yet again. This time the rains did not stop, so that by midnight all roads in and out of the village were completely blocked and impassable, as were many other roads in the area. The water in St. Leonards Road was lapping up to the edge of the high part of the roadway in front of the houses, and the railing at the brook was completely submerged. To help clear some of the ditches Essex County Council sent out a large 20-ton lorry with a grab crane on the back, but it was marooned in St. Leonards Road until it was towed out at 7.45 on the Monday morning. Considerable structural damage was done to 27 houses, four of which were to remain uninhabitable for more than six months. One of the flood wardens who tried to reach some of the waterlogged householders in Hoe Lane was swept off his feet by the force of the floodwaters streaming down the road, and managed to save himself only by grabbing an ornamental chain decorating the edge of a front garden.

Although not as severe, there was more flooding on Sunday/Monday November 5th/6th and again on Saturday/Sunday 11th/12th November. Some people wondered if there was some peculiar reason why the floods always seemed to happen over a weekend.

Utilities

As Nazeing developed after the First World War utility companies saw the opportunity for new custom. By 1939 water, gas, electricity, and telephones had reached most parts of the village. People moving in from the London suburbs and elsewhere found some of the facilities that they were used to but brought pressure for others such as street lighting to be introduced.

Water

The Herts & Essex Water Company had begun to operate in Nazeing in 1908, but did not reach all parts of the village immediately. Bernard Pegrum recalled the arrangements at Curtis Farm:

> The household water was obtained from a pump over the sink in a large, brick-floored room known as the wash-house. (We always pronounced it "washus".) Given the opportunity – which was not often – I would try to work the pump but could never move the handle fast enough to make the water gush forth like my father could.

After the First World War the tenants of Walnut Tree Cottages were still obtaining water for washing and cooking from a pond in the back garden.

In the 1930s people at the Red House had to collect water from a stand-pipe in Back Lane but, as Enid Brent recalled: "That was quite convenient compared with walking half way up Common Hill to get a couple of buckets of water...My Uncle Ernie used to have this yoke with two buckets hanging either side of him on chains". In 1938 mains water reached Nazeing Common and the trustees of Nazeing Wood or Park paid "a moiety" [half] of the cost of laying on water to the Pindar's House.

If there were complaints about the company, none was recorded until 1934, when its water was said to be "hard and dirty". In August 1935 its failure to give adequate service meant that Walter Hargreaves had to close the Convalescent Home and send the patients back to Tottenham; other people complained as well, some voicing particular concern about water supply in case of fire. After the war there were complaints constantly about supply throughout the village; in 1947 a breakdown meant that the company had to provide Dobbs Weir with stand-pipes and water-carts four times a week.

In the early 1950s the colour and taste of the water "left much to be desired", a problem said to be caused by "heavy seasonal demand from glasshouses which caused a seesaw motion of water through the mains". P. Hills and Councillor R.G. White both made graphic demonstrations of the problem by producing bottles of the offending water. In response to complaints from the parish council and numerous villagers the company carried out tests that proved its water 100 per cent pure, so the parties had to agree to differ.

In the hot summer of 1959, although the Herts & Essex Water Company blamed problems of water shortage and unreliable supply on the drought, it still agreed to install improved plant. By 1965 water was being supplied by the Lee Valley Water Company, which became part of the Three Valleys Water Company around 1980. Problems with low pressure continued, particularly on higher ground such as Banes Down in the long hot summers of the 1990s.

Electricity

Electricity came to Nazeing before the First World War in the form of private generators, the first of which was at Goats Farm. When Archdale Palmer built Rookswood in 1913, he had a generator installed to serve his house and the two new cottages. It was housed at Rookswood Garage (now Homefield), where later George Cordell, his chauffeur, did the maintenance.

After the First World War there was clearly scope to extend mains electricity to rural areas, so in 1921 the Nazeing and District Electric Supply Company was established by two electrical engineers, a haberdasher, and a greengrocer, all of whom lived in Tottenham. The company's name was the most impressive thing about it, for two years later the Board of Trade reported that it had never done any business and was defunct.

In 1923 the North Metropolitan Electric Power Supply Company applied to Epping Rural District Council for powers to lay mains in Nazeing, intending at first to supply only Keysers Estate. The parish council, clearly irritated by this preferential treatment for what it regarded as "the isolated Western portion of the Parish", urged the district council to insist that "Nazeing Lower Gate should form the terminus of the mains for the present". Presumably the company intended to lay a cable from Broxbourne, but it is unclear exactly when this happened. In 1927 the Electricity Commissioners promoted a Special Order that authorised the company to lay mains to Nazeing and other villages in the Epping district. Initially only the Nazeingbury area was covered, and the company bought from David Pegrum the land south of 4 North Street for an electricity sub-station.

Gradually the company extended the supply of mains electricity throughout the village. It reached Nazeing New Road in 1931 and Bumbles Green in 1933. In 1934 Archdale Palmer paid for cabling to bring electricity to Upper Nazeing. There was no electricity at Nazeing Common until after the Second World War, so Peter Brent built his own generator. When at last the mains supply was laid on Peter and his neighbour at Kingswood Chase had to pay for a branch cable to be put in.

By 1958 the Eastern Electricity Board had taken over from the North Metropolitan Company. Soon after moving into Nazeing Bury, John Gervis wanted to disconnect an unsightly box housing old electrics and the EEB gave him the go-ahead. Having removed the box, he proceeded to cut the cable, when there was a mighty flash and bang that plunged the house into darkness. Fortunately John was wearing rubber boots but he was still flung across the room, with a wooden handle of the melted saw in his hands. His mishap blew the streetlights also, so the EEB agreed that the cable was not dead and cordoned off the surrounding area.

Street lighting

Early in the twentieth century there was still only one form of street lighting in Nazeing. Its source is indicated by the provision that in winter evening services at All Saints' would be held only on the Sunday nearest to the full moon. As late as 1923 the inaugural meeting of what became the Nazeing Branch of the British Legion was deferred until "a later date, when the evenings are somewhat longer". In 1926, when it was known that mains electricity was to be supplied to Nazeing, a suggestion that street lighting should be installed at Riverside was defeated in a special poll of electors. Over the next thirty years there were several similar proposals for various parts of the village but, as it was necessary to obtain the support of a majority of ratepayers, this was never forthcoming.

Under the Parish Councils Act of 1957 parishes were empowered to install street lighting on small estates without reference to the ratepayers. Soon after the Act came into force Nazeing Parish Council voted in favour of lighting but, as there was known to be opposition in the parish and a new council was about to be elected, councillors postponed the implementation of the decision in order to consult the ratepayers. A public meeting was held on 1st May 1958 at the Chapel Hall, where a plan of the proposals was on display and information sheets were handed to each of the 200 people present. The opposition fell into three categories. Some who had lived in the village for many years said that they had never needed street lights before and that they still did not. Some argued that a few widely spaced lamps would merely provide individual pools of light interspersed with large areas of darkness, which would be of no help to pedestrians or motorists and perhaps more dangerous than nothing at all.

A few objectors were those scheduled to have lights right outside their houses, although some of these supported the broader arguments. Despite the strong opposition, the majority of the meeting felt that the scheme would reduce the number of traffic accidents, so it was adopted on a show of hands by an estimated 150 votes to 50. It was perhaps an early example of the conflict between natives and newcomers that was, as usual, won by the latter.

The new parish council established a Street Lighting Sub-committee, which accepted a tender from the Eastern Electricity Board to install thirty lights at a total cost of £1,186. This required the raising of a 6d rate. By January 1959 the lights were being installed and already the parish council had received complaints about their location. One light was due to be installed immediately outside Trevone and Newlands but, on the insistence of Connie Reynolds, it was put on the other side of Middle Street. Another was placed wrongly in the front garden of 78 Western Road and a long-running saga shifted the blame from the parish council to the Essex County Council highways department to the Eastern Electricity Board, which finally moved the light to its correct position on the pavement.

As the village continued to expand the lighting network expanded with it. The parish council attempted to meet the objections of those who thought that the lights would be too widely spaced with a rolling programme whereby eighteen new lights were installed every three years. It negotiated sensible arrangements with the county council and with builders to share the costs of installing and maintaining lights. The council's meetings were twice plunged into darkness by power-cuts and on both occasions it was, by an appropriate coincidence, discussing street lighting.

Refuse collection

By 1934 there had been a private refuse collection at Keysers for some time; otherwise residents were advised to "take their own steps by means of an incinerator or other methods". Then Epping Rural District Council accepted a tender from a Nazeing man for a fortnightly collection covering the whole parish, for which he charged £104 a year plus 7s 6d per house at Carthagena.. At first the scheme worked quite well but in 1937 the parish council complained that collections were too infrequent and many houses were not covered at all, so the district council took over the service, which it extended and improved.

For many years two dustcarts solemnly trundled up the avenue to Harold's Park Farm, one to serve the farmhouse and cottages, which were then in Waltham Holy Cross Urban District, and one to serve the new bungalow which was in Nazeing and therefore in Epping and Ongar Rural District. This less than efficient arrangement ended when Epping Forest Council was created in 1974.

In 1967 there were so many complaints about the untidy state of the village that the parish council began to employ its own street cleaner for 20 hours per week. For a while Epping Forest District Council took on the responsibility and Dennis Hutchings of Long Green did the job. Then, in 1977, as part of a general reduction in cleansing staff, the council dispensed with his services. He was a popular figure and a petition in his support was signed by well over a thousand people. The district council was adamant, however, so the parish council employed him. In 1981 it made a point of expressing its appreciation of his services but when he reached retirement age in 1988, he was unable to agree the council's offer of part-time work, so that sadly his employment ended in some acrimony.

When Dennis Hutchings (left) retired, the Nazeingbury Residents' Association presented him with a leaving gift and he showed committee member David Pracy how the job was done.

In the 1990s the district refuse service was privatised. With environmental matters much more prominent in the public mind, the district council introduced two recycling schemes, although they did not extend to all parts of the village. Garden rubbish was collected in special bags, and paper and tins in blue boxes provided for the purpose.

Shops and post offices

The fortunes of the village shops, and of the post offices with which they were sometimes combined, ran in broad parallel with the overall development of Nazeing. For many years each of the scattered hamlets had two or three shops which usually carried a huge variety of stock. Some of the shops and their owners were long-established village institutions, while others were transitory and made little impression. Documentary sources and reminiscences have provided a considerable amount of detail of which the following is a brief summary.

The longest established shop in Nazeing was at present-day Mayflower. Thomas Argent had opened it by 1841 and was still running it forty years later, aged 85. On the 1891 census his daughter Mary Ann was described as "Keeper of Village Provision Shop", but by 1898 John H. Ashby had taken over. Evidently shopkeeping at Mayflower was a healthy occupation, for after he died his widow Eliza Annie ran it until she was at least 80. Their granddaughter Marjorie was a dressmaker who later reopened the shop as a specialist drapers until, in 1960, she took one

Mayflower in Middle Street, where there was a shop (here just visible as the right part of the building) for more than a hundred years.

242

of the new shops at Nazeingbury Parade and the old premises were incorporated into the private dwelling.

There were other shops in Middle Street. Before the Second World War, Alexander Charge ran a hairdressers and toilet requisites business at the corner of "High Street" (Hoe Lane) and Middle Street. This was turned into a grocers by the Rumseys, whose son Basil was killed in the V2 tragedy, and later taken on by the Umneys. Around 1930 Charles Drane opened a shop and post office in Middle Street at what later became Thaxdene. In 1992 the post office moved to Nazeingbury Parade and the shop closed shortly afterwards.

John and Eliza Ashby, who ran the shop at Mayflower in the early twentieth century.

Peter Daniels recalled that his grandfather, George "Dicky" Banks, was a fishmonger who lived at Whitehall Farm, where Peter was born.

When Squires' grocery at 45 North Street closed, the Fowlers opened their General Stores next door at no. 47. It survived until about 1990.

243

Though blind, George was "able to conduct his business in a most efficient manner mainly due to the guidance he received from his old horse. It was his proud boast that he was never once 'diddled' by anybody in the village because of his blindness." George's wife worked at the St. Leonards House laundry in Laundry Lane, and obtained Ralph Bury's permission for her grandchildren to go into the woods and fields to collect nettles and other fodder for the rabbits which her husband sold. Opposite Whitehall Farm the Pearces had a dairy at 45 North Street, which later became a grocery run by the Squires family.

The first shop at Bumbles Green was opened by Thomas Pegrum around 1860. According to his grandson Bernard, he was also a coal merchant and hay carter, so he should have been comfortably off but as he was "addicted to 'the bottle', the all-too-handy King Harold's Head took a considerable profit from him". Marjorie Sykes recalled that after Thomas's death the business was run by his son "little Alf Pegrum and his wife Sarah, [...who] was certainly a character and very definite of speech". When they gave up the shop, it was taken on by Jimmy Brent who ran it as a butchers and general store.

Around 1890 Frederick Cook established a post office and shop almost opposite Thomas Pegrum's. Initially they were perhaps a sideline, for he was a shoemaker by trade and described as such on the 1891 census. Marjorie Sykes, who thought that "shops were so much nicer in the country than in the town", summoned up the magic of his shop for a girl growing up before the First World War:

> The post office was run by old Fred Cook; and his daughter, red-haired Em Cook, sold stamps and sweets. Some people said Em read the postcards to keep herself informed on affairs of the village. I'm sure this was untrue; but of course all village people are interested in other people's affairs even in our enlightened days... I always thought Em was Fred's wife, until after the 1914 war when she married Harry Mead who worked on the staff at Nazeing Park...The stamps were in a wooden folder beside the small scales for the weighing of letters, and a pile of letters was lying there ready for the afternoon delivery. Letters cost a penny for home mail, twopence halfpenny for foreign. Postcards could be sent for a halfpenny.

> But the interest for us was on the right side of the counter where the large glass sweet jars displayed attractive wares. There were all sizes of bulls' eyes, the largest as big as tennis balls. There were also aniseed balls which had a very strong taste. But the best value for us with our halfpennies and farthings were the smaller sweets. You could get four ounces for a penny

but our mother would not let us buy those, they were too cheap to be any good; of those at two ounces a penny we were not allowed to eat the green ones because they were said to contain arsenic which was poison. We hated to waste these lovely green sweets. Other very popular sweets of the time were in the shape of sea shells in a pale washed colour that was very realistic and attractive; they tasted very nice too, but they did not last very long, as they were soft sweets.

Fred died in the early 1930s, his daughter Emily Mead took over the business. When she retired, the post office moved to Brent's Stores, and was run by Ivy Brent. The Meads' shop was no longer be simply "The Post Office", so Emily chose the name "Cranbourne Cottages", since her son Dennis was stationed at an RAF spitfire base at Cranbourne outside Salisbury, Rhodesia. The shop continued to be run by "Midge" Johnson, wife of Dennis' cousin Laurie Johnson, until 1987. The shop over the road also closed and became a private residence called "The Old Post

Upper Town Cottage, off Betts Lane, was a post office for about eighty years. Built around 1500, it is the oldest house in Nazeing that survives in virtually its original form. The postman is emptying the post box and his van is by the gate.

245

Office". Bumbles Green was now without its own shop for the first time since old Thomas Pegrum had set up more than a century earlier.

In the 1890s Fred Cook's father David, also a shoemaker, had opened another post office at Upper Town Cottage, just off Betts Lane. It too was a general shop where fizzy drinks and other commodities were sold. Having been run for a few years by Mr and Mrs Charles Lewsey, it was taken over by Mr and Mrs Henry Starling and then by their son Harold and his wife. After they died it was run by their daughter Adelaide until 1972, when she retired and it closed. In 2001 she was still living in the house that had changed little since her birth 96 years earlier. In Upper Town there was also, from 1902 to 1950 at least, a general store at the Mill House run by Adelaide's cousins, the Savage family.

In the 1930s Charles and Kate Marshall had a shop in Nazeing Road, possibly at 6 Tatsford Villas, where in 1945 there was a "Sweets & General Store". This probably served the Aerodrome and is unlikely to have survived it for long. In the late 1920s Winifred Wynner opened a ladies' hairdresser at 6 Kingsmead, where a hairdressing business continued until about 1990.

The original 1908 plans for the new Keysers Estate included shops, several of which opened in Old Nazeing Road during the 1920s. No. 123, the one on the corner of Keysers Road, was at one time kept by David Raithby; Edna Miller remembered receiving some ham "off the bone" as a welcome gift when she moved in. No. 86 was a butcher's shop run by Frederick H. Jones and his son-in-law, Ralph Cook; later it was used by a chiropodist. The Post Office and General Store at no. 88 was at first owned by Arthur Button, who built Buttondene Crescent, and then for many years by Mr and Mrs Thomas Turton. When Mr Turton, died Ray and Ruth Brown took it over but later gave up the post office and ran the business down. When they left, Riana Kitchens used it for a while. Opposite No. 88 there was a hut where Gladys Jones and her sister Grace Nash initially sold hardware but later ran a more general store where the young mothers met. It was replaced by a modern building, which had been a shop selling ski clothing and then became a general store/post office until the manager defrauded the Post Office of a large sum of money. Edna Miller and Doug Ball remembered there being no money to pay their elderly relatives' pensions. By the 1990s all the shops had closed and been converted into residential accommodation.

Earlier in the century, many of the shopkeepers increased their trade by taking their goods to the customers by horse and cart. Bernard Pegrum recalled that before the First World War Horace Pemble visited Queens Cottage weekly, delivering one order and taking the next. The round of a Roydon baker named Herbert Mansfield included the Red House, where he fell in love with Nellie Starling and later married her and moved in. Their daughter Enid married Peter Brent, whose father Jimmy travelled all round the area by horse and cart until he "got an old T-type Ford van, which really was a dodgy thing to work because its ignition was by a tremor-box and it had no gear lever".

Between the wars cycling was a popular recreation and hundreds of cyclists used the route from Epping across Nazeing Common and on

The tea room at Jacks Hatch was one of the enterprising ways in which Nazeing people catered for the interwar cycling boom. Remarkably, the photograph also preserves a record of Rumsey's grocery van, which was wrecked by the 1944 V2 rocket.

through Bumbles Green to Waltham Abbey. Local residents were quick to take commercial advantage. A cycling club met regularly for teas in a room at the back of the King Harold's Head and several cottages advertised Hovis Teas, Eldorado Ice Creams, and R. White's Lemonade.

247

At Jacks Hatch, next to their petrol pumps, the Faux family had tea rooms in their thatched cottage until it was burnt down accidentally in 1939.

Another enterprising family were the Johnsons of Long Green. Laurie Johnson recalled those summer weekends and Bank Holidays. At the bottom of what is now Bumbles Green Lane, then only a grass bridle-way, his father erected a small portable black hut with a drop-down counter, and produced his own ice cream in a double walled churn packed with ice. Laurie cycled to Broxbourne station to pick up a crate of ice from where it had been left on the platform; he remembered that it needed at least an hour's hard work turning the churn handle to mix three to four gallons of ice cream. This was an entirely speculative venture but on good days it was sold out in cornets, wafers, and walnut whips. Occasionally, if any ice cream was left over, it was taken up to Nazeing Common Cricket Club.

The last landlord of the Red Lion was Henry Croudson, a famous theatre organist. In the 1960s, he installed and played a Compton organ there. Curtis Farm is visible further along Middle Street.

Doubtless the cyclists were among the many who quenched their thirst at the local pubs. The twentieth century saw many more outside visitors and the resident population of Nazeing grew sixfold, so it is perhaps surprising that the number of pubs fell, albeit only by one. The Sun, the King Harold's Head, the Crooked Billet, the Coach and Horses and the

Crown all existed by 1800 and were still flourishing two centuries later. The only casualty was the Red Lion (now The White House), which had been a pub since the early nineteenth century but closed in 1967.

The post for Nazeing came through Waltham Cross, except for Riverside which was served by Broxbourne. In the 1920s there were regular complaints about the poor quality of the service and the parish council suggested that a motorcycle might be used to get post to Nazeing more quickly. In 1928, when his Langfield Estate development was well under way, David Pegrum asked via the parish council for an additional post-box near Nazeingbury crossroads and this was soon installed. Around that time two more post offices were opened, to serve the rapidly developing Keysers and Nazeingbury areas. In 1949 the Post Office refused to place a pillarbox at Pound Close because there were others within half a mile and people were allowed to hand letters to the postman. By 1953 the Nazeingbury post office in Middle Street had probably become the busiest of the four because, unlike the others, it was allowed to have a stamp machine. Eventually it was the only one to survive.

In 1997 birds nested in the pillar box opposite The White House in Middle Street, and kind-hearted Post Office staff provided an additional box so that the birds would not be disturbed. Less kind-hearted were the thieves who in 2000 stole the box and a similar one in Betts Lane for their antique value.

The greatest single change to shopping in the village came in 1960 with the building of Nazeingbury Parade, which was described in a county council report as an "intermediate shopping centre with a fair range of choice". Originally it and the neighbouring houses were to be called Nazeingbury, which is why the numbering starts at 6, but this was found to be confusing and the word Parade was added early in 1961. Plans for a new shopping parade had been mooted as early as 1951; when they came to fruition there was great interest among potential shopkeepers.

Much of the original lineup could be discerned forty years later. No. 8 was still a chemist, although it and no. 6 had been knocked together and the hardware shop which was there originally was replaced by the post office. Charlie Stonnall, a greengrocer from Broadley Common, moved to no. 10 and, although the business changed hands several times, it thrived until the mid-1990s when various problems caused custom to drift away, so that sadly the last owners had to close in September 2000 through lack of support. Cricks of Broxbourne took on No. 12, which as Nazeingbury News remained a newsagent, confectioner, and tobacconist after they gave it up. No. 14 began as an electrical shop but changing leisure patterns meant that in the 1980s it switched to video hire. At no. 16 were Rudgewicks the butchers, who, by December 2001, were the only family who could claim to have been there from the outset. Marjorie Ashby moved from Mayflower to no. 18 but was forced by ill health to give it up and Dayrose Cleaners took over. Braithwaites the bakers, a family firm based in Wormley, had no. 20a from the beginning but closed all their shops in July 2001 when they could find nobody who wanted to get up at 2.30 am to bake the bread. No. 20b began as a wet fishmongers, a trade that continued in a mobile van on the forecourt, but later became a fish and chip shop. Originally a shoe shop, No. 22 became an off licence which for a while had the rather inappropriate name of Drinkwaters. No. 24 began as a traditional grocer's and was later converted into a small supermarket, which in 2001 combined with the off licence to form a single shop. Above the grocer's there has always been a hairdresser's.

As early as 1927 David Pegrum and Arthur May stated in their publicity brochure that "Tradesmen from Hoddesdon, where there are excellent shops, call at Nazeing daily". They did not even mention the local shops, which they evidently considered beneath the dignity of their potential customers. Between then and 1960, however, more shops opened in Nazeing than closed, so presumably the incomers used them enough for most of their owners to make a reasonable living. Nazeingbury Parade gradually had its impact on the small shops and the last of them closed in the 1990s. Doubtless they were also affected by the rise of car ownership, supermarkets, and out-of-town shopping, which eventually contributed to closures at the Parade too.

Telephones

In 1912 a line of telegraph poles was erected through a field at Carthagena and by 1917 the telephone had reached Nazeing. The General Post Office ran the service and the first Nazeing exchange was a board hanging on the living room wall at Fred Cook's post office in Bumbles Green. Only the wealthy could afford a home telephone so that initially there were just nine numbers, including Nazeing 1 for the post office itself, 2 for Rookswood, and 7 for Nazeing Park. Cook's grandson, Dennis Mead, was born and brought up in the post office. He recalled that the first exchange became inadequate in the mid-1920s. "My grandfather was thrown out of his bootmaker's shop and a proper exchange was put in. Until electricity was laid on in 1935 it was powered from a battery shed in the back garden."

In those days the operation was entirely manual. The subscriber would wind a handle which caused an "eyelid" to drop in the exchange where the operator would put in a plug, and then a second plug to contact the person required. To phone a local exchange outside Nazeing, operators plugged in and asked the staff at the Hoddesdon manual exchange to get the number, while longer distance calls were routed from there via London. "My mother was a stickler for confidentiality," recalled Dennis Mead, "but you still couldn't help knowing what was going on!" When Emily Mead took over the business, she employed his cousin Rhoda Johnson as a daytime operator. "At other times members of the family operated it as and when, running in when the bell went, although I don't think we often had to get up in the middle of the night. For every call we had to write down who was making it and the length of time, then send it off to the Post Office for billing - it was bedlam trying to do that when we were busy." The Post Office received telegrams also; these were dictated over the telephone and written out by hand. Dennis Mead often took them round on his bicycle, sometimes as far away as Claverhambury which was covered by the Nazeing exchange, but "no one seemed to mind a ten year old delivering their telegrams".

Most people relied on using phone boxes. When in 1932 the post office started closing on Wednesday afternoons, the parish council did not object, provided that the "Public Call Telephone Office" and the ordinary telephone service were maintained. In 1936 a telephone kiosk was installed in Betts Lane, later achieving listed building status because it was one of the comparatively few remaining examples of Gilbert George Scott's classic design. In 1941 a new exchange was built at Bumbles Green, allowing the installation of additional private lines. The existing 120 lines were prefixed with a 31 or 21 so that Nazeing Park, for example, became 3107.

After the war telephones were in short supply so that many people had to share a line. In the early 1950s Desmond and Valerie Day of Newlands in Middle Street had to share with Shadwalkers opposite and divide up a single bill. As late as 1965 Colin and Prudence Dauris were told when they moved into Goodalls that they might have to share a line. In May 1958 a shortage of cable meant that residents of the new dwellings in Western Road and Shooters Drive had to go on a waiting list for phones; by September they were being installed but a kiosk outside the Middle Street Post Office was still needed. As telephone boxes continued to be essential, twice in the late 1960s the parish council asked for one at Nazeingbury Parade, expressing its willingness to pay for the installation if the GPO refused. In the 1980s, however, a kiosk installed between the wars at Keysers was removed when the Browns gave up the post office.

Betts Lane is in the Nazeing and South Roydon Conservation Area, and the phonebox there is not out of place.

Once electricity had come to Nazeing, wireless sets with valves could replace the cat's whisker receivers which some people had. Radio became a vital means of bringing the outside world into the village, as wartime reminiscences indicate. In the 1950s houses began to sprout television aerials, so it is probably no coincidence that some of the recreational activities described in chapter 9 began to decline at that time. Although by 2001 satellite dishes, mobile phones, and the internet had become commonplace, earlier means of communication still had their uses: a carload of young people lost in the Betts Lane area were obviously very relieved when told that they were within a hundred yards of an old-fashioned phonebox.

Celebration at the opening of an extension to the Princess Louise Convalescent Home in 1924. The woman holding the flowers is Lydia Hargreaves and the men on the extreme right are Frederick Green and Walter Hargreaves. The building on the left was next to the Red Lion (now The White House) in Middle Street. Walkers Hill is in the background.

Two postcards of Nazeing. Above is The Coach and Horses in 1912. Below is Nazeingbury Parade in 1961, shortly after it was built.

CHAPTER 7

"THROUGH SUMMER SUNS AND WINTER STRIFE"

Farming and horticulture

In his 1933 report Professor Adshead wrote:

The lands north of Waltham Abbey are as unspoiled and as primitive as any in England... The Lea Valley and its wide spreading marshlands are wonderfully attractive, and may be seen from many vantage points. The descent from Roydon down to Nazeingbury presents a particularly fine panorama. But this very hilly area offers other and equally fine views of park and homestead... Here is English landscape at its best; pretty farms, corn and grassland, fine elm-trees and peeps of distant blue...An area of small farms, little churches and practically no towns...

The Nazeing landscape in 2001 could scarcely be described as "unspoiled and primitive", yet it remains predominantly rural and Adshead would certainly recognise it. Although comparatively few Nazeing people work in farming now, it still takes up most of the total acreage of the village. To appreciate the factors that influenced twentieth-century farming patterns in Nazeing it is necessary to take a brief look at an earlier period.

Agriculture

The First World War and before

Five miles from everywhere relates how the Nazeing economy was, as in most of rural England, based on agriculture. In the vast majority of households the wage earners were either farm workers or engaged in farm related activities; as late as 1912 the parish council described Nazeing as "a purely agricultural parish". The romantic perception of life in the English countryside before 1914 was of brawny, weather-beaten farmhands steering the single furrow wooden ploughs behind heaving shire horses, corn seed being broadcast by hand over a tilled field, muscular arms rhythmically swinging scythes through the ripened corn, and jovial families enjoying their beer, cider, bread and cheese at the foot of the haystack when haymaking was finished.

But these idyllic snapshots of pastoral tranquillity were only part of the story. In reality there was much hardship. Working hours often extended from dawn to dusk and in all weathers. Agricultural labourers were usually poorly paid and living conditions were often primitive and cramped. In spite of some mechanisation there was much hard physical labour. Bernard Pegrum recalled running to the end of the orchard at White House Farm to watch a threshing engine at work in the yard of neighbouring Church Farm while the farm boys carried drinking water and milk in pails suspended from a wooden yoke over their shoulders.

Although smallholders had at least some independence, theirs was a tough life, having to eke out a living growing and tending a wide range of crops and livestock to balance the inevitable failures from diseases and pests. For them, and indeed for the larger farms and landowners, crop yields were derisory compared with those of today.

In 1912 the New Domesday recorded a wealth of information including the names of owners and occupiers, the amounts of rent, rateable value, land tax, tithes, and a market valuation, which took into account the value of the land and items such as standing timber, buildings, and structures. Some of the properties were the subjects of a few pithy comments. Lodge Farm, then 241 acres, was owned by Ralph and Archdale Palmer and rented to their bailiff, Walter Brown, for £312

Lodge Farm in about 1912 when the New Domesday recorded: "Land very heavy. Most is poor."

256

per annum; it was described as "Land very heavy. Most is poor." Nazeingbury Farm (336 acres), owned by Sir Herewald Wake and rented to Joseph Pegrum, had buildings described as "old and inconvenient". The Common is listed as covering 480 acres with a gross value of £8,250, just over £17 per acre.

Until the early years of the First World War the country had total confidence in the ability of the Royal Navy to protect the two-thirds of its food supply which was imported by sea. That belief was shattered by a single event which some commentators believe to be the origin of British agricultural policy in the twentieth century, the introduction of the submarine. At the outbreak of war it would have been reasonable to expect a Government Order stipulating that a percentage of grassland had to be ploughed and switched to arable crops, but the approach from Whitehall was fairly muted, in spite of the introduction of guaranteed prices for wheat, oats, and potatoes.

By 1916, as the German blockade was beginning to take effect, County War Agricultural Committees were set up in an attempt to increase home production. A survey carried out by Essex's committee in December 1916 revealed that permanent grass still predominated on all Nazeing's farms, a trend that had begun in the 1870s (*Five miles from everywhere*, p131). The total farm acreage in the parish was 3,200 acres of which 2,662 acres were permanent grass (83 per cent). The survey lists 42 farms in the parish, ranging from Allmains Farm of five acres to Harold's Park Farm with 440 acres. Other farms with over 300 acres were Langridge (423) and Nazeingbury (by then increased to 370). Stock numbers included 1,361 sheep, 887 cattle, and 242 horses. The total permanent labour force, excluding the farmers themselves, numbered 58, of whom, surprisingly, only two were listed as shepherds. No doubt the overall labour force had been depleted by enlistment in the armed forces.

Marjorie Sykes, who often visited her Pegrum relatives, recalled that time:

> Hay-making was in its last stages in the back field. Instead of the jolly crowd of hay makers with their hoary old jokes and field picnics, with the beer brought out to them, four old men: uncle Alf, Mr. Perry, Mr. Jim Pegrum and another were loading up the final wagon, two on top of the load, two forking it up so that the stack could be made up ready for the winter feed.

With the appointment of David Lloyd George as Prime Minister in December 1916, the Government became more interventionist. On 30th

257

July 1917 the Essex War Agricultural Committee sent a letter to all landowners in the county drawing attention to the serious shortage of "bread stuffs". The Government needed three million acres, then under grass, to be ploughed and switched to arable production. Essex's share was deemed to be 85,000 acres. It was pointed out that the committee had "extensive powers, but preferred voluntary co-operation". In 1918 a call went out for a further 80,000 arable acres for wheat, oats, barley, peas, and beans. There is no written record of the response of Nazeing farmers to these edicts but, according to Brian Coleman, David Pegrum "made enough money from a field of oats to buy Greenleaves". He is unlikely to have been alone in putting permanent grass under the plough, thus heralding a return to mixed farming.

Between the wars

The post-war period was a significant one for farm sales in the village. In May 1918, even before the war had ended, the auctioneers Crawter of Cheshunt put the freehold of five agricultural properties under the hammer. They had belonged to the late Edward Jones Williams, an absentee landlord who had owned more land in Nazeing than anyone except the Wake, Palmer, and Bury families. Before they were sold off all the properties had been let, producing a gross rental of £333 7s per annum, from which tithes had to be found. Ninnings, quaintly described by the auctioneers as "an old fashioned cottage residence" with outbuildings and 10 acres, had been let for an annual rent of £23 and sold for £1,000. Little Profits Farm, let for £20 a year, was in reality a smallholding comprising a three-bedroom house, various outbuildings, and "2½ acres more or less", which sold for £460.

As with some of the other properties, the large five-bedroom house and "commodious" outbuildings of Perry Hill Farm, which had been let for £67 a year, seem out of all proportion to the modest 42 acres which is all the farm comprised. Edward J. Fowler of Mamelons bought the property which, with a greatly increased acreage, remained in his family until it was broken up in 1989, a few years after the death of his son, Edward Fowler. David Pegrum paid £1,350 for Greenleaves, described by Crawter as a "picturesque, old-fashioned, country residence". The sale included a large number of outbuildings and 38 acres. David bought Darmers also, together with its 31 acres, for £925.

Wartime food and labour shortages temporarily strengthened the

258

Sale particulars of the Williams estate which in 1918 was the fourth largest in Nazeing.

position of agricultural workers and their union, which formed a Nazeing branch in October 1918. The inaugural meeting at the Crooked Billet was crowded and many gave in their names for membership but, as there was no tradition of militancy in Nazeing and none of the leaders lived in the village, the branch soon withered. In the 1920s, despite promises made during the war, Britain returned to a free market in agriculture. The Agricultural Wages Board which had been created in 1917 was abolished in 1921 and the slump meant that the pay of agricultural labourers, like that of other workers, fell by a quarter. The experience of the pindar of Nazeing Common was typical: his wages rose steadily from 16s per week in 1914 to a peak of 48s in 1921 before dropping back to 36s, where they remained until the Second World War brought about a return of inflation and wage rises.

Farmers were affected just as badly, so that many hedged their bets by adopting mixed farming practices. In 1921 William Graham, one of the pioneers of grassland farming in west Essex since coming down from his native Ayrshire in 1887, left Harold's Park Farm, where he had been the tenant-farmer, and bought the 240-acre Church Farm. Three years later his son, David, paid Archdale Palmer £4,500 for Lodge Farm, where the family farms still. John Graham, William's grandson, recalled life at Lodge Farm in those difficult times and contrasted it with life today:

> We had cows, sheep, pigs, chickens, horses to do the heavy work and just one tractor. Nazeing Common was rough grazing and available to rightholders from April to September. Most of the work was manual, which meant employing several farm labourers. We farmed 170 acres for which we employed eight men. Today we have one full time employee and a part-timer for 1,200 acres which include the Common.

Another farmer who came to Nazeing from Scotland was James Gray. His is an incredible story. Before the First World War, Scottish weather permitting, he put his Masham lambs out to grass until January and then fed them on turnips, before selling them to farmers further south for fattening. He decided to seek his own grazing in the south and sent the sheep by boats to London. They were off-loaded at Limehouse and, starting out at 1.00 am, were driven through the streets to Hyde Park and Green Park. The sheep remained in London throughout the spring and into June, when the best were sold, either directly to private butchers or at Caledonian Market in Islington. The remainder were dipped in Hyde Park, close to Peter Pan's Statue, and then sold in October.

In 1918 Gray decided that it was time to make a move south. He rented 600 acres in Broxbourne, where shepherds brought down from Aberdeenshire tended the sheep. In 1926 he moved to St. Lawrence Farm and in the following year was farming over 500 acres at Harold's Park. By 1928 he had built up a flock of 1,500 in-lamb ewes grazed at St. Lawrence Farm, at Harold's Park, and on the Common. His sheep again became a feature of London parks, being transported from Scotland this time by train. They were grazed in the parks until 1942 when the removal of the railings for the manufacture of munitions brought an end to the enterprise. After the Second World War Gray adopted a policy of mixed farming but his was still the largest wool crop taken to Thomas Piper of Redbourn, the wool merchant for the area. Sheep remained the main enterprise of the business, as indeed they still were under the owners in 2000, James Gray's son-in-law Mac Moncur and Mac's son James.

At the end of the 1920s world events precipitated another agricultural depression. The Wall Street crash of 1929 and the ensuing slump of the early 1930s brought about the wholesale growth of interventionism and the development of new ways to support farming. In Britain most food imports from Empire sources were exempted from duty. It was a depressing time for Nazeing farmers with prices and therefore incomes falling. However, piecemeal solutions such as deficiency payments, the introduction of producer controlled marketing boards, and tariff and trade agreements with Denmark, Argentina, and the USA brought about a gradual recovery.

The Second World War

As war clouds gathered over Europe in the late 1930s the experiences of the First World War, particularly the vulnerability of overseas supplies to submarine attacks, prompted comprehensive plans for the production and distribution of staple foods. These included guaranteed prices for all agricultural products and rationing and price controls of consumer purchases. After war broke out, county War Agricultural Committees were set up again, with powers to regulate every aspect of production. The Essex "War Ag", for example, offered 1d per tail for dead rats. By June 1940 Germany controlled most of Europe and imports to Britain had become severely restricted, so it was essential to increase home food production. John Graham recalled the edict to plough up grassland to meet the target of a 50 per cent increase in the national arable acreage. As more grass went under the plough, the landscape changed. Of the 511 acres at Harold's Park Farm 491 were given over to arable production, with heavy crops of wheat being grown following draining, ploughing, and liming.

Members of the Women's Land Army made a major contribution on the farms. The nature of their work is indicated by reports that sometimes they were not allowed on buses because their clothes were dirty. The electoral register shows that thirty women of voting age were housed at the Golf Club House, the Princess Louise Convalescent Home, and a special hostel in North Street. Others aged under 21 may have been accommodated on the farms where they worked or in private houses such as Little End in Hoe Lane. Some married and stayed in the village. Prisoners of war worked on the farms and in the nurseries; after the war one married a local girl.

Clearly a treasured photograph of the Land Army girls.

In 1942 a Government farm survey was carried out with the intention of maximising food production. It listed Lodge Farm as 161 acres of which 113 acres were grass supporting 63 head of cattle, 93 sheep and lambs, and three horses. The arable acreage was split between wheat (22.5 acres), oats (12.5 acres), and smaller acreages of beans, potatoes, mangolds, and kale. At that time David Graham employed four men, although the survey noted that he needed more labour, which he received when prisoners of war and conscientious objectors were drafted in. New machinery was almost unobtainable and, although the Grahams did manage to obtain a second tractor in 1942, they had to convert horse-drawn implements to tractor draw-bars, which diminished their useful life severely. In the early years of the war most of the work was done by horses, which required land to be set aside for grazing, winter hay to be provided, and a field of oats to be grown for winter feed. The initial shortage of tractors to tackle the ploughing of permanent grass on heavy soils meant that on Lodge Farm the conversion of fields to arable production did not take place on any appreciable scale until 1943, when more new machinery began to arrive.

The 1942 survey revealed that, as in 1916, much of Nazeing's agricultural land was down to grass. Edward J. Fowler was farming Mamelons, Perry Hill, and Byners, 145 acres of grass. At Brewitts Farm, W.J. Hollow had 127 acres of grass, out of a total of 166 acres, supporting 64 head of cattle. With a staff of 22, G.W. Chapman at Langridge Farm was farming 584 acres, of which 379 acres were grass. Cattle numbered 146 and there was a large poultry unit with 1,180 birds. His principal arable crops were oats (95 acres) and wheat (34 acres).

At St. Leonards Farm Ralph Bury employed seven full-time farm workers including, in his words, "an 83 year old pensioner and a half-wit". He took the opportunity to point out also that "the army had taken 10 acres", presumably for the Outer London Defence Line. In 1939 he had withdrawn from his public activities in order to concentrate on food production for the war effort but, as his view of what was needed did not coincide with that of the War Agricultural Committee, his contribution was not appreciated. Of his 212 acres 180 were pasture for mowing or grazing; the compiler of the survey reported that "He makes little use of his arable land for feeding his milking herd. He has no wish to plough the land for the purpose. He does not appear to endeavour to make a success of the arable land, of which he is quite capable."

The spirit of the school report was not limited to the activities of Ralph Bury. Farmers were graded A, B, or C, according to performance. Top of the class was James Gray, who still retained some pasture at St. Lawrence Farm. For a while keeping sheep proved impossible as the army dug unfenced trenches for the Defence Line, destroying most of the fences and hedges in the process. Later Gray

… ploughed up grassland for oats. The management of newly ploughed grassland on purely grazing land is excellent and a great improvement has been made by draining, ditching, and hedging. In view of the number of fat bullocks and sheep fed on this land, the need for fertilizers is largely reduced.

Most farmers were graded A with the occasional positive comment, as for Arthur Nicholls who had "only recently taken over Sturtsbury Farm and was showing improvement". Remarks about those graded B included "old and insufficient interest", "lack of initiative and ability", "too much attention paid to milk round", and simply "not a farmer". Only one man was graded C, for displaying "Obstinacy and lack of cooperation and lack of knowledge".

Post-war

Britain's wartime agriculture has been described as "a success story for both consumers and farmers". There was a determination that this success should continue and that farmers should not feel betrayed, as they had after the First World War. A national advisory service was established and successive governments continued to support agriculture with complex arrangements embracing guaranteed prices and assured markets. These measures, together with the introduction of new technologies from both industry and Government funded research, ensured that Nazeing's largely mixed farming was in a healthy state. In the early 1960s, however, the Government introduced linked price guarantees to fixed output volumes, a move which was highly unpopular with farmers. In the 1960s there were still 600 people in Nazeing and Roydon employed full-time or part-time in agriculture and horticulture, but already foreign competition meant that numbers were in decline.

In 1973 the United Kingdom joined the European Economic Community. The biggest beneficiaries of the Common Agricultural Policy which was imposed then were the "cereal barons" with their vast acreages, a type unknown in Nazeing. Support from the heavily funded CAP improved the incomes of most farmers for a few years, but in the 1990s there was a gradual decline in farming profits. Farmers were advised to seek alternative crops and to diversify, and even to cut production by leaving land fallow. One alternative crop whose acreage increased enormously was oilseed rape. Yellow swathes of it became a familiar sight to travellers using the road over the Common.

Diversification took many forms. The Arnold brothers, Bert and Reg, ran a butcher's shop at Camps Farm in Hoe Lane. At Harold's Park Farm

George Mackie expanded his range of Christmas trees and converted farm buildings to stabling for horses. The Moncurs at St. Lawrence Farm opened a retail outlet supplying straw, hay, and animal feedstuffs. On several farms surplus outbuildings were let as units for a variety of small businesses. Some fields were fragmented, with owners of horses and ponies buying or renting the land for grazing.

These measures, however, fell short of compensating for the poor returns received from mainstream farming. Over-production in the European Community, the reduction in farm support, the ravages of BSE (Bovine Spongiform Encephalopathy. Brain disease of cattle that can affect humans in its variant form, Creuzfelt-Jakobs Disease), the deregulation of milk, and massively increased bureaucracy were just some of the factors that contributed to a substantial downturn in farming. As the century closed British agriculture was in crisis, with total farm incomes down 40 per cent from 1995. While the retail price of milk in supermarkets was 47.5p per litre, farmers, needing 20p per litre just to break even, received only 17p or 18p. The price of wheat in 1995 was £100 per tonne but by 1998/99 it had fallen to £60 per tonne, when the break-even figure for East Anglian farms was £90 per tonne. In November 1996 lamb fetched £1.10 per kilo but four years later it was selling for 77p per kilo. All this happened against a background of ever increasing prices for fertiliser, diesel, and many other commodities essential for crop and animal production.

At the beginning of the century the writer Rider Haggard visited Nazeing on his journey through rural England (*Five miles from everywhere*, chapter 7). The effects of the recent agricultural depression were still being felt and Joseph Pegrum, who was then farming 600 acres in the parish, told Haggard that "things could not look worse". For farming it would seem that the century ended as it began.

Nazeingwood Common

The most obvious example of Nazeing's switch from grassland to arable is also its most enduring open space, which covers over 400 acres in the north-east of the parish. It has justifiably been described as "a glorious sweeping vista which proves that Essex scenery is not always flat and boring". Nazeing Wood or Park is the legal name of what is now more generally known as Nazeingwood Common, Nazeing Common, or simply the Common. These other names are misleading since the area of land is effectively owned by its freeholders, the present owners of 98 ancient properties designated by an Act of Parliament of 1656 and in the schedule of the current Act, the Nazeing Wood or Park Act of 1947. (See *Five miles from everywhere*, pp 69-70, 99-100.)

The Common until 1947

In about 1930 the London and North Eastern Railway published *Rambles in Essex* (price sixpence). The paragraphs on Nazeing in the chapter entitled "The 'Long Green' Country, Waltham Cross to Epping" read:

> Nazeingwood Common is an unusual type of common, being administered by trustees under a special Act for the benefit of a few commoners. Part of it is used as a golf course in order to provide a revenue for its upkeep but, apart from this area, the Common looks uncared for, though the commoners' sheep scattered about and the birds that frequent it give it a certain wild charm. Nazeing lies just off the route, beyond the north-west corner of the Common, and is a scattered picturesque village.

Though the writer was misinformed about the exact way in which the Common was administered, his description fits in with what we know of it. Its story up to 1914 is covered in *Five miles from everywhere*, and between the wars it changed little. It was still grazed, mostly by sheep, but its slow decline continued, so only the molehills and the Golf Club flourished.

Maurice Coleman recalled:

> The midnight milkman [carried] out his second milking of the day after he had partaken of his supper at approximately 9.30 p.m., often by oil lamp guidance. After milking, [he] would drive his cows along the road, some twelve or more of them, and would tie a red lamp on the tail of the trailing beast, as he drove them to their night's pasture on The Common. He was in fact a right holder…

> During holidays and weekends, when not at school, … the local lads, of which I was one, to act as "gate-openers" for passing horses and carts, motor cars, cyclists, and horse riders… just wide enough, so that the drivers etc. would be able to place in our hands the half pennies - the usual charge for those passing through, unless it was the Chairman of The School Managers on horseback, when, by devious means, and "Bush Radio", his approach would become known, and the gate openers would disappear to ensure he had to get off his horse, open the gate, lead his horse through without the gate closing on him, and then re-mount with considerable difficulty.

**Alfred James Pegrum, "the midnight milkman" with his niece who later, as
Marjorie Sykes, recorded her memories of Nazeing. About 1904.**

Although grazing and golf were suspended when the dummy airfield
was created, there would have been no reason why they could not have
been resumed after the war. On 2nd August 1941, however, the
Chairman, Archdale Palmer, told his fellow-trustees that the Essex War

267

Agricultural Committee had sent him a formal notice of its intention to take over the Common for food production. A labour force of several dozen Women's Land Army girls, billeted in huts on the Common and in the deep shelter at Lodge Farm Road, helped with clearing scrub and other tasks. John Graham remembered the employment of tractor drivers who, at considerable expense, ploughed up the Common to grow wheat, potatoes, and sugar beet, the first 200 acres in autumn 1941 and the remaining 200 when the dummy airfield was dismantled the following year.

In 1941 James Gray become a trustee of Nazeing Wood or Park, replacing Arthur May in a behind-the-scenes deal that was not brought before the freeholders. Archdale Palmer reported that

> Mr E.J. Fowler had arranged to transfer to Mr James Morrison Gray some cottages in Middle Street to which is attached Common Right No.85 [Walnut Tree Cottages] to qualify for being appointed - and it was resolved that Mr J.M. Gray be proposed and seconded as a Trustee of Nazeing Wood or Park, subject to the completion of the transfer named - at the forthcoming General Meeting of Freeholders & Copyholders, any legal costs being borne by the Trust.

Although it made obvious sense for the trustees to have such a resourceful farmer amongst their number, they may soon have regretted their stratagem. On 26th January 1943 Palmer wrote to Gray "enquiring whether a rumour...to the effect that he had been appointed to the management and whole control of the Common was correct or otherwise, and indicating...the undesirability of Mr Gray occupying this dual position". This referred to Gray's appointment to the "War Ag", which was managing the Common. At the next annual meeting of the freeholders H.H. (Harry) Watts of Curtis Farm was elected a trustee in place of Gray. Evidently there were no hard feelings, for in 1946 Watts resigned because of ill health and on Palmer's suggestion Gray was elected, remaining a trustee until his death in 1952.

As traffic increased, the gates to the Common Road were usually left open. In order to ensure that they retained ultimate control of the road, however, the trustees instructed the pindar to close the gates once a year, on Good Friday. It is said that on one occasion he failed to carry out this duty and so the gates were never closed again. One of them is now at Smalldrinks and the other is stored in a barn at Upper Town Cottage, a service for which the trustees pay a rent of £1 a year.

The 1947 Act and after

When the war ended, the land was in a good state of cultivation and it was clear that the Common could never be the same again. The Nazeing Wood or Park Act of 1778 still governed the running of the Common but presented an insurmountable restriction, as there was no provision for the use of the land for ley farming (the alternation between arable and dairy use of land) either by the freeholders or, more importantly, by letting. The freeholders therefore sought a new Nazeing Wood or Park Act to regularise the situation and were most fortunate in that Ralph Bury was a trustee and an experienced King's Counsel. He was authorised at the June 1946 meeting of the freeholders, by 75 votes (22 owners) to one, to arrange for a new private Act of Parliament to be drafted. This passed into law on 6th August 1947, repealing and replacing the 1778 Act.

The one vote against the proposal was cast by Essex County Council, which held several common rights. It attempted to purchase the land on the grounds that it would, under the new Town and Country Planning Act, enhance the value of the land. Bizarrely, Essex used a second vote in favour of the bill. Bury managed to frustrate the council's efforts but its intervention proved costly. Despite his assistance in keeping down the expense, the opposition caused the cost of the new Bill to rise from £550 to £1,610. At a special Parish Meeting in February 1947, 61 people had supported the Nazeing Wood or Park Bill, although many of them may have been among the 44 individuals who held common rights and therefore have had a vested interest. Only eleven had wanted Essex to acquire the land for communally owned common and playing fields. It is unclear whether Essex intended to implement this request or to turn the Common into a housing estate for Harlow. If the latter had been the case, the unique legal status of the Common being governed by Act of Parliament would have made such a development almost impossible.

The "War Ag" controlled the land until 29th September 1950, when the Ministry of Agriculture and Fisheries finally de-requisitioned it. The trustees advertised for tenants and let 215 acres in the north-east to David Graham of Lodge Farm, 60 in the south-west to Arthur Nicholls of Sturtsbury Farm, and 125 in the east to Harold Lauritzen, who was then living in Harlow but later built a house at Epping Long Green and used parts of the Common as an apple plantation. Various changes took place subsequently but, when Bert and Reg Arnold gave up the south-western end in 1983, John and Robert Graham, son and grandson of David, became the tenants of almost the whole of the cultivated arable land and then of the Pindar's House, which was refurbished. In June 2000 the Common's net annual income, rents and investment income less management expenses, provided each of the freeholders with a gross income of £390. In addition to this regular windfall, many freeholders found an indefinable and priceless pleasure in partly owning such an historic tract of land.

The continuance of the switch from grazing to arable is the most obvious post-war development but there have been others. During the late 1950s and early 1960s the volume of traffic across Nazeing Common grew rapidly, mainly because of the expansion of Harlow. The narrow road with no double white lines and the even narrower bridge at the cascade were causing accidents, so in 1960 Essex County Council began negotiations with the freeholders to enable the road to be widened. This led to a number of protracted and often heated discussions at the Annual

The bridge over the Cascades on the Common Road between the wars. The road was widened in the late 1960s.

General Meetings in 1963 and 1964 and at a special meeting in November 1964. There was a threat of a compulsory purchase order and eventually, for the princely sum of £1, the trustees conveyed to the county council the existing road and sufficient land to provide for its widening. Most of the old pound and the forecourt of the King Harold's Head were lost to the scheme, although the freeholders did manage to squeeze from the council a number of conditions, including the erection of a new pound opposite Back Lane and the provision of oak rather than concrete fence posts alongside the road.

This was a turbulent period when, not for the last time, the term "Blazing Common" was used. It contrasts greatly with the position before the First World War, when often the only people present at the AGM were the five trustees, who simply proposed, seconded, and voted for their own re-election. Over twenty freeholders made a formal call for a special meeting which was held on 7th May 1964. Initially a highly critical agenda was proposed and, although it was later toned down, it nevertheless included an item "To consider the estate management of the Common in all its aspects". A vote of censure was passed on the clerk to the trustees, J.M.A. Edmundson, who resigned. This marked a major break with the past, for he was the senior partner of Jessopp & Gough, the Waltham Abbey firm of solicitors which had been involved with the Common since its reorganisation in the 1770s. The clerkship was taken over by Arthur Ellaway, a Wormley accountant, although for some years Edmundson continued to act as legal advisor to the trust. When, in 1973, Maurice Coleman was appointed clerk, he was the first Nazeing resident to hold the post.

It was perhaps inevitable that with the regime under the new Act there would be some outspoken disagreements while the new pattern of management became settled. This coincided with a period when the great majority of rights had come to be held by individual house owners. Most of them, even newcomers, felt involvement in and obligation to the community in which they lived, but such feelings became less evident after the social changes that followed the Second World War. Further, from the late sixties onwards the management became less controversial. The concerns of the trustees were with occasional changes in the letting of the farmland and fluctuations in farm incomes, with licences to use small parcels of land (mostly on the north-western side of the common), with the pylon issue in the late 1960s (see page 175), and with the laying of a gas pipeline in 1997. The late twentieth century was one of the comparatively quiet periods in the history of Nazeingwood Common.

Many common rights go with ancient timbered farmhouses and cottages surviving from the sixteenth and seventeenth centuries, themselves on the sites of mediaeval houses (see *Five miles from everywhere*, p 38), but others are attached to more modern replacement

Typifying the changing ownership of common right houses, Nazeing Park Cottage has been transformed from the dilapidated tied cottage shown above in the early 1900s, into the attractive owner-occupied house shown below.

buildings on or near the original sites. Most are still attached to a single property but eight have been divided between pairs of relatively new houses, and the one attached to the former Curringtons has been split three ways. Even where farming continued, the reduction in the work force in the last fifty years has meant that only a few common rights are now attached to remaining working farms and cottages such as St. Lawrence Farm in Waltham Road. During the decade or so after the Second World War the position reverted to that in the eighteenth century when few owners held more than one right. The difference is that in those days they rented the houses to tenant farmers and cottagers who put their stock on the common, whereas by the late twentieth century the owners lived in the houses and, although under the Act they still had the right to put out stock for grazing, they derived an income from the letting of the land instead.

Horticulture

In the 1960s the Ministry of Agriculture produced a film featuring the Lea Valley glasshouse industry entitled *Sea of Glass*. An aerial view of the area showed the justification for this description, but even then the area of glasshouses was shrinking. It had reached the height of its expansion in the years before the Second World War when the total area was about 1,400 acres, giving rise to the claim that it was probably the greatest concentration of glasshouse nurseries in the world.

Pioneers

The industry was pioneered by the Rochford family, who had a nursery at Tottenham. In 1882 they bought eight acres at Turnford; within six years they owned 86 acres of nurseries in the Lea Valley. The industry developed rapidly and by 1914 many families destined to become household names in the horticultural field had established nurseries along the Valley, from Ponders End through Enfield Highway and Cheshunt to Wormley.

These bewhiskered, bowler-hatted, far-sighted entrepreneurs were persuaded to move north from the Lea's lower reaches by plentiful supplies of water, level land, and suitable soils. The location was still within horse and cart distance of the ever expanding London market, from which seasonal labour was readily available. The earlier nurseries were sited on the sandy loams and soils of the flood plain around Cheshunt and

273

Turnford; others followed on the gravel soils near Hoddesdon. The first glasshouses east of the river were erected on alluvial soils in the years before and immediately after the First World War. In Nazeing the development later spread to the higher slopes where London clays and boulder clays predominate. The plentiful supply of stable manure still available from London at that time played a significant role in this development, making possible the rapid structural improvement of the heavier soils.

From the 1920s Nazeing was a major player in the industry. *Kelly's Directory* for 1914 listed just one tomato grower but by 1933 there were sixteen nurserymen; four years later the figure had grown to 23. Growers employed a substantial labour force and glasshouse hands earned one pound for a six-day week, with the average working day lasting ten and a half hours. More Nazeing people worked in the Lea Valley glasshouse industry than commuted to London, and Adshead attributed Nazeing's rapid inter-war growth to the industry. The ownership of a house at Tatsford Villas exemplifies this. In 1928 it was bought by a perhaps unusually prosperous "farmhand" from Belchers Lane. When he died in 1949, he was described as a "nursery hand" and his family sold the house to another nurseryman, who moved from Edmonton and stayed until he died in 1977.

Glasshouses were concentrated mainly in Paynes Lane, Nazeing Road, Nursery Road, Sedge Green, Pecks Hill, and Hoe Lane. The Co-operative Wholesale Society owned a large nursery at Pressfields and the Enfield Highway Co-operative Society had Rusheymead. Another valuable horticultural product was the watercress grown in many of the shallow streams that ran alongside the main river.

On the whole the industry was accepted as bringing a degree of prosperity to the village, although in the late 1930s some of the more traditionalist members of Nazeing Parish Council regarded it as something of a menace. When part of Hoe Lane collapsed at an extremely dangerous corner in 1937, the council blamed the damage on lorries which it said were serving the nurseries and "cutting up Hoe Lane terribly". The council objected formally when the draft Town Planning Scheme proposed expansion towards All Saints' and other previously unaffected areas, arguing that glasshouses should not be allowed in parts zoned for agriculture.

Arthur Harknett, who had a nursery in Hoe Lane, was well respected in

Nazeing. He wrote poetry for his own pleasure. This witty verse captures the trials of his occupation:

As a nurseryman I spent my life, through summer suns and winter strife.
The compensations were as such - sometimes nothing, sometimes much.
One night I dreamed about the strife - and that time wanted back my life.
My eyes were closed expectantly, I wondered what time had in store for me.
Weightless I travelled with the Fates, to the fast locked pearly gates.
St. Peter when the bell I plied, said "O.K. Arty, step inside.
How you have lived," he said, "We must know, and then decide which way you go.
You say you've been a nurseryman? Ah now we fully understand,
Your fate is easy to decide, 'Tis heavenwards that you must ride.
Step inside the lift old chap; I'll press the bell - my God you've had your share of hell!"

Acreage in decline

Unfortunately there are no really accurate historical records of the year on year trends in the area of land covered by glasshouses in the Lea Valley. It is estimated that in 1932 there were 500 nurseries in the Lea Valley but by 1970 their number had shrunk to 300. It seems unlikely that this 40% decline in the industry was reflected in Nazeing where housing development made only minor inroads. By contrast, in Cheshunt a large number of nurseries were pulled down and replaced by housing and industrial estates. The total acreage fell from the inter-war peak of 1,400 to 1,100 in 1950 and 720 in 1962. This steady decline continued so that in 1999 no more than 300 acres remained. In addition to the encroaching urbanisation, a shortage of skilled labour, competition from imports, and a lack of capital investment all contributed to this decline. Therefore some nurseries closed and others moved to places such as the south coast, which was smog-free even before the 1956 Clean Air Act.

In the early 1960s local Ministry of Agriculture horticultural advisers estimated that of the 720 acres of glasshouses in the Lea Valley 220 acres (31 per cent) lay within the boundaries of the parishes of Nazeing and Roydon. An area of this magnitude meant that the industry was a significant local employer, which it remained until the late 1970s. In 1970 150 acres in Nazeing and Roydon were under glass, growing mostly tomatoes and cucumbers. In Nazeing there were 58 nurseries, a figure which is unlikely to have changed dramatically since the late 1930s. By 2001, however, there were only 35 nurseries in the parish.

Over the years, nursery ownership changed dramatically. Before the Second World War, and for a decade afterwards, virtually all the nurseries were family businesses, most of them run by local people. They included Dutch, Danish, and Norwegian immigrants whose surnames became part of our village heritage. In the late 1950s mounting labour shortages resulted in the recruitment of workers from Italy. Initially their living conditions were poor but, by dint of hard work for low wages, some of them became nursery owners. Today in Nazeing, as elsewhere in the Lea Valley, growers whose family roots are Italian own approximately half the glasshouse businesses.

All steamed up!

Since the early days when the pioneering entrepreneurs moved northwards from the lower Lea, the changes in glasshouse production methods have been vast. Today crop yields have reached levels that those earlier growers would have considered unobtainable. Plant breeders, glasshouse designers, heating engineers, and research workers in both the public and private sectors have all had an important part to play in the huge technological advances which have affected all sections of the industry. For example, in the absence of any significant crop rotation, soil sterilisation used to be the norm throughout the Lea Valley, to combat soil-borne diseases. Those Nazeing residents who remember the 1950s will recall seeing clouds of steam billowing from dimly lit glasshouses, when the commonly practised night steaming was in progress. And the car drivers among them will undoubtedly recall crawling along Nazeing Road behind one of the very slow moving "mobile" steam boilers en route to a nursery. For all but a few crops steaming is largely a practice of the past because inert growing media and soil-less composts have replaced soil.

From the early beginnings until 1939 the range of crops grown on Nazeing nurseries largely mirrored those of the Lea Valley as a whole. Tomatoes were the major crop, followed by cucumbers and the occasional crop of lettuce. Chrysanthemums were the most widely grown flower crop, but carnations, roses, and some bedding plants were grown also. With the onset of the Second World War the picture changed dramatically. Controls were put in place under the jurisdiction of the War Agricultural Committees. Only essential food crops were permitted which, under glass, meant tomatoes. The growing of cucumbers, which have lower nutritional values than tomatoes, and flower crops on any reasonable scale was prohibited. Tomatoes were marketed at guaranteed set prices. The war years were probably among the most profitable for the industry.

At the outset of the war the Lea Valley Growers Association had to convince the Government that two proposed orders should not be implemented, as they would restrict output severely. They called for all glasshouses to be shaded to prevent reflection by moonlight, and for all glasshouse crops to be grown without heating in order to preserve coal stocks. The Association's opposition to these bizarre proposals was successful and for the duration of the war growers received reasonable tonnages of anthracite, as its export to Canada ceased.

For several years after the war tomatoes continued to be the dominant crop. One of the main Nazeing producers was G. & C. D. Chapman, who owned four nurseries in the area. Their five and a half acres of heated glasshouses at Langridge Nursery in Paynes Lane had been cropped with tomatoes each year since it was built in 1927. During the war it was one of several Lea Valley nurseries to have suffered extensive bomb damage.

The Chapman lorry at Paynes Lane, c1990.

Nazeing – a leading player

Nazeing glasshouse growers have often been among the first to adopt new techniques. From the 1950s through to the 1970s they could hear

277

first hand accounts from research workers and others who spoke at the winter monthly meetings of the Nazeing and Roydon Growers' Discussion Group. Held at The Crown, it was the only forum of its type in the Lea Valley. Another organisation, which attracted support from both commercial and amateur growers, was the Nazeing Chrysanthemum Society, which held regular autumn shows in the years after the Second World War. A founder member and treasurer was James Jones, the director of Muraltones wallpapers, who created a unique garden at Elham, the house in Middle Street which he built in 1939.

It is important to put the acreage loss in perspective. By 2000 actual production had increased to a point where the 300 acres in mainstream glasshouse production probably yielded more than the 1,100 acres did in the post-war years. From the late 1950s, as the total glasshouse acreage declined, so too did the area devoted to tomatoes. Forty years later it was estimated that only ten acres of the crop were grown in the Lea Valley.

There were also two large fruit farms within the parish boundary; one close to Epping Green and the other, well known in its heyday for its "pick-your-own" facility, in Paynes Lane. By 2001 both had closed and the only nearby fruit growing on a commercial scale was a soft fruit holding at Broadley Common, which offered a wide selection of crops for customers to pick.

In Nazeing cucumbers became the preferred crop but it was other developments which turned the horticultural spotlight on the village. During the 1990s new glasshouses were built in Paynes Lane and in the Sedge Green/Meadgate area and others were planned, on a scale not seen anywhere else in the valley. The production of young plants, particularly for bedding, became an important part of the local economy. From the mid-1980s, investment was considerable, with some Nazeing nurseries going over to natural gas in the late 1990s. In 2001 there were an estimated 60 acres of commercial glasshouses in Nazeing, with a combined annual gross turnover of £5.5m. Other significant sectors of the industry were peppers for the supermarket trade and mushroom production on farms in Hoe Lane and Laundry Lane. Mushrooms had become among the most valuable horticultural crops with a countrywide annual output equal to the combined outputs of all the salad crops grown under protection. Otherwise, some nurserymen diversified into garden centres. Thus in 2001 horticulture remained the village's principal industry, with Nazeing probably the leading player in the Lea Valley.

Nazeing Horticultural Society

The society was founded in 1946, perhaps by returning servicemen keen to enjoy healthy outdoor recreation and grow their own produce at a time of severe food shortages. The first flower show was held in 1952 and the society organised a competition as part of the Coronation celebrations. In 1954 a competition for council house gardens produced a poor response and was not repeated.

In the early days only one flower show was held each year, in the late summer. Not only members took part in exhibiting their produce but also local growers and nurserymen could enter in an open class. Inevitably much rivalry occurred but this added to the excitement of winning a first prize. Silver cups were donated to the society by local members and industries, including Wrighton furniture makers. As the society progressed and the number of exhibits increased, so more silver cups and trophies were donated. All the awards were decided by qualified judges, some of them from various national societies. The first shows were held in a marquee, where the forecourt of St. Giles' Church now stands, and later at the Chapel Hall. Since St. Giles' Church and Hall were built in 1964, all functions organised by the Nazeing Horticultural Society have been held in the hall.

As the population grew the society membership increased and an Early Summer Flower Show was introduced. Support increased and the showing of dahlias at the Late Summer Show became one of the most colourful exhibits, filling at least one third of the table space allotted to hold all the exhibits. In 1976 the committee instituted a members only Spring Flower Show with no 'open' classes, held on an evening early in April. The three Flower Shows have been held annually since then, with 26 major awards, each retained for one year by the exhibitor.

On 1st September 2001 the Nazeing Horticultural Society held its 50th Late Summer Flower Show, which was filmed by the BBC for its *Joy of Gardening* programme. Although that film was not broadcast, an item about society stalwart Bernie Lanham and his allotment was shown.

Enthusiasm for active gardening has waned perhaps, with competition from other pastimes, but Nazeing Horticultural Society is still able to hold its three Flower Shows with great success. The society provides also a place for making friends and has developed an equally successful social side. Well attended monthly meetings offer a variety of speakers on topics related to gardening. The society arranges coach outings to places of interest, such as stately homes and gardens of particular interest, and weekend breaks and short holidays abroad. With these additional activities as a further incentive, the society has well over 400 members from Nazeing and Broxbourne, which makes it one of the largest in the village.

Clifford Derek Chapman (behind) at Langridge Nursery with three prisoners of war who had been drafted in to work there. Their countries may have been at war but they seem to be a happy group.

CHAPTER 8
"EXCELLENT RESULTS IN DIFFICULT CIRCUMSTANCES"
Education

In the twentieth century there were four schools in Nazeing. The church school at the junction of Betts Lane and Hoe Lane was opened in 1854. It closed in 1878 when the Board School at Bumbles Green opened but re-opened in 1891, finally closing in 1947 (*Five miles from everywhere*, pp127-8, 162-3). The Bumbles Green school closed when the County Primary School in Hyde Mead opened in 1958. These were all for Nazeing children, but from 1952 to 1995 Essex County Council had a special needs school at Nazeing Park for children from all over the county.

The Betts Lane school

The school was reopened by the vicar, Thomas Goddard, in 1891 to serve children from the Broadley Common area, who could walk across

The Betts Lane school around 1910.

the fields to school. Initially the average attendance was 66 but by 1907 there were 97 children on the register. Enlarged by voluntary subscription, it was a substantial brick building with a classroom 20 feet by 18 feet, by 15 feet high, plus a lobby and WCs. Although by then Essex County Council were the freeholders, the vicar and churchwardens managed the school. The building was deemed to belong to them and much of the cost was borne by the church. Although later the Government made an annual grant, money was still tight, so in 1927, when the roof needed urgent repairs, the vicar had to write to people who might be willing to give a subscription for the upkeep of the school. Lack of funds was a constant problem: when in 1936 it was decided to lay water into the building, painting, and decorating had to be held over.

There were only two classes, infants and seniors. At the beginning of the 20th century the headmaster was Alfred Phillips, who was followed in the 1920s by Jane Jeffery. Both lived at Ravens, in Back Lane. On Miss Jeffery's retirement, Miss Robertson was appointed as temporary head. From then until the end of the Second World War the headteacher was Sydney Margaret Rowley, who is still remembered by her pupils from the Betts Lane school and from the Bumbles Green school, where she taught too. She married Arthur Bassett, who was fifteen years her junior, but outlived him and died in 1992 aged 101. For many years the headmistress took the seniors and Adelaide Savage, who lived at the Mill House opposite the Triangle, taught the infants. Both Miss Savage and Miss Jeffery took advantage of the opportunity to buy their houses from Archdale Palmer. The brightest girls were taken on at this and other schools as infant teachers with no formal training whatsoever.

As it was a church school, knowledge of the scriptures was important. The vicar visited weekly and the Diocesan Inspector once a term. From 1932 to 1948 the inspector was the vicar of Waltham Abbey, A.V.G. Cleall. Children were examined on their religious knowledge and certificates were awarded.

In 1939 the number of pupils at the school was boosted by the arrival of evacuees, some of whom stayed until the end of the war. When it was decided that the large windows could prove dangerous during an air-raid, the school authorities reinforced the Vicarage cellar, and made a secondary exit. Everyone went to this shelter when the warning siren sounded and stayed until the "All clear", but getting children from the school to the Vicarage was hazardous, so later a shelter was built on the playground. The school had two near misses: a high explosive bomb dropped on the tennis court across the road at Buttfield and an incendiary bomb fell on the playground. The last headmaster was Mr Bates from Harlow, who stayed until the closure in 1947.

The interior of Betts Lane school, c1900.

When the building ceased to be a school, it became the church hall and was used for meetings of the Parochial Church Council, for the Sunday School, for church functions, and by the Women's Institute and some other organisations. Sir Hereward Wake, the freeholder, offered the reversion to the PCC in 1961, an offer that was refused because St. Giles' Church and Hall were already being planned. When they were built, the old school was returned to Sir Hereward "for demolition", but it survived to become first the privately owned Dormarlyn Hall and later a private house.

The building of the Bumbles Green school

The logbooks of the Bumbles Green school show that for eighty years it was one of the hubs of the village. Early entries in particular give a vivid picture of Nazeing in the late nineteenth and early twentieth centuries. Hundreds of children passed through its doors and most of the inhabitants, whatever their status, would have visited the school building at some time. The influence of the teachers and what they taught, as well as the example set by the managers and the visitors, must have had a great effect on the village as a whole, setting standards in thought and behaviour. In order to appreciate fully the role of this school it is necessary to understand how it started, functioned, and evolved before the beginning of the First World War.

In the first two-thirds of the nineteenth century most children received some form of education but its provision was unstructured and could come in a variety of ways. As the industrial revolution gathered force, radical changes took place in the country. In 1800, 80 per cent of people in England and Wales lived in villages but by 1900 a mass exodus to find work had reversed these proportions, so that 80 per cent were town dwellers. While poor living conditions caused unrest, education was seen as a calming influence, teaching behaviour and respect. Forster's Education Act of 1870 recognised education as a public service and divided the country into *ad hoc* districts similar to Poor Law Unions. Each was administered by an elected board, partly maintained by special rates; there were also local boards to run individual schools. A further act of 1876 made education compulsory.

Nazeing, which came under the Epping Board, was then a predominantly agricultural community of some 780 inhabitants. Most of the children went to the Betts Lane school, which was remote from most of the cottages and homesteads, making the journey to school long and tiring for many of its pupils. As there were ninety children at Betts Lane, it was recommended that a new school to take forty children should be built in a central part of Nazeing, preferably as near as possible to the road to Broxbourne. Initially a site near Nazeing Gate was suggested but in 1874 Henry Tyrwhitt, the vicar and chairman of the newly elected school board, proposed that there should be one village school built to take 130 children. This would relieve the church of the running costs and be more economical than maintaining two buildings, each with its own staff. So, in 1875, a piece of "waste" ground was found at "Brimmers Green", only 100 yards from the Lower Recreation Ground and with a frontage on two highways.

Early days

When Nazeing Board School opened on 30th September 1878 no one could have imagined the changes that were to take place, many of them reflected in the life of the school. Not least was the population growth, which in 1958 necessitated the building of a larger school at Hyde Mead.

The first master was Robert Hicks Brown and the assistant was Mrs. Harriet Brown. With few exceptions husband and wife teams constituted the staff until 1933. In the early years they were assisted by a monitress, who was paid a weekly salary of between a shilling and half a crown. Generally she was a young girl such as fourteen year old Alice Ashby, who in 1895 had finished her schooling and helped with the infants.

According to the 1870 Act, Board Schools were to be secular and undenominational, although an amendment to the Act permitted boards to provide religious instruction. The Nazeing Board, perhaps influenced by the vicar and by its strong Chapel element, did so. A consignment of Bibles ordered in 1878 was sent back by the master because the print was too small. Instruction must have been fairly rigorous, as children read Genesis, Exodus, Joshua, Judges, I and II Samuel, the four Gospels, and the Acts of the Apostles. Psalms as well as hymns were taught.

The former Council school at Bumbles Green, c1960.

The school buildings were cramped and, by later standards, uncomfortable. The master's house had an inside water tank, which had to be pumped out periodically, when the water became offensive and stagnant. Adjoining it was the school with two classrooms, the main room for juniors measuring 20 feet by 45 feet and the infants' room 20 feet by 18 feet. There were three porches, the girls' 12 feet by 19½ feet, the boys' 6 feet by 18 feet, and a smaller one 4 feet by 6 feet. Both the house and school rooms were heated with coal and lit by lamps.

Maintenance and repairs were the concern of the Board, as was the delivery of stationery, pencils, books, and slates. In 1880 it cost 3 shillings for sweeping the chimneys, 1s 10d for fuel, 5 shillings for cleaning the school, and 2 shillings for "fluid".

Across the yard were separate boys' and girls' "offices", bucket lavatories, which over the years caused many problems. They were often referred to as being in need of a "flushing" and in one case as being "very offensive". This is not surprising as the number of children seldom fell below 90 and sometimes reached more than 120. In the 1920s sewage from the school was dumped on the Lower Recreation Ground and the Lee Conservancy Board prosecuted Essex County Council because pollution was contaminating the Nazeing Brook. For flush lavatories to be provided it was necessary for Epping Rural District Council's sewerage scheme to be extended along Middle Street as far as the school, but Alfred Barratt informed the 1946 Annual Parish Meeting that this would be too expensive. In 1948 Connie Reynolds told the local press that the children were still using bucket lavatories. Barratt complained to the parish council because he was a school governor and thought that her comments reflected badly on him. The council took no action. Following the outcry in the press, Leah Manning raised the issue in Parliament and flush lavatories were installed in April 1951.

His Majesty's Inspectorate (HMI) inspected the school annually but the management was by the local board, which met monthly. The board members, who could make many decisions regarding the day to day running of the school, were drawn from the leading men in the village. The first chairman was Charles Bury, who held the post until his death in December 1897. Other board members in the early years were James Pegrum, George Nicholls, and William Nicholls, all of the Chapel. When George died in 1888, he was replaced by Harry Bugg, who farmed at Mansion House Farm and later became a parish councillor and overseer of the poor. Regular visitors were Robert Henty and the Misses Henty, who leased Nazeing Park from the Palmers.

Charles and Anna Bury played a large part in the life of the school and made regular visits. He "examined" the children and checked the attendance register, she brought materials for the girls' needlework and generally showed interest in their work. From their own pockets they provided treats for the children, and they distributed apples and made gifts of sweets, biscuits, and nuts to encourage good attendance. At Christmas they supplied a tree and a tea, which at first comprised plum cake and tea but was gradually extended with small gifts and cards until it became "liberal" with Christmas cards and bonbons. In 1896 there was a conjuror from London and a display of fireworks by Ralph Bury. The following year there was a Punch and Judy Show and the usual tea provided by Mrs. Bury despite the recent death of her husband.

After the passing of the 1902 Balfour Education Act, which empowered local councils to provide primary and secondary education, the Board School became the council school. The Board members became the Managers, with the addition of Alexander Frogley. Later

The Council School, formerly the Board School, in about 1905.

Ralph Bury became chairman of the managers and had a great degree of say in the running of the school. Well into the twentieth century the headmaster had to get permission from Bury on many matters, some seemingly quite trivial.

287

In the absence of a village hall the Board allowed the use of the school room for outside activities, such as a "Musical Entertainment and Reading by Students of Cheshunt College" in 1879 and a concert in aid of local charities of the parish for the Coal and Clothing Club in 1880. The school building was used for a variety of public functions including parish council meetings, political meetings, collection of allotment rents, whist drives, private parties, and concerts. Evening classes held over the years included needlework, dressmaking, basketry, carpentry, shorthand, electrics, and wireless. It was, and still is, used as a polling station for parliamentary and council elections.

Until 1891 parents had to pay a small fee, which was set by the Board. There is no record of the levy at Nazeing apart from 1879 when it was agreed that pupils living outside the parish were to be charged three pence a week; Nazeing children would probably have been charged two pence. This would have been a drain on the incomes of many villagers, particularly where families were large. Some parents could not or would not pay the required fee and did not send their children to school, which resulted in a visit from the attendance officer. Occasionally parents were taken to the Epping court and warned or, in bad cases, fined. In 1887 one quarter's school fees paid to the Epping Board amounted to £6 4s 5d. With the passing of Lord Salisbury's Education Act in 1891, fees were abolished and schooling became free.

Attendance was of great concern to the Master and the Board, because money to run the school depended on the number of pupils and a good annual report on the progress of the children in reading, writing, arithmetic and drawing. Of even greater importance than the numbers of children who attended was the percentage, so on the few occasions when attendance was over 95 per cent or reached 100 per cent, the Masters were jubilant. Low attendance and/or low scholastic attainment meant a low grant, so annual grants varied. The HMI report in 1896 stated "the Teachers appear able to make the needed improvement in school method and in the attainment of the children; and the continuance of the present scale of Grants must be considered as conditional on such improvement." That year the grant was £59 17s 0d but the next year, after a good report, it rose to £75 6s 0d.

There were incentives to encourage school attendance. When the percentage was high, a half-day school holiday was given and prizes were awarded at the December "treat" for children who had managed full attendance. In 1892 three children were given two shillings each and four one shilling each, all in new coins. There were, however, many reasons why children could not get to school, severe weather being one of the most frequent. The brook often caused problems and flooding was commonplace; children were sent home before the water became too deep or, if they lived in Lower Nazeing, did not arrive at school at all. Heavy rain or snow could reduce the numbers; once only twelve out of 102 children were present. On really bad days the register would not be taken and on occasion the Board would close the school, sometimes for days. In good weather numbers would rise but there would still be absences due to helping at home, haymaking, gleaning, gathering acorns, and "collecting for Guy Fawkes".

School life before the First World War was tough. For children who lived some distance away getting to school would have been arduous. Many had poor footwear; as late as 1910 two children could not attend school as they had no boots. With so many children in the building, disease was rife: hooping (*sic*) cough, measles, influenza, ringworm, chilblains and, in 1887, an outbreak of typhoid are recorded. When an illness reached epidemic proportions, the Medical Officer of Health closed the school.

Every so often death touched the school and the children were affected. A half-day holiday was given in 1883 so that they could attend the funeral of Col. George Palmer, and in 1897 most of them attended the funeral of Charles Bury. In February 1905 one of their teachers, Mrs. Webb, died of cancer and on the day of the funeral, the school was closed so "children may follow". Illness took some children, including George King after a week's illness in 1883, three children from measles in 1892, George Barnard, aged four, from a cold in 1896, and Ernest Perry from pneumonia in 1906. Health was of concern from the outset and in 1905 the Relieving Officer came from Epping to see whether any children were underfed. Happily he reported that there was no anxiety on that score.

Examinations in reading, writing, and arithmetic took place regularly. Good results were important, as the grant depended on satisfaction in each subject throughout the school. As time went on, the syllabus expanded. History and geography were taught, and there were talks on hygiene, first aid, and the cottage home. Girls did needlework and the boys agriculture; then older girls were allowed to do agriculture and drill was tried. In 1904 slates were abolished, and the Master noted "now we've enough paper, neater and better results are obtained". There must have been great excitement when in 1907 Mrs Bury presented two dozen hockey sticks and a ball to the school.

There was some interchange with the church school. In 1909 seven older girls went to cookery classes there. Some of the children from Betts Lane, accompanied by the vicar's wife and one of their teachers, attended hygiene lessons at Bumbles Green. On 30th May 1924 both schools joined together when 54 children, with some mothers as helpers, went to the British Empire Exhibition at Wembley.

Learning by rote was usual. In 1902 Standards (classes) I and II had to learn *Somebody's Mother* (48 lines), Standard III *Sunshine & Showers* (60 lines) and the oldest children (Standards IV to VI) Tennyson's *The Revenge* (120 lines). Songs learnt that year were: *Now Pray We for Our Country*, *Fan Song*, *Merrily the Cuckoo*, *Love at Home*, and *Hearts of Oak*. Infants had to master *Babyland*, *Past 8 o'Clock*, and *Mrs Bond*. Children also studied a curious subject known as "Object Lessons", which had to be approved by the Inspector. Topics included: for infants, donkey, lion, tea, bread, things for washing with, and setting the tea table; for Standards I to III, paper, cork, the fox, monkeys, and feet of birds.

Despite what appears to have been rigorous tuition in overcrowded conditions and with a high ratio of pupils to teachers, inspectors over the years record that "teaching is kindly and effective". Nevertheless, pupils were occasionally caned and "a big incorrigible boy" was expelled for swearing and molesting children, mostly girls and little ones. Dinner children were also subject to intimidation; on one occasion a telegraph boy caused trouble and threw mud at them and the school wall. A hedge was broken too.

Holidays were limited. The Board allowed one week at Christmas and for the Easter holiday only Good Friday and Easter Monday and Tuesday. The four-week summer holiday was known as Harvest Holiday because it coincided with the harvest. There were additional days on big national occasions such as the Relief of Mafeking, for which there was a day's holiday. On Empire Day, after a lesson on the Empire and citizenship and singing patriotic songs, a half-day was given. Three royal celebrations each warranted a week's holiday, the Golden Jubilee of Queen Victoria and the coronations of Edward VII and George V. For the Jubilee, a public subscription provided tea, sports, and fireworks. Another holiday was earned when the National Anthem was sung for the Proclamation of

George V, perhaps because Ralph Bury, as High Sheriff of Essex, did the proclaiming.

Outings were not numerous. In 1882 "Sir Foxwell Buxton, Bart., sent an invitation to 50 scholars to attend his private stand to witness the Queen's visit to Epping Forest". It must have been a right royal expedition, for they had flags provided by Robert Henty, rosettes given by Anna Bury, and wagons lent by Charles Bury and James Pegrum. There was an outing to the Crystal Palace and in 1913, at Ralph Bury's suggestion, children were taken to see the hounds meet at Common Gate.

Little is recorded about the Boer War but children were aware that it was happening. Fifteen shillings were collected from children in November 1899 for the War Fund for Widows and Children, and the Master noted that he sent a postal order for one pound. John Banks, who was then Chairman of the Board, explained the meaning of "relief" and impressed on the children the duties and lessons of patriotism. An evening hymn was sung nightly and *O God Our Help in Ages Past*, *All People that on Earth Do Dwell*, and *Now Thank We All Our God* were taught as being useful in the "present War and Troubles".

Thrift was encouraged, with 31 families having Savings Bank Books. In 1896 one family was over-enthusiastic, for their book had been tampered with and amounts put in that had not been received. The master indignantly stated that they "were not in my handwriting", and the affair was referred to the Board. A School Club involving 33 families and 70 children seems to have been a Christmas club, as money was given out at the end of November. In 1899 £35 had been banked for the year and £5 was given away in bonuses. The bonus was apparently awarded according to attendance, another incentive for parents to send their children to school.

The First World War

By 1914 Nazeing Council School was firmly established. Older girls went to cookery classes and the boys were taken in a conveyance to a woodwork centre in Harlow. Gardening classes began in that year, with Mr Bullock, Assistant Horticultural Instructor for the County, making an inspection; perhaps that was an early *Dig for Victory* campaign. The inspector, the medical officer, the school nurse, and the attendance officer all visited.

When the war started the master in charge was Noah H. Bevan, who served from 1906 to 1919. In 1912-13 he had been allowed a year's absence for training and was replaced by three temporary masters. He made very few references to the war in the school logbook. At that time Nazeing was still an agricultural, fairly insular community but the children must have been very aware of family and friends who had gone to fight, some of whom did not return. On Friday, 16th April 1916, the infant classroom was taken over as a Guard Room, perhaps by soldiers on exercises in Nazeing, with the result that the children had to be taught in the playground. A similar event occurred during the Second World War, when in May 1941 the school was closed at midday for some Grenadier Guards to be billeted overnight.

Two night air raids in January 1918 meant a low attendance the following day. In March Major Ralph Bury gave a talk on *The Causes of War* and Miss Herrington explained what her OBE decoration meant and how she had obtained it. The school was closed on Armistice Day, 11th November 1918, when it was hit by the influenza pandemic which killed more people in Europe than four years of fighting, but happily all the Nazeing children survived. In subsequent years Armistice Day was remembered with two minutes' silence, as it was throughout the country. To celebrate the Peace the summer holidays in 1919 were extended by one week.

Between the wars

Over the years the number of children on the register fluctuated, sometimes being as few as 90 but often rising above the stipulated 130. An HMI report for November 1921 noted that

> The conditions of work here are by no means easy, as Standards I – VII (juniors) numbering 77 on the books, are all taught in one room, with no partition or space to separate the different groups from one another. This involves considerable strain on the teachers and the powers of concentration of the children and it makes good oral work particularly difficult. In spite of these drawbacks, however, the teachers are managing very well and the general level of attainment is satisfactory.

On becoming headmaster in 1924 Bernard Swinden was convinced that the school could not work properly without a partition dividing the main room. Eventually a curtain was provided but, not surprisingly, it proved unsatisfactory. It took until 1930 for a moveable glass and wood partition to be installed, making two junior classrooms. Peter Brent thought that Swinden might have suffered from shell shock, for he would often stare out of the window oblivious to what was happening in the class.

For many years the rooms at the school were heated by coal fires but in very cold weather it was difficult to keep them warm. Children were often away with chilblains, which suggests that neither home nor school was heated adequately. Perhaps in earlier years staff and children had been less complaining, for it was not until February 1929 that the headmaster recorded the extent of the cold, when there were two months of low temperatures due to the inadequacy of the fires. In 1932 the recorded temperature by the window was 44° F and two years later, in December, after lighting the fires early it was only 43° at ten in the morning, "below the danger line". Central heating was installed in 1938 but on really cold

Pupils of the Council School, c1920. Back row from the left: Unknown, Albert Perry, "Piper" Mansfield, John Mansfield (not related). Middle row: Ben Bridgeman, Maurice Coleman, John Lawrence, Len Standingford, Noel Hale, Reg or Jack Mansfield (Brother of "Piper"), Sid Smith, Frank Coleman, Len "Tiddler" Hale (not related to Noel), Arthur "Tubby" Parker, Herbert "Dat Toes" Johnson and Charlie Johnson (Cousins). Front row: Annie Myson, Dulcie Perry, Connie Smith, Eva May, Mary Bridgeman, Jean Verrall, (niece of Headmaster), Eileen and Enid Webb (twins), Bertha Brace.

days there was no improvement. At 39° it was too cold for the children to write and by midday had reached only 50° with the windows closed.

Although the school was fairly central, many children had long distances to travel. In 1924, 35 of the 97 children had to come through water when the roads were flooded. Some would come across the fields so fathers put "blakeys" (studs) on boot soles to give small feet a grip on wet soil and to save wear. These made the children liable to slip and fall on the smooth playground. Those children who lived a long way from school brought a midday meal with them, which prompted the headmaster to start a cocoa scheme for 45 children. The infants had theirs at 10.30 am and the dinner children theirs at midday. From 1926 a few children arrived by bus and 2,757 tickets were sold at school in February 1934. Others had cycles and by the late 1930s the local policeman inspected them regularly. As the number of children with bicycles increased, these inspections became routine, as did cycling proficiency classes, tests, and road safety talks, a practice which takes place still.

As well as "the three R's", history, geography, and art were taught. There was a wireless receiver by 1939, when the school used the *B.B.C. Handbook for Schools* and listened to the Remembrance Day Service from the Cenotaph. H.M.V. gramophone records augmented the piano in music lessons. Good groundwork, to equip the girls for work in the home and boys for tasks on the land, was deemed important. Girls did cookery and needlework, learning to mend and cut out and sew garments (quite a feat in a crowded classroom); boys were taught woodwork, agriculture, and gardening. A wider range of books became available as the County Library van called regularly.

The school garden was established in 1914 and continued after the war. The Assistant Horticultural Instructor for the county travelled from Chelmsford to give advice and, at intervals, a sub-committee from Epping made inspections. The plot was producing potatoes, broad beans, runner beans, and parsnips, with the children keeping diaries on their activities, which included cleaning and oiling their gardening tools. Some idea of the importance of the garden is seen in the report of the Horticultural Instructor in 1926: "Considering local conditions and the present season, the appearance of this garden is distinctly good. The crops are of more than average promise and denote much care and attention in culture. Correlation is being effected as far as possible and the notebooks examined were of quite outstanding merit." The heavy Nazeing soil must have been a handicap, as it was suggested to the managers that the bad drainage needed attention. Nevertheless the boys were given a sound training in vegetable and flower culture; at one point, a three year course in rural science was envisaged but it never happened. In 1923 the Ministry of Agriculture offered scholarships for sons and daughters of agricultural workmen and details were posted on parish council notice boards. No response was recorded.

After 1918 ancillary health services became routine, although some parents objected to medical examinations. One mother whose children were found to have nits was so cross that she threatened to send her children to school in Hoddesdon. When medicals took place in the school it led to complete disorganisation of lessons as the infant room was used, leaving the children to spend the morning outside. To encourage dental hygiene three dozen toothbrushes were sold at sixpence each in 1926.

Better communications meant that children were able to travel further afield. They competed in the Dagenham Music Festival and the Epping District Sports, and played cricket and football against Roydon School and Harlow Common School. The girls played netball and stoolball, an old game resembling cricket. Visits extended to the Tower of London, Westminster Abbey, and the British Museum, and in May 1937 Ralph Bury provided a coach so that 40 children could see the decorations for the coronation of King George VI.

Until her death in 1933 Anna Bury and her son Ralph continued the practice of Christmas "treats", which she had started with her husband Charles in the 1880s. In 1934 the managers joined a hundred children at the tea, for which they provided 100 oranges, 1 lb tea, 9 dozen crackers, 6 lbs sugar, 4 lbs jam, 4½ lbs butter, 1½ gallons milk, 100 fancy cakes (good), 120 fancy cakes (cheaper), 100 half-cakes, slab cake (4 shillings), and 30 lbs of bread. Parties continued on this basis until 1941, when rationing and the large numbers of children involved made it necessary to have class parties after school on separate days. Food was provided by the parents and pooled. Their generosity resulted in a surplus of butter, sugar, tea, and cake, which was sent to Hertford Hospital. Prizes for good attendance were handed out at Christmas. Again the Bury family appear to have supplied them until about 1930; afterwards they were provided by subscriptions from the managers.

The population of Nazeing was rising by about fifty a year and with it the number of children on the register. By 1934 there were 148 children so that the three classrooms were overflowing, with mixed ages in each class. The school name was changed for the third time and it became the Nazeing Council Junior Mixed and Infant School. Those over eleven left to go to senior school, usually in Waltham Abbey, so that by September a more manageable 97 children were left. Enid Brent remembered this time: "We had a double-decker bus with a conductor and we went to Waltham Abbey, the boys on one bus and the girls on the other, very prim and proper."

County Minor Scholarships were being offered for places at selective schools. In 1931 Peggy Coleman became the first pupil in the history of the school to win such a scholarship and four years later Dennis Mead was the first boy to gain a place at Newport Grammar School. External examinations for selective secondary schools continued until the early 1970s. By the 1930s all the juniors were tested in arithmetic, reading,

Pupils from the Council School, c1940. Back row from the left: Ken Judd, Billy Martin, Michael Welch, Brian Coleman, Richard Hale, Raymond Seymour, Maurice Tillbrook, David Cleaver, Miss Beatrice Pulham. Middle row: Muriel Welch, unknown, June Bilton, Iris (surname unknown), Violet Starling, Kath Barrett, Marjorie Mead, Molly Hollow. Front row: Jean Rogers, Morvyth Perry, Mary Albiston and unknown.

composition, recitation, spelling, dictation, and grammar, with history and geography added on for the two upper classes.

One of the best-loved infant teachers of the twentieth century was Beatrice Pulham. She was a pupil at Nazeing Board School, leaving in 1898 and returning as a monitress in 1899. She resigned in 1904 but returned in 1930, being well established when Marcus Hills became headmaster in September 1938. Although she never received a formal college education, she had great natural gifts with children and many Nazeing natives will still remember her. Paddy Hutchings recalled that, although unmarried, Miss Pulham was one of the most reassuring and motherly people she has ever known, helping countless young children to overcome the terrors of their first day at school. Michael Hills, the younger of the headmaster's sons, remembered that often in his pre-school days he sat on her lap while she taught. When she retired in 1946 she was presented with sixty guineas in appreciation of her services. Mrs Bassett, formerly headmistress of the church school, replaced her as infant teacher.

Beatrice Pulham's grandfather and father were James Pulham and Son of the Brickworks in Station Road Broxbourne, which manufactured ornamental garden features. Her father, W.A. Pulham, had moved to Nazeing by 1924, when he bought Burnt Hall in Middle Street, where he had been Archdale Palmer's tenant. After he died, Beatrice and her brother Bert lived there until her retirement and Bert's death. Then she had a bungalow built in Middle Street where she lived until she died, on 2nd January 1969, aged 85.

The Second World War

War brought many changes which disrupted the children's education and must have been difficult for the teachers, especially Marcus Hills. With the threat of war looming he was disturbed to find that there were no plans for the safety of the children; on contacting the chairman of the managers he was advised to "sit tight". By February 1939, however, the district council and the police had advised on the provision of trenches and "safety first" lessons for the children.

At the onset of war in September the school opened a week late due to evacuee problems and the provision of additional school accommodation. By then all children over eleven went to schools outside the village but difficulties arose when senior pupils returned to Nazeing from the boys' and girls' schools in Waltham Abbey. When the school did open, there were, as well as the original infants and juniors, nine Government evacuees, eight voluntary evacuees, and six others. By October the seniors had arrived and from then on numbers were high, reaching more than 170. In a school originally built for 130 and already cramped, this was unworkable. A "double shift" system was tried in October, infants and juniors attending from 8.30 to 12 noon and seniors from 1.30 to 4.40, but this was soon reversed. Staff from the Waltham Abbey schools and South Woodford Boys' School taught the seniors.

As numbers crept up other solutions had to be found; by Easter 1940 the Chapel Hall had been rented and equipped to take the seniors. When the tenancy expired in November, all the children were due back under one roof at Bumbles Green. Within a fortnight, however, the Chapel Hall was in commission again.

On 9th November 1940 a bomb landed just outside the front door of the school house. Fortunately no one was injured, as the bomb fell at seven in the evening and Mr Hills' wife and family had been evacuated. There was damage to the roof and walls of the house, ceilings in the school were rendered unsafe and the chimneystacks of both house and school had to be demolished. The electric light cable installed in 1939 was severed but as the windows had been "netted" not one was broken.

Repairs went ahead and by the beginning of December 160 children were back at school. The headmaster recorded that difficulties included standing to write in the middle of the room, standing in shelters, and there being no room for a blackboard in front of class. "We can 'manage' but teaching suffers," he commented. Damage to the school building occurred in January 1940, when a violent explosion at the Waltham Abbey Gunpowder Factory caused showers of dust from the roof but no structural damage, and in October 1940, when the ceiling fell in after a land mine exploded at Long Green.

Amidst all this the lessons went on. Older children took entrance exams to senior school, teachers attended courses, and the library bus called. Visits were made to dental and eye clinics, children were immunised against diphtheria, and there were medical and cleanliness inspections. As part of the war effort boys helped with potato picking and, at Ralph Bury's request, children were sent on cabbage planting and on farm work. For relaxation a travelling circus visited and there were outings to Whipsnade Zoo, St. Albans, and the Roman site of Verulamium.

But war was never very far away. In 1941 it was decided that in the event of a local disaster the school should become an emergency rest and feeding centre. Everyone carried gas masks, which were repaired or replaced periodically, and there were Red Cross meetings. A "Make Do and Mend" van visited the school, helping collecting and saving to become a way of life. Spurred on by a talk by Mr Goddard from the Ministry of Supply, 1,500 books were collected (35 cwt. of paper), together with salvage of iron, rubber, rags, and bottles. Children who collected the most salvage received an award. By the autumn of 1942, when emergency feeding equipment had been delivered, work started on the "kitchen", which was in the cycle shed, while a cloakroom cupboard became a food store.

War savings and special collections were important. When a Penny Savings Bank was opened at the school in 1939, 105 children enrolled. The school bank traded every day during *War Weapons Week* in May 1941, when 44 Savings Certificates were bought and £40 3s 3d was deposited. For *Warships Week* in March 1942 the children raised the large sum of £53 10s, in recognition of which they were given an extra day's holiday. *Wings for Victory Week* in 1943 far surpassed the target of £60 and raised £186 18s 11d, although a drive to form a flight of the Air Training Corps brought no response, despite the displaying of posters and the notifying of eligible candidates. In 1944 *Salute the Soldier Week* raised £101 19s 5d.

The greatest catastrophe to hit both Nazeing and its council school was the V2 rocket which fell at St. Leonards Road on 12th November 1944. As the village came to terms with the deaths and devastation few children went to school on the Monday morning. Two boys from the school, John Weare and Basil Rumsey, were killed outright; later William and David King died in hospital. Five other children, Cyril Hall, Hector Hall, Don Newton, Robin Pallett, and Fred Sewell were hurt but mercifully recovered. A Rest Centre was opened in the Chapel Hall, where homeless children received eggs and fruit, in short supply in wartime. Each November 12th until the 1960s children from the top class took flowers to the Rocket Memorial in All Saints' churchyard.

In May 1945, just six months after the rocket fell, there were celebrations for VE Day. Both the school and the house were decorated with flags and every night for a week they were floodlit, which would have been illegal during the black-out. There was a street party in Allmains Close and sports, dancing, and a bonfire on the recreation ground. Further celebrations took place for Victory Day in June 1946, when the school rooms were packed with 400 children enjoying tea and a cinematograph show; no doubt this was a hot and steamy occasion, as the rain came down and the intended sports were abandoned. The shadow of war lingered until December 1949, when the repair of bomb damage was completed.

School dinners

School dinners started during the war. Although this would have helped the mothers because their rations would go further, it must have been a great trial for the teachers. The three classrooms became dining rooms for the lunch hour and from noon to 3.30 the cloakroom served as a kitchen. As over 100 children were staying, inevitably there was overcrowding; frequently there must have been chaos. Dinners were delivered from Roydon and were sometimes unsatisfactory. On one occasion in 1944 the recently installed telephone wires became hot when "immediate action" was called for. Action was not immediate and for a while there was no dinner service, although it must have resumed, as in 1945 it took a lorry to deliver canteen equipment consisting of one saltcellar.

It became obvious that with school dinners firmly entrenched a separate dining area was a necessity. Although sanctioned in 1943, the canteen was not built until 1948 and even then its start was inauspicious: the first consignments of building materials from Hackney were returned twice, as there was no builder on site to receive them. In 1947 canteen equipment had started arriving in dribs and drabs - a doormat by rail on 1st August, two dusters and two oven cloths by registered post on September 12th, a scourer worth sixpence by registered post on 2nd December. The canteen opened finally on 21st March 1949, when all but ten of the 127 children stayed to dinner.

A school milk scheme had begun before the Second World War, paid for by the parents. Occasionally the Epping Voluntary Association paid for milk and in 1926 six children were recommended by a doctor to receive this "free" milk. In 1934 seventy children had daily milk and the total amount of money taken for the week was fifteen shillings. In 1940

Prime Minister Winston Churchill, who declared that "there is no finer investment for any community than putting milk into babies", gave instructions that free milk should be distributed at school to all children throughout the country; from 1942 it was available in the holidays as well. It was discontinued in 1980.

The final years at Bumbles Green

Although only five to eleven year olds were attending Nazeing School, overcrowding was becoming an insoluble problem by 1950. The new council estates and some private houses had been built, so that the population was increasing by an average of 150 a year. With 161 pupils the school was bursting at the seams; in September 1951 parents were informed that there would be no intake of new children that term. As a temporary measure the deputy headmaster, David Merry, took one class to Waltham Abbey.

The parish council suggested the possibility of an extra classroom in the Women's Land Army hut or in the Chapel Hall; in September 1952 the latter was brought into commission yet again. Forty-two infants travelled by bus to the hall to be taught by Eileen Merry and Mrs Winch. Eventually, as the number of infants reached the hundred mark, the room behind the chapel was used as a third classroom and the then teachers, Kathy Barrett and Mrs Tilsley were assisted by a welfare helper, Peggy Hollow. On the first Monday when the church room was used, the ladies of the Women's Fellowship turned up for their meeting unaware of the situation. The class had to move out for the afternoon.

School life at the Chapel Hall was not easy. As other activities took place there out of school hours, all school equipment had to be put away every night and brought out the following morning. A curtain divided the hall and heating was provided by two metal stoves which the teachers had to keep stoked up; even so the room was often cold. On really cold days the children were allowed to put their bottles on the fender to warm the milk. Dinner arrived in large containers and, once the curtains were drawn back and the tables arranged in rows, the adults distributed the food. As there were few facilities, teachers took the children up Perry Hill on nature walks, showed educational films, sang, and read stories. They took a boat trip on the Thames, had a sports day on the field next door, and put on a Nativity play for the parents.

301

By 1956 there were 288 pupils. There were three infant classes in the Chapel Hall and three overcrowded junior classes in the original building at Bumbles Green. A fourth junior class was in the canteen and, despite the objections of Nazeing Parish Council, a fifth was at Epping Upland school, having moved from Waltham Abbey. The HMI report noted in detail all the organisational difficulties and the opportunities denied to the children, but that the school was nevertheless a happy place; the inspector commended its "excellent results in difficult circumstances". There were extracurricular activities and educational visits to places such as the Geffrye Museum, London Zoo, Kew Gardens, Madame Tussauds and, in 1951, to the Festival of Britain exhibition. In the summer of 1957 six hundred adults and children went on a memorable outing to Clacton and Walton.

Although the school did an excellent job in most respects, it seems to have been responsible for a myth about Nazeing that has persisted into the twenty-first century. Generations of children accepted without question the assertion that Nazeing was the second biggest village in England. At nearly 4,000 acres it is indeed "a vast and scattered parish" but it has never been even the second biggest village in the Epping district, much less in the whole country.

School transport

The imbalance caused by having the school at one end of the village and increasing numbers of children at the other led to major transport problems. After the closure of the Betts Lane school in 1947 children were transferred to the Bumbles Green school, so that some had much further to travel. The parish council's request to the school managers and the education authority to provide transport for them was refused. In 1950 children were "refused boarding the bus when there appeared to be room", and there were complaints that they had to leave school early to be sure of catching the bus home. Children were often left at the crossroads and points further along the route because of overcrowding, so the vicar asked the London Passenger Transport Board to put on extra buses at 8.50 am and 3.50 pm. The education department rejected the parish council's suggestion of a special service because it could be provided only for children living more than two miles from the school. The council replied that many of them did.

In September 1953 the bus service was described as "totally inadequate". 120 children were attending the main school and another forty the annexe at the chapel, with more expected from Palmers Grove, which was being built. As the result of a slight accident a conductress refused to take any children over the authorised number and one mother declared that "if her child could not go by bus she would keep her child at home and face the consequences". By 1955 up to one hundred children were getting off the bus at Bumbles Green. Sometimes thirty or forty were left behind at the crossroads, according to the attitude of the "conductor/ress" and whether they allowed three children per seat or only two. The provision of a special bus for children from Keysers alleviated the problem. By 1957, as there were 336 children on the register, five junior classes were being bussed to Priory, a vacant new school in Harlow.

Older children attending schools further away also had problems. Until the building of the Harlow comprehensives in the 1950s, girls who won grammar school places were admitted to the Herts and Essex High School in Bishops Stortford, but Essex children could not normally attend Hertfordshire schools, so scholarship boys had to go by train to Newport twenty miles away. There were complaints about poor train service and requests that morning buses should leave Nazeing earlier because when they arrived at Broxbourne Station the boys had only two minutes to scramble on to the Newport train. A special bus took children to schools in Waltham Abbey, but ten children from Upper Nazeing had difficulty even getting to the coach. In 1955 there was a complaint that the 393 bus could not accommodate all the children attending various secondary schools in Harlow, who either had to wait half an hour or walk. Maurice Coleman took up the matter with J. Tillett of the Forest Divisional Executive of Essex County Council Education Department, which had issued free bus passes to thirty Nazeing children but not ensured that there were buses on which they could be used; on one occasion Coleman sent a private car to Netteswell school for his children and a bill to Tillett for the cost.

Hyde Mead

The life of the Board School was drawing to a close. In 1949 Essex County Council began a census of all its schools and within two years identified the urgent need for a new building in Nazeing. After Epping Rural District Council had acquired the Hyde Mead site by compulsory

Hyde Mead School built in 1958.

purchase in 1953, the county council announced its plans for the new school in the following year. At first it came up with a rather half-baked idea whereby three classrooms would be built and more added later but Nazeing Parish Council argued that "the new school should be big enough to take all the children for the foreseeable future". Essex duly revised its plans to provide the nine classrooms that would be necessary for the 360 children expected. Then in 1956 it hedged its bets with a press report hinting that because of "the Chancellor of the Exchequer's economy measures" there might be only seven classrooms. The parish council wrote to the county in "the strongest possible terms of protest at the continuing cost of sending classes out of Nazeing to other schools" and, although it took another two years, the nine classrooms were provided.

When the new school opened in September 1958, 336 children were admitted, even though it was by no means finished. Set in extensive playing fields, it had a main hall, which could be used as a dining room, and an on-site kitchen. A new family meals service, which was filmed for inclusion in a television programme, engendered a great deal of interest. As headmaster since 1938, Marcus Hills had seen many changes and taken the school through the war and into Hyde Mead. To mark his twenty years as head he was presented with an illuminated address and £100 from the village of Nazeing. He retired in December 1961 and soon

304

afterwards was replaced by Russell Haynes, who also completed twenty years as headmaster.

As Nazeing expanded, an increasing proportion of the population worked outside the village, which retained much of its rural appearance but no longer had a strong agricultural community. Some of the old Nazeing surnames could still be found in the register but many were now "outsiders" and the population was more mobile. At the same time there was for many a rising standard of living, which was reflected in the school and its amenities. In 1960 it was proposed to build a swimming pool and a school sale, which was to become an annual event, raised £475 for the venture. It was decided to have two pools, a small courtyard pool for the infants (no longer there in 2001) and a larger one for juniors. The first swimming gala took place in 1961.

The range of activities increased steadily. In 1959 older pupils had the

Pupils from Nazeing County Primary School at Hyde Mead in 1959. Back row from the left: Roger Cook, John Coleman, Michael Brent, Terry Hayward, Christopher Raithby, David Nicols, Leonard Bayford, David Muhley, Barry Wells, Michael Thornton, Hugh Bradbury. Middle row: John Price, Graham Smith, Marilyn Jarman, Shirley Harvey, Christina Tasker, Wendy Mansfield, Barbara Hutcheon, Sheila Smith, Susan Fauvelle, Rachel Cole, Jennifer Crook, Russell Joyce, Peter Pennal. Front row: Trudy Yore, Linda Sullivan, Manda Waterman, Jennifer Mills, Jacqueline Everitt, David Merry (deputy headmaster), Marian Smith, Judith Tant, Carole Pring, Marian Traveller, Jean Spouncer.

chance to go abroad on a school trip, thanks in no small measure to David Merry who managed the arrangements and fought what he called "the Battle of the Fares" to obtain the lowest possible price. With great excitement, and with flags and bunting fluttering from the newly erected council houses opposite, children of class 9 set off for Denmark. Later there were trips on school cruise ships and fly cruises. Sadly David Merry died young of a heart attack.

A tape recorder and cine projector were used in the classrooms and by the early 1970s children could have extra tuition to play musical instruments. There were clubs for music, art, dance, science, stamp collecting, and after school games. Christmas events regularly included a Nativity play, Christmas dinner, parties for infants and juniors, and carol singing round the Christmas tree.

A new school building did not, however, solve all problems. An extra junior classroom was added in 1966 but two years later pupil numbers reached 397. The parish council considered that the residents of Crooked Way "were getting a raw deal" because of the large number of pupils using the footpath through to the school. Over the next few years concern was expressed frequently over the continuing lack of space. By the 1970s there were two movable classrooms sited near the infants' playground. There appears to have been quite a turnover of staff at times due to teachers' marrying, taking maternity leave, or leaving the district. The expansion of Harlow New Town and increasing population within the divisional education authority area added to the difficulty of getting both new staff and supply teachers, so that the existing teaching staff were sometimes very stretched. In several cases council houses were allocated to teachers.

At first the building of the new school eased the difficulties with transport but by 1967 there were problems in getting children from Riverside to Hyde Mead. One bizarre episode involved the Forest Divisional Executive (FDE), Nazeing Parish Council, and Redlands Gravel. In response to complaints about "the deplorable condition of the roads" caused by debris from its lorries, Redlands provided an expensive piece of sweeping equipment. About the same time, according to the parish council minutes, the FDE "refused to alleviate the difficult situation of Riverside children despite telephone promises when trying to avert militant parents' action", thus displaying "a lack of local knowledge and remoteness". For some unexplained reason the FDE chose to contact

Redlands about this "vexed question", so the company took umbrage and withdrew its agreement with the parish council. The 1968 Parish Meeting resolved that "militant action should not be discouraged if some sympathetic consideration were not forthcoming". The problem was solved soon afterwards, however, when the county councils of Hertfordshire and Essex introduced a more flexible policy in allowing primary school pupils to cross the boundary.

The school building programme in Harlow affected the secondary education of Nazeing children. It became general policy to transfer eleven year olds to particular Harlow schools and the old method of admission to selective schools by examination in maths and English was scaled down. By the mid-1970s this exam was replaced by Verbal Reasoning Tests, which were taken if parents wished, but by 2001 tests for children entering secondary school from Nazeing had virtually

Ron Hickman invented the world-famous Workmate after a do-it-yourself mishap at his new bungalow in Banes Down. The tool's versatility was demonstrated in 1968 when two benches he gave to Nazeing County Primary School attracted press photographers. From the left: Mark Tracy, Barry Crowe, Michael Thorn, Deborah Knott, J Spence (caretaker), Russell Haynes (headmaster).

disappeared. The cross-boundary policy was extended and many Nazeing children went to Sheredes and other Hertfordshire secondary schools.

The Hyde Mead School became involved regularly with the local community. In 1970, with financial help from the parish council, thirty young mothers initiated a successful Summer Play Scheme which, although not happening every year, became well established. Children visited Hyde Mead House and members of the Elderly and Handicapped Association were invited to school performances. Through the 1960s and 70s regular collections were made for Dr. Barnardo's Homes, with a visit in 1979 by their regional officer, who presented an embroidered pennant to the school for outstanding service.

Several special occasions were marked in the 1960s and 1970s. In July 1965 the school was closed for the 750th anniversary of Magna Carta and the 700th of Simon de Montfort's Parliament. It closed again in 1972 for the Queen's Silver Wedding Anniversary and 1973 for the wedding of Princess Anne. For Elizabeth II's Silver Jubilee in June 1977 a fête was arranged, which raised nearly £500 for children's organisations. The Centenary Celebrations of Nazeing School were held on 22nd June 1978, when an exhibition was staged in the school. Unfortunately the actual day was very wet and all outside activities were postponed until 3rd July, which was cold and windy but dry.

Nazeing was fortunate that strikes rarely disrupted the running of the school. The most notable withdrawal of labour took place when the school kitchens were closed in opposition to cuts in the school meals service. In November 1980 the members of the Epping Forest Branch of the National Union of Public Employees withdrew their labour, so 223 children had to eat sandwiches.

Although in the early years there was a small amount of vandalism, the last quarter of the twentieth century was to see less respect for people and property throughout the country; Nazeing School was not exempt. In 2001 closed circuit television deterred vandalism and inappropriate use of school grounds.

In the 1990s further changes took place in the management of the school. Although the managing body had been drawn from local people, the local authority had always carried much of the responsibility. This changed when, following the 1988 Education Act, Local Management of Schools began in 1991. The managers became a Governing Body, which had greater responsibility for the school, including its premises, finance, and curriculum. After 1999 it was made up of four parent governors, three local education authority governors, a representative of the parish council, four co-opted members from the local community, one teacher, one member of staff other than a teacher, and the headteacher. There had been yet another change of category in April 1999, when Nazeing Primary School was designated a community school.

The National Curriculum, which was introduced in the 1990s, by reviving an emphasis on literacy and numeracy, ensured that Nazeing children still received a good basic education. The children who started at the Board School in 1878, however, would scarcely have been able to imagine the classrooms of 2001. They would have been pleasantly surprised by the carpeted floors, the range of brightly coloured books, the work exhibited in the classrooms, and the amenities available. They would have been astonished and perhaps bewildered by the information technology area, connected to the National Grid for Learning, where children would be able to send and receive their own e-mail. What the 1878 children would have recognised was their successors' having to learn to read and do sums, although modern technology was enabling more interesting methods to be used.

The shell logo

The logo of Nazeing Parish Council is a red scallop shell, the emblem of St. James, who is the patron saint of pilgrims. The scallop was worn proudly by pilgrims in the Middle Ages. Those who went to the Holy Land were known as palmers (Latin *palmifer*, palm-bearer) because they received a consecrated palm branch to take home. It was assumed therefore that the council had adopted the shell for its logo as a tribute to the Palmer family. In the 1997 edition of *Nazeing Round and About* Nicholas Wood suggested a different and very convincing version of its origin.

When he first attended Nazeing School, his school uniform included a green cap and blazer, both of which displayed the red scallop. This he believed to have been introduced by Marcus Hills. In the school hall was a large oak plaque carved with the scallop and the school hymn, *Who Would True Valour See*, each verse of which ends with the line "To be a pilgrim". The hymn was celebrating the pilgrim tradition which in Nazeing was continued by John Eliot and other Puritans, who sought

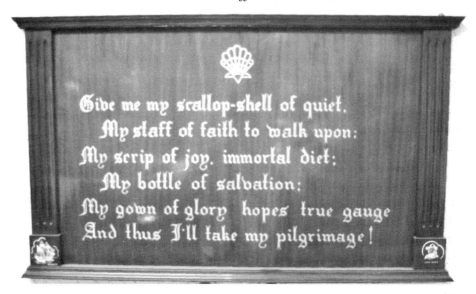

The oak plaque with scallop shell at Nazeing County Primary School.

freedom of conscience in America in the seventeenth century. The plaque disappeared but after many years it was restored to pride of place in the school hall.

Thus it was the parish council which borrowed the shell logo from the school rather than the other way round. It is a happy coincidence that two major threads of Nazeing's history, the Puritan tradition and the influence of the Palmer family, are united in a single symbol.

Nazeing Park School

Before the 1944 Education Act, special education had generally been restricted to children with physical and mental handicaps. In Britain and America it began to be recognised that there was a category of otherwise normal children who were showing behavioural problems which were often caused by broken homes and, more seriously, physical abuse of all kinds. Little structured effort had been provided for such children, but in the decade 1945 to 1955 there was considerable expansion of provision for maladjusted pupils.

When Sir Walter Hargreaves left the village, Essex County Council bought Nazeing Park and its stable block, together with four cottages and surrounding grounds of some seventy acres. Nazeing Park School was opened in 1952 as a residential school for upwards of forty children of primary school age, who had special educational needs related to social and emotional causes. The principal object of the school was to provide a warm and caring environment in which the pupils might overcome their social and educational difficulties, with the aim of returning them to mainstream schooling.

The ground immediately surrounding the school, a playing field, a football field, and some of the woodland were retained for school use. The remainder was let to local farmers for grazing, the land between the house and Common Road often being characterised by flocks of grazing sheep. The appearance of the land changed little, except for the loss of many mature elms to Dutch elm disease. Four further houses were built in the grounds for staff and the main house was linked to the stable block to provide domestic facilities and further space for classrooms. Many of the non-teaching staff were recruited from Nazeing. Under the aegis of Essex County Council the school had its own governing body, which sometimes included Nazeing residents. The school remained at Nazeing Park until 1995, when the children and many staff moved to premises at Chigwell.

The estate was sold by the county council and reinstated as private property. The unsightly additions to the house were removed and it was restored as closely as possible to its original state. In 1998 owners Jim and Jayne Egan and architect Steve Kuschel won Epping Forest Council's annual award for heritage and conservation.

Nazeing Park around 1900 when it was a private house. In 1952 it opened as a residential school for forty children with special educational needs. By 1998 it again became a private house and has been restored to an extremely high standard.

Two Nazeing celebrations. Above is an outing from Nazeing in
1924. The shield on the charabanc reads "Prince Henry,
Knowler Bros. Waltham Abbey. Below is a "street party" at
Nazeing Bury celebrating the 50th anniversary of VE Day.

CHAPTER 9

"ALL NAZEING GATHERED TOGETHER"

Recreation

The topic of recreation in Nazeing would be enough to fill a book on its own, so this chapter can be only a summary. It looks first at the communal buildings and places that were used for recreation, then at the various activities and the organisations that ran them, and finally at some special events that brought the village together.

"The tin tabernacle"

The first parish hall was situated near the junction of Betts Lane and Hoe Lane, opposite the entrance to what is now the Old Vicarage. Aptly nicknamed the "tin hut" or "tin tabernacle", it was built in 1891 by Thomas Goddard for a Sunday School on land owned by the Wake family. Since at that time the Church was still a part of local government, the vicar and churchwardens had a lease at a peppercorn rent, ten shillings per annum. In the aftermath of the First World War there was for a while a real desire to put aside the petty squabbles that had marked the pre-war years and to develop a real sense of community in the village. Sir Hereward Wake and the vicar and wardens agreed therefore that the hall was not a church hall but the parish hall of Nazeing, which could be let for community events and entertainments as well as for church meetings.

Originally the hall measured 18 by 55 feet but it was enlarged to 29 by 76 feet. It had a lean-to store at the back and a frontage to Betts Lane of only three feet. It was constructed of corrugated iron, painted red, and had a urinal and two earth closets. Mains water was not laid on until early 1934; the costs of the installation and of the provision of a sink were met by Walter Hargreaves. At the same time Frederick W. Green presented a pianola piano to replace the piano, which had become practically worn out. Later that year electric lights were installed, paid for by Archdale Palmer who had expressed his concern about the dangers of the oil lamps. In 1936 James Sutherland and the churchwardens, Archdale Palmer and Cyril Chapman, asked Sir Hereward if they could be relieved from the hall's management. Sutherland seemed particularly anxious to be freed from any responsibility for it. It seems that Palmer was willing to support

NAZEING. PARISH HALL

REGULATIONS
FOR HIRING THE PARISH HALL

SCALE OF CHARGES

No.	Class of Hire	Hours	Period of Year	Price
				s. d.
1.	Socials	From 6.30 p.m.		
	Concerts	to Midnight		17 6
	Whist Drives			
2.	Women's Institute	Up to 6.30 p.m.	May to September inclusive	6 0
3.	Wedding, etc., Receptions		October to April inclusive	8 0
4.	Afternoon Teas	Up to 6.30 p.m.	May to September inclusive	2 6
			October to April inclusive	4 6
5.	Church Socials, Concerts, etc.	Up to 6.30 p.m.	May to September inclusive	5 0
			October to April inclusive	7 0
		From 6.30 p.m. to Midnight		10 6
6.	Missionary and Church Meetings other than No. 5.	Up to 6.30 p.m.	May to September inclusive	4 0
			October to April inclusive	6 0
		From 6.30 p.m. to Midnight		7 6
7.	Women's Sewing Club	Up to 6.30 p.m.	May to September inclusive	2 6
8.	Women's Fellowship		October to April inclusive	4 0

NOTE.—The above Charges cover the provision of Lighting, Firing (during the period October to April inclusive), and Hot Water; and the services of the Caretaker in preparing the Hall.

PAYMENTS.—The Fees for hiring must be paid to the Clerk of the Parish Council— Mr. A. Coleman, of Howards, Middle Street—to whom alone application for the use of the Hall must be made at the time of booking it.

WASHING UP.—In the case of Meetings where Refreshments are served, the washing up and tidying must be undertaken by the party hiring the Hall.

NUMBERS.—When the Hall is hired for Evening Whist Drives, Dances, etc., the numbers to be admitted must be limited to 100, exclusive of Band.

INTOXICANTS.—When the Hall is hired for profit, and/or is the subject of a payment for admission, INTOXICANTS must not be introduced for consumption on the premises.

LENT.—The Hall will be available for any of the purposes set out in the above Scale of Charges during the season of Lent.

By Order of the Parish Council,

A. COLEMAN,
Clerk.

The regulations for hiring the Parish Hall, issued when the parish council took it over in 1936, indicate the wide variety of social events held there.

him but that he was opposed by Chapman, for apparently it was only after pressure had been applied that Chapman agreed to the proposal that Nazeing Parish Council take the hall over. It is indicated in the Parochial Church Council's minutes that several members shared Chapman's unease about the transaction, particularly concerning furniture and fittings, such as a lot of chairs donated by Walter Hargreaves, all of which had been given for the hall and intended for the use of the Church's congregation.

Sir Hereward continued the agreement to let the hall for ten shillings a year and the parish council spent £33 on repairs and new equipment. In 1934, when Richard Andrew was a churchwarden, the Upper Nazeing Women's Institute had asked the PCC unsuccessfully for a reduction in its hiring fee but had been invited to raise the matter again. Aline Andrew, the treasurer, did so on the WI's behalf in 1938, when her husband was on the parish council, but had no better luck, for the councillors voted unanimously to refuse the request because the hall was running at a loss. For the same reason the council refused "free use of the Hall at a forthcoming Entertainment for two highly deserving Charities".

At the outbreak of the Second World War the Parish Hall, like most places of entertainment, was closed on safety grounds. Soon it was realised that this lowered the morale of civilians without enhancing their safety, so the policy was reversed. Mrs. Andrew and Mrs. Simmons supervised the blacking-out of the Parish Hall and it was reopened for entertainment. If air attack were threatened, the officer commanding the Engineer Unit on Nazeing Common would telephone Col. Richard Andrew, Chairman of the Nazeing ARP Committee, who lived at Buttfield near the hall. He would warn people there of the impending danger. All users had to sign an undertaking to carry out ARP instructions in the event of an air-raid, observe black-out arrangements scrupulously and, when they had finished, extinguish lights and secure the premises.

Despite the sanitary facilities, rather coyly described as "not adequate", the hall was well used. In 1943-4 it was let 62 times. Apparently organisations were charged according to the contribution they were deemed to be making to the war effort. No charge was made to the Parish Invasion Committee, nor when the hall was used as an emergency rest centre for people rendered temporarily homeless by war damage. Dr. G.F. Wilson, Medical Officer of the Essex Western Area ARP, attended occasionally and had to defray only heating costs. When the Upper Nazeing Women's Institute and Joan Baker of the Fruit Preservation Centre used the hall for jam-making, they obtained a special rate of 3s 6d, but for their Thursday evening entertainment the Women's Land Army had to pay 12 shillings, later reduced to 7s 6d.

During the war the hall made a small annual loss, varying between two and ten pounds, but immediately afterwards extensive repairs were necessary and the deficit jumped to £25. There were complaints that the stove smoked, so electric radiators were installed at a cost of £27 10s; these proved unsatisfactory too. In 1950 it was agreed that "as the Hall was very little used, the Caretaker be dispensed with". Furthermore, the hall was far from the growing centres of population at Nazeingbury and Riverside. Serious consideration was given to its closure but the long-awaited extension of the bus service and de-rationing of petrol meant a reprieve. A new caretaker was employed and received a special payment of a pound for an initial clean, which suggests that the hall had become somewhat grubby.

The hall was used for meetings, dancing lessons, and whist drives; a performing rights licence was obtained. The parish council ran special fund-raising dances which produced £22. With £10 from the Nazeing Amateur Theatrical Society and £2 5s from the Square Dance Society added, this was enough to purchase a gramophone with loudspeakers.

The old piano became beyond economic repair, so a second-hand one was bought; as this suffered from damp, it was fitted with its own electric

A fancy dress party at the Parish Hall, c1943.

heater. Improvements included the provision of a new slow combustion stove, six wall lanterns, and a concrete path. The Young Conservatives requested a reduction in the hiring fee because certain facilities were lacking, but this was refused because other improvements had been made and more were envisaged. The continuing post-war shortage of materials was demonstrated as late as 1951 when the Upper Nazeing WI asked whether their cupboard "could be extended with the spare wood from the dismantled Jam Centre and Library shelves". The parish council agreed, "provided there was wood to spare after the Gents' Cloakroom door and frame had been made".

In 1953 the rent was increased to a still less than crippling 12s 6d per annum. By then, however, the hall was beginning to show signs of its age and the parish council voted 4 to 2 to pay £300 on improvements but, as quotes for the repairs were too high, nothing was done. In 1956 the WI complained that the doormat was missing and, apparently as a less significant afterthought, that the lavatory accommodation was unsatisfactory. Councillor Douglas Ragg suggested therefore that the hall be closed but his proposal was not supported. In 1958 the County Architect reported that the hall would need extensive and costly repairs, so the parish council took an immediate and unanimous decision to close it down and rent it out for storage.

The photograph of Archdale Palmer rescued by Brian Hills, who commented: "Something of his real gentleman character is evident - and the kid gloves say it all."

In 1961 the landlord refused the parish council's request for change of use and sold the hall to Len Davis, who applied to build a bungalow on the site. On a snowy morning in January 1962, a young district council planning officer came to inspect the application site, only to find that the hall had been demolished already. Brian Hills, the son of headmaster Marcus Hills, as a boy had been driven round the village delivering Poppy Day materials for Archdale Palmer. He recalled what happened next:

> ...kicking through the rubble heaped up on the site, I chanced upon a small picture frame broken in pieces, glass all smashed, but inside - the unmistakable smile of Archdale Palmer showed through the dirt! I couldn't bear to leave the picture lying there and rescued it...

The photograph "knocked about" in his garage for the next 37 years and inevitably it deteriorated. Now it has been restored to make a splendid record of Archdale Palmer as many remember him.

The Chapel Hall and St. Giles' Hall

Throughout the twentieth century the village was dependent for any major events on using halls owned by the two churches. The Chapel Hall was closer to the centre of Nazeing than the Parish Hall and remains the largest in the village. It was the venue for events as varied as the 1935 Jubilee celebrations and the 1958 meeting about street lighting, as well as the church's sporting activities. Among the organisations that used it were the British Legion, the Lower Nazeing Women's Institute, the Nazeing Village Association, the Footlights drama group, the Guides, and the Evergreens Club for older people. Its use declined after St. Giles' Church and Hall was built at Nazeingbury crossroads, which had become the centre of the village. Opened in 1964, St. Giles' Hall was soon the venue for many organisations and for most public meetings.

Bumbles Green Leisure Centre

Under the 1861 Nazeing Enclosure Award the piece of land where the Leisure Centre now stands was recognised as "a place of exercise and recreation for the inhabitants of the Parish". In 1919 it was "used by children and youths for cricket and football"; fence repair costs were paid out of the income from letting the grazing rights. Like the nearby Common, it suffered from molehills and thistles, so in 1937 Archdale Palmer gave instructions for them to be cleared as much as possible.

By the end of the Second World War bomb craters and molehills had made the field unusable, so a bulldozer was brought in to level it. Memory of its original use was almost lost and it was let to Arthur Nicholls who complained about wilful damage to its gates and fences. Councillor Leonard Archer was asked to check for "any mention in Enclosure Award of purposes for which the so called Recreation Ground was intended". When he reported back, Nicholls was given notice to quit. Nazeing Football Club was allowed to use the ground provided that it took "all necessary steps to make the ground fit for play". In 1948 Essex County Council enquired about hiring the ground for use by the school and a contractor was employed to level it. As he left it in a worse state than before, it was deemed "utterly useless for recreation". Mechanical methods having failed, Councillors James Gray and Arthur Nicholls greatly improved the condition of the ground with the more traditional remedy of grazing their sheep on it. In 1950 the county council put the ground in order and shared the cost with the parish council. School sports were held "up the Rec.", as it was known. Although it was considered suitable for "all sorts of recreation bearing in mind its small area", it was used mostly for football, by the school and by teams such as the Nazeing Minors, who played in the East Herts League.

This 1950s photograph of Nazeing Football Club shows the wooden pavilion in the background. Standing from the left: Bernie Pegrum, unknown, Eric Reynolds, Vic Clarke, Arthur Springham, Alec Edwards, unknown, Fred Myson, Bernie Brooks, Jim Robertson, unknown, Jimmy Brent (President). Middle row: Larry Ward, Ralph Thurlow, Ted Nettle, Ivor "Bubbie" Brent, Frank Turner, Ernie Hutchins, Dennis Mead. Front row: Ralph Bayford, Ben Penn, Willie Hampton, Eric Ashby.

319

Soon after buying Harold's Park Farm, John Mackie generously permitted use of the fairly flat rectangular field next to the Avenue for football and a wooden pavilion was erected. In 1959 he tackled the fact that the parish recreation ground was too small and offered an adjoining piece of land "to assist the football club", so the parish council expressed its "unqualified appreciation" of the proposed gift. The council and Mackie shared the cost of new fencing; later he made a further offer to "put the areas subject to flooding into perfect order by turfing". The council decided to include the Bumbles Green allotments in the ground and to improve those in Middle Street as compensation.

Footballers still had to change in a cloakroom over the road at the Village Centre, formerly the Bumbles Green school, so the parish council began to consider building "a pavilion with lavatory facilities" on the recreation ground. In 1964 Councillor George Compton was asked "to submit plans in a professional capacity not exceeding £2,000" and soon afterwards it was agreed that "no further time should be lost in the provision of a pavilion". The matter lay dormant until 1972, when the possibility of a building to house a pavilion, village hall, and library was suggested. Although this seems to have been considered too ambitious, it

The Leisure Centre at Bumbles Green was built in 1975.

did serve to revive interest in the more modest proposal of the pavilion and caused the parish council to make a firm decision to build it at a cost of £2,800. There were the inevitable delays and additional costs but by the end of 1975 it was complete and the parish council declared it "a fine building". As it was more than a football pavilion, it would be known as the Leisure Centre. Local residents argued that this breached the original conditions on which planning permission was granted and complained about noisy events going on as late as 1.40 am. They sent a petition to Epping Forest Council but the parish council submitted a successful application for "occasional community use", which has continued ever since. The building was extended in 1981.

The village hall that never was

As the Nazeingbury area developed, it became the obvious place to locate a new village hall and recreation ground. When the 1939 Town Planning Scheme was published, the parish council asked that a large field of several acres near the centre of the village should be set aside for recreation, although there was no suggestion of a hall. In 1945 eight people requested a playing field in the area and a joint committee of councillors and petitioners suggested that a piece of land should be scheduled in the revised Town Planning scheme. The following year Ralph Bury offered a one and a quarter acre field behind present-day St. Giles' for a hall, provided that another field behind it could be acquired as a recreation ground. Grants towards both projects were available and the parish council seemed confident that they would go ahead, but they had to be put to the vote at a parish meeting, which was held on 7th November 1946. The Nazeing Ratepayers' Association opposed the scheme on the grounds of "excessive cost" and Carthagena residents did so because of the "scattered nature of the district"; not even the original proponents of the scheme supported it.

In 1949 the newly-elected parish council returned to the idea. It set up a fund for the purpose and a sub-committee to work on plans. In January 1950 a large number of residents attended a special parish meeting and voted unanimously in favour of the plan. Full support to the venture and to the fund soon came from the Lower Nazeing Women's Institute (£112 18s 1d), Nazeing Amateur Theatrical Society (ten guineas), the Nazeing Conservative Association (25 guineas), and the Nazeing Labour Party. The Nazeing Parents' Association organised three successful fund-raising carnivals, attended by hundreds of people, at which parades were followed by displays of children's dancing and demonstrations by Scouts, Guides, and other organisations. The site that later became Nazeingbury Parade was identified as suitable and the plan was that the hall should be next to the shops. Enthusiasm was such that the parish council established a separate bank account for the Village Hall Fund (£180), because it was larger than the council's general account (£170). The British Legion had promised £250 which, together with the £180 already raised, would have been enough to purchase the site. Plans were circulated at the Parish Meeting in April 1951 and everyone seemed optimistic that the project would go ahead.

Already, however, problems were developing. Essex County Council had bought the land in 1938 for its proposed Lea Valley Road and, although that plan had been altered, various

HUNDREDS TURN OUT FOR NAZEING'S CARNIVAL DAY

CROWDS of Nazeing people on Saturday watched the carnival organised by the Nazeing Parents' Association and saw a police car lead the way for the colourful procession.

The carnival procession itself was led by Lady Godiva (in reality Girl Guide Alison Hitchin on her white pony " Barney ").

Immediately behind Lady Godiva was the Hoddesdon Town and Fire Brigade Band, then came the Cubs, followed by the Girl Guides with their Colours, led by Lieut. Trixie Finch, all on foot.

The first of the decorated lorries carried a tableau by the Scouts depicting a camping scene, complete with a " fire " and raw sausages.

The Nazeing Pixies' lorry was decorated with coloured paper streamers and carried the Maypole and all the Pixies in their gay paper dresses.

There was also an impressive display by the N.A.T.S., showing a scene from their recent show and a peep into the future.

The Carnival Queen, Miss Jean Weare, was sitting in state surrounded by her six maids of honour on a gaily decorated platform lorry, and other tableaux were " Where the rainbow ends ", " Load of Mischief ", " St. Leonard's Home Farm " (featuring live piglets and ducklings, etc., instead of children), and " Market Garden " and " Hungarian Dancers ".

Humorous touches were provided by other tableaux.

There was a canoe with a crew of three sailors, two decorated cycles, and a decorated car entered by the organiser of the carnival, Mr. Douglas Ragg, and one lonely pedestrian, Miss Rosemary Hall, in her Ascot fashions.

Also in the procession were the Haileybury Boys' Club and Army Cadet Force, a new ballast lorry entered by the St. Albans Gravel Co., and a large articulated tanker waggon by F. W. Berk and Co., of New Oxford Street.

The organisers would have been unable to put on the carnival without the support of many owners of transport.

Later, in the garden of Trevone, Children's Day was staged in front of an audience of about 750.

Entertainments included displays by the Nazeing Pixies (dressed and trained by " Brown Owl "), acting nursery rhymes; sylvan dances and ballet by pupils of the Alwyn School of Dancing, trained by Sylvia Hayward; a physical training display by the Haileybury Boys' Club and Army Cadet Force, under their instructors, H. Bell and J. Davis; the Nazeing Brownies, singing and acting the " Vipper Klinger Folk Song " in Danish, and Brownie dances, ending with the Grand Howl; Chief Brownie Clare Trenow read a translation (by a member of the Youth Hostel) over the loudspeaker before the Danish dance, which had been taught by Mrs. Toettcher; a " surprise item " by the Nazeing Boy Scouts demonstrating first-aid training, arranged by their instructor, Mr. A. Brown; a jungle dance by the Cubs; international dances by a group of Nazeing girls attending Waltham Abbey Secondary Modern School, trained by Mrs. Toettcher and Mrs. Puddephatt; and three Maypole dances by the Nazeing Guides, who were trained by Mrs. Widdicombe (Brown Owl).

The grand finale (by request) was " The Holy City ", sung by Sylvia Murrant, accompanied by Jimmy Wootton and the Singing Scouts.

This was followed by the ceremony of the uncrowning of the Nazeing Carnival Queen by Mr. L. O. Archer, chairman of the Nazeing Parish Council. Mr. Toettcher, chairman of the Nazeing Parents' Association, thanked Mrs. Reynolds for organising a very successful day and for allowing her house and garden to be used.

Refreshments, soft drinks, ices, and teas, served by the Women's Institute, were on sale throughout the afternoon, and Mrs. Leah Manning, vice-president of the Nazeing Parents' Association, arrived in time to watch the latter part of the programme.

This was the last of three very successful events sponsored by the Nazeing Parents' Association to raise funds for the proposed village hall.

A picturesque group showing the Nazeing Queen and her attendants in a sylvan setting.

A press cutting describing "the last of three very successful events sponsored by Nazeing Parents' Association to raise funds for the proposed village hall", c1952. The picture shows the "Carnival Queen, Miss Jean Weare" with "her six maids of honour".

council departments were said to be considering other uses for the site. Rumours were rife, so that at the parish council meeting in May 1951 Connie Reynolds reported "considerable unrest in the village due to lack of public information as to the progress of negotiations". A figure of £5,000 for the hall was suggested but it was agreed that this would involve heavy loan repayments, so a cheaper form of building should be considered. At a public meeting in July representatives from some organisations expressed dissatisfaction with the progress made and with the lack of guidance from the parish council.

In November 1951 Nazeing Parish Council received a letter stating that the county council was thinking of building a new school in the village and that the old Bumbles Green school might become available as a village hall and community centre. This meant that the parish council had to choose between the Nazeingbury site and the old school, a decision members felt unable to take without broader consultation. A county council officer told the parish council that, by a quirk of the regulations, only village associations were eligible for grants towards community centres, although parish councils could raise a rate to contribute to such associations. The parish council therefore met representatives of village organisations and the Nazeing Village Association (NVA) was born. A further meeting between the parish council and the organisations failed to make a firm decision about the site, and the county council informed the parish council that the middle portion of the Nazeingbury site was no longer available.

In May 1952 a new parish council was elected. The former chairman, Leonard Archer, had not stood for re-election but instead became chairman of the NVA, which soon had a formal constitution. Whereas the parish council minutes have a detailed record of the negotiations from 1949 to 1952, those of the NVA, which would have covered the later period, have not been traced. Passing references in the parish council minutes and elsewhere give only a rather sketchy idea of what happened.

The NVA decided immediately to abandon the Nazeingbury option and to wait for the old school to be vacated. It played an important part in the village over the next few years, for example with a successful fund-raising handicrafts exhibition at the Chapel Hall in 1955. In 1958 the new school was opened and the NVA took on the old one, renamed the Village Centre. The parish council closed the Parish Hall in Betts Lane because the building was beyond economic repair, but the opening of the Village Centre as an alternative venue for communal activities may well have influenced its decision. Certainly the council transferred its village hall funds and 45 chairs from the old hall to the NVA.

By 1961 the NVA was facing financial problems. During the 1960s the parish council gave "sympathetic consideration" to various NVA requests for financial assistance. Eventually, however, it declared that "owing to altered circumstances the Nazeing Village Association was not

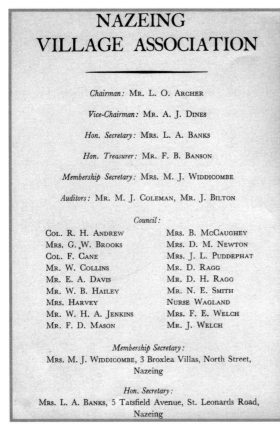

NAZEING
VILLAGE ASSOCIATION

Chairman: Mr. L. O. Archer

Vice-Chairman: Mr. A. J. Dines

Hon. Secretary: Mrs. L. A. Banks

Hon. Treasurer: Mr. F. B. Banson

Membership Secretary: Mrs. M. J. Widdicombe

Auditors: Mr. M. J. Coleman, Mr. J. Bilton

Council:

Col. R. H. Andrew	Mrs. B. McCaughey
Mrs. G. W. Brooks	Mrs. D. M. Newton
Col. F. Cane	Mrs. J. L. Puddephat
Mr. W. Collins	Mr. D. Ragg
Mr. E. A. Davis	Mr. D. H. Ragg
Mr. W. B. Hailey	Mr. N. E. Smith
Mrs. Harvey	Nurse Wagland
Mr. W. H. A. Jenkins	Mrs. F. E. Welch
Mr. F. D. Mason	Mr. J. Welch

Membership Secretary:
Mrs. M. J. Widdicombe, 3 Broxlea Villas, North Street,
Nazeing

Hon. Secretary:
Mrs. L. A. Banks, 5 Tatsfield Avenue, St. Leonards Road,
Nazeing

**The Nazeing Village Association in its prime
was no mean organisation, as this listing of
its officers shows.**

functioning in the best interests of the village". In November 1968 a special parish meeting approved the council's proposal that it should take over the Village Centre and set up a committee, consisting of parish councillors and former NVA officers, to run it. The parish council took over the financial affairs of the NVA, including "a number of urgent financial payments".

It is not entirely clear what went wrong. In 1958-9 Leonard Archer and Douglas Ragg died and Lilian Banks moved away. Others who initiated the project may also have died or moved away, so that it lost impetus. As the Village Centre had been built almost a century earlier for a completely different purpose, the cost of maintaining it must have been considerable. If this was the case, the NVA had lost sight of its objective, because the hundreds of pounds raised in the 1950s had been intended for capital investment in a hall that would be owned by the whole village, not for dribbling away on an unsuitable building which still belonged to Essex County Council.

At the time there were rumours of financial mismanagement or even corruption, and perhaps the disappearance of the minutes and accounts of the NVA supports this suggestion. In 1972 the parish council was asked what had happened to the Village Hall Investment Fund after the demise of the NVA The council replied that the money was in the hands of trustees, who were not named. No explanation was given as to why the funds did not revert to the parish council which had provided them latterly, nor do the minutes mention the matter again.

When the Bumbles Green Leisure Centre was opened in 1975 the parish council saw it as taking over the functions of the Village Centre, although neither of them can be described as being a centre in the geographical or social sense. With the benefit of hindsight it is easy to argue that the NVA's decision to plump for the Bumbles Green school represented a missed opportunity, but even at the time there were dissenters. In 1953 the Chairman of the British Legion pressed the NVA to purchase the Women's Land Army hostel at 88 North Street. It consisted of three blocks, one suitable for a modest village hall, another consisting of three committee rooms, and a third of bathing and toilet facilities; in addition there was a good air-raid shelter which might be converted for use. The parish council recommended that the NVA should buy the hostel for £1,500 but the proposal was "turned down by a small majority at a poorly attended public meeting", because the buildings were too expensive and already deteriorating. They were sold privately and demolished later to make way for present-day 88-88c North Street.

When a new proposal for a village hall in the Nazeingbury area was put forward at a parish council meeting in 1961, Councillors Wally Bradbury and George Compton criticised it on the grounds of the "prohibitive cost of land and building" and the motion was withdrawn. Two years later, with the support of the parish council, the Church of England bought a piece of land from Compton and built St. Giles' Church and Hall, which is central and by default fulfils some of the functions of a village hall.

At this time the parish council, declaring that the Bumbles Green playing field was "too far from the centre of population", made persistent and vigorous efforts to find a piece of ground in the Nazeing Road area "to satisfy an urgent and essential requirement in the village"; it was thwarted by the scarcity and high cost of suitable land. In 1974, however, the parish council did secure a 999 year lease from Compton on the one and a half acres behind what was later Elizabeth Close. This became a play area but it was only when the Lee Valley Regional Park Authority opened Clayton Hill Country Park in 1978 that at last Nazeingbury obtained a large recreational area.

In 1973 the Nazeingbury Residents' Association requested a new community centre in its area. The matter was deferred for the attention of the new parish council, which resolved to hold a referendum because "the cost of a Community Centre would fall on the whole parish". The referendum was held in 1975 but only 780 of the 1,495 eligible to vote did so, and of them a majority opposed the scheme. The parish council chairman deplored the low turnout, which he attributed to the "prevalence of apathy", but with the Bumbles Green Leisure Centre almost completed and with only 23 per cent of the total voting population in the village supporting the scheme it was obviously a non-starter. In 1989 the association revived the suggestion of a village hall but, as opinion at a public meeting was equally divided, the matter was taken no further. One lady recalled "a big event with floats and other attractions designed to raise money for a village hall", probably one of the Nazeing Parents' Association carnivals. "What happened to the money we raised then?" she wondered. It was a very good question.

Footpaths

Before the Second World War, Nazeing's fine network of public bridleways and footpaths was well used by villagers going about their normal activities, so few problems were recorded. When, for example, Bernard Pegrum's family moved from Queens Cottage in Back Lane to Curtis Farm in Middle Street, his father simply carried him across the fields to his new home. Then came an increase in car use and the influx of new residents, who did not learn as children where the paths were and did not need to use them in their daily lives.

Under the Access to the Countryside Act of 1949 county councils were obliged to prepare definitive maps showing rights of way and in 1952 local people carried out the necessary survey for Nazeing. The network was on the whole in good shape, although many directional signs were in need of repair. A special parish meeting resolved unanimously that where footpaths were superfluous they should be closed or diverted, and that old area and road names which had fallen into disuse should be reinstated. In 1955 three old footpaths were extinguished, three new ones created in exchange, and two diverted.

By then several well-known paths had been ploughed or blocked deliberately; over the next few years the situation deteriorated rapidly. The path from St. Leonards Road to Clappers Weir was blocked by barbed wire and the Co-operative Wholesale Society built nurseries across the one from Pressfields to Stoneshot. Edward J. Fowler gave instructions that the footpath at Ploughed Garlands, from St. Leonards Road to Perry Hill, should be left open. The gap was too narrow, however, so he responded to complaints with the comment: "Although the field is set with corn, there is nothing to stop pedestrians using the right of way if they so desire." The path next to the Bumbles Green telephone exchange was repaired "to prevent it slipping into the adjoining ditch". The route from Goodalls to the church, formerly called Church Lane and later known as the Burial Path, was ploughed up. Two footpaths on the Common were closed, one in error and one deliberately, but, after a vigorous campaign by Nazeing Parish Council, they were reopened. In 1960 the footpath from Banes Down towards the church was blocked, a situation unchanged forty years on.

The next survey in 1961 found that most paths were "open and passable but not too well defined due to little use". There were broken bridges and stiles, overgrown entrances, and "two or three apparently deliberate attempts by owners to stop rights of way". The clerk wrote to "horseriding establishments" asking them to refrain from using public paths. Nazeing Parish Council regularly drew the attention of Essex County Council to these problems. The intention was that the county should take action when the Definitive Map was issued. That did not happen until 1963 and even then there was no improvement. In 1967 David Cook of North Street reported "attempted closure and misuse of footpaths", five of which were impassable, so the parish council wrote to the owners and to Epping and Ongar Rural District Council. Two years later the Women's Institute found the paths "in deplorable condition, blocked, overgrown, wired up, no stiles, and worst no signposts".

In 1980 the Nazeing Conservation Society organised three autumn walks, which attracted a total of 90 participants. Colin Gibbons, who arranged them, found: "It was still difficult in many cases to establish where a path started and where it ended." In response to many requests he wrote and published on behalf of the society a booklet entitled *Walks In and About Nazeing*.

Other problems were caused by the failure of the county and district councils to do their job properly. Essex omitted inadvertently from the 1963 Definitive Map a short stretch of path off Hoe Lane and in the 1980s, around the time of a failed application for housing development on nearby Green Belt land, a concrete fingerpost disappeared; the path is therefore a matter of dispute. A path from Waltham Road to Middle Street was blocked at Bumbles Green Farm, and no action was taken to clear it. Epping Forest Council granted permission for a wall to be built across a footpath at Paynes Lane but did not make provision for an alternative route. At the new golf course between Middle Street and Back Lane one of the conditions imposed in 1989 by the appeal inspector was that the footpaths crossing the course should be re-aligned; twelve years later nothing had happened despite an appeal to the Local Government Ombudsman and innumerable meetings involving the county, district, and parish councils, the golf club, and the Ramblers' Association.

In law a footpath continues to exist until an order is made to close or divert it. Even though no such order has been made in any of these cases and without doubt the public footpaths exist, walkers do not have the unhindered freedom to use these sections of the network whenever they wish. Nazeing Parish Council planned an updated walks book which was written in 1997 but four years later the problems seemed as far from resolution as ever, so it remained unpublished.

All is not gloom, however. Epping Forest Countrycare, a small department of the district council which is considerably more effective than some of its larger counterparts, works with volunteers and local groups on maintenance of the paths network throughout the district. Although its responsibilities are enormous and its resources limited, activities such as the clearance of badly overgrown paths and the installation of stiles and bridges have made a real difference. Working parties of Nazeing people, organized by Ed Borton, have carried out similar tasks. The Lee Valley Regional Park Authority has made some excellent improvements on its land near the river. Much remains to be done, but the Nazeing footpaths network is probably in better shape than at any time since the 1950s.

The Nazeing Triangle

Like the Bumbles Green ground, the Upper Recreation Ground came to the parish under the Enclosure Award of 1861. The New Domesday noted in 1912 that "the area includes a large Pond from which the villagers used to draw their water". After the First World War the "Dunking Pond" was regarded as dangerous and the parish council decided to fill it in. Archdale Palmer offered at his own expense to "lay out the ground in an attractive manner [as] a place of rest and recreation", provided that one end of it was available for children at the nearby school to play cricket and other games.

Willows grown there were often sold to cricket bat makers such as W.J. Breeder, whose premises were close to the old Essex County Ground at Leyton. In 1928 eight willows were found to be diseased and the parish council authorised Palmer to arrange for their disposal at his own cost, retaining such timber as would be of use to him. In 1931, when a further sixteen diseased willows were removed, Palmer donated four golden willows and four horse-chestnuts. In 1945 the problem recurred, so he had those diseased trees cut down, this time distributing the timber to neighbouring cottagers.

As the area had deteriorated, in 1946 the parish council dismissed it as "incapable of development". The hedges had become dangerously overgrown and had to be cut back. In 1956 it was described as "very wet and bad...a shallow depression used only for grazing", the rights for which were still let for £1 a year, as they had been fifty years earlier.

For a while there was even some doubt as to whether the parish council owned the area. Then suddenly, in 1961, councillors awoke to the situation and resolved that the land should "cease forthwith to be used as a sanctuary for Water Rats and be restored to its former recreational use". In 1963 the council decreed that the land would in future be known as Palmer's Green, a name which seems never to have caught on outside council meetings, perhaps because it is far better known as that of a north London suburb. Although it wanted the land to be "left as natural as possible", it rather contradicted that aim by voting for "the hedges to be grubbed out and replaced with a low post and chain fence". There were objections to these proposals immediately: the hedges stayed.

In 1988 Epping Forest Countrycare installed a kissing gate, seat, and stile, and in 1990 it took on the management of the Triangle. In 1999, after an estimated 537 hours of work, the Triangle was opened officially as a nature reserve. Countrycare began a redevelopment that included a boardwalk over the pond for wheelchair access and an information panel, which featured artwork by pupils at Nazeing County Primary School. In December 2000 Countrycare announced that the area was to become a Local Nature Reserve, one of only six in the Epping Forest district.

Down by the riverside

The fact that Nazeing's western border is the River Lea has proved a mixed blessing for the village. Nazeing people have easy access to a wide range of leisure facilities but those same facilities attract large numbers of outsiders, many of whom bring cars, noise, and even anti-social behaviour. The advantages and disadvantages of proximity to the river can be illustrated by reference to three institutions, the Crown Hotel, the Broxbourne Rowing Club, and the Lee Valley Regional Park Authority (LVRPA).

Crown Hotel Broxbourne.

The Crown from a postcard posted in 1914.

The Crown, with its creeper-covered walls and adjoining pleasure gardens, was a great draw for day-trippers from London in the late nineteenth and early twentieth centuries. The New Domesday described it and explained its decline:

> The property has a long frontage to River. House - very old rambling low pitched contains 1 Attic, 9 Bedrooms and Boxroom. At one time a very noted House, much patronised by Anglers & others; but since new Road from Broxbourne to Nazeing has been opened, the House is little used.

The Crown could no longer collect tolls for the nearby bridge, so the old tollgate became derelict and "served no kind of purpose except to be an obstruction and a source of danger". In 1929 the Essex and Hertfordshire County Councils took the bridge over but it remained insecure and dangerous. Describing the "continued inaction" as "altogether scandalous", Nazeing Parish Council complained strongly so, after two years, the tollgate was removed and the bridge rebuilt. For many years it was known as the Black and White Bridge, from the paint used by the two counties on their respective halves.

In the 1930s the Crown was rebuilt and the gardens were abandoned. The clientele became more diverse, so that in 1937 the parish council asked for additional policing to control weekend traffic and rowdyism at the river. From 1948 onwards there were frequent complaints about traffic congestion and "weekend holiday trippers". Perhaps in order to discourage such visitors, the parish council opposed the building of a public convenience at the Crown and in 1952 it asked Charringtons to pull down a "delapidated [sic] building" behind the Crown which was being used "to satisfy lavatorial ambitions". There were also complaints about people camping at the Crown, who were "noisy until 1a.m. and then up again at 4.30". The Camp Controller promised that he would attempt to abate the noise but added that it was a matter for the local police. Charringtons solved both problems neatly by converting the hut into a proper public convenience.

On fine weekends in the warm summer of 1955 the area was inundated regularly by daytrippers, many of whom made nuisances of themselves. There were cases of hooliganism, bad language, and assaults on residents who remonstrated with offenders. Some bathers walked through from the road, undressed on private lawns bordering the river, and treated them as public land. Congestion from parked cars blocked roads and on one occasion Hoddesdon Fire Brigade vehicles were seriously delayed in getting through to a fire in Nazeing Road. On the August Bank Holiday a "vast and scattered crowd" congregated along the banks of the Lea and the police were conspicuous by their absence. Seventy residents, supported by the parish council, submitted a petition to the Essex Police, requesting adequate police patrols and parking facilities. The police promised to do all they could, although they were "considerably under strength [and] restricted by limited manpower". They advised the parish council to "provide 'No Parking' signs on a liberal scale" and to ask the Crown and boatowners to improve their own parking facilities.

No problems were reported in 1956. That was probably because the wet summer dampened the spirits of even the most ardent hooligan, for in 1957 there were complaints about daytrippers once more. It was a "general condition during summer Sunday afternoons" for Old Nazeing Road to be "totally blocked by cars", so that fire engines could not have got through. Few complaints are recorded after that, perhaps because, as leisure patterns altered, the problems eased. Many who live there, however, might suggest that little has changed.

Despite its name, the Broxbourne Rowing Club is in Nazeing. It was formed in 1847, shortly after the coming of the railway made it possible to offer boating facilities to visitors from further afield. The Crown provided a handy hostelry for refreshment and accommodation, and in 1860 a boathouse was built nearby. A second boathouse, erected on Currant Tree Island in 1897, burnt down in 1905 and was rebuilt within a year. Access was only by permission of the landlord of the Crown, at a cost of one guinea per annum. The club affiliated to the Amateur Rowing Association in 1897 and reached its heyday in the 1920s, when crews rowed at the Henley Royal Regatta and membership stood at 170 with a waiting list. The club purchased the freehold of the site from Broxbournebury Estates in 1923 and the Lord of the Manor of Broxbourne, Major Smith-Bosanquet, was president of the club from 1908 until his death in 1939.

The club suffered a decline in numbers during the depression of the 1930s and merged with Broxbourne Sailing Club to form the Broxbourne Yacht Club. This continued to function during the war and held a regatta and swimming gala in 1944, at which prizes were presented by Mrs. F.

The Broxbourne Yacht Club boathouse from a postcard posted in 1949.

Wrighton. After the war a cadet section was formed, the club flourished, and by the 1950s it was competing again in regattas and races. In 1953 the club entered an eight for the Head of the River Race in a hired boat coxed by Harry Sykes, the well-known licensee of the Crown and the proprietor of a boat building and hire business. Subsequently Sykes became president of the club and presented it with an eight of its own. In 1962 the club reached the semi-final of the Wyfold Cup at the Henley Royal Regatta and achieved successes at open regattas in 1966 and 1967.

In 1965 the clubhouse burnt down and the sailing club moved to the disused gravel pit in Meadgate Lane. Meanwhile the rowing club, still based at the Crown, was housed in a temporary building moved from the Hoddesdon Precinct Development. In 1974 the two clubs separated, with funds divided according to membership while the freehold land and buildings were retained by the rowing club. In 1989 it had a record season with 53 wins at open regattas and heads.

In 1996 the rowing club's proposals for a new clubhouse encountered strong opposition from local residents who, supported by the parish council and Nazeing Conservation Society, feared an increase in noise and traffic. The club dismissed the objections as scaremongering, claiming that the new building would provide a valuable sporting facility for the area and be far more pleasant to look at. After the club had made various modifications to the plans, Epping Forest Council passed them but the club failed to secure a £650,000 National Lottery grant that would have helped pay for the project. Nevertheless, in 1997 it celebrated its 150th anniversary, still thriving and competing with success.

The idea of a Lee Valley Regional Park to reclaim derelict industrial land and act as a "green lung" for London was first proposed in 1944. Finally established in 1967, it stretches 23 miles from Ware to the Thames. Even before the park was set up, Nazeing was seen as a "regional recreation area", and the LVRPA seems to have had a penchant for proposing new schemes that would encourage the twin bugbears of noise and traffic, thus triggering off the campaigning instincts of Nazeing people. In 1988 the park authorised a programme of 28 motorcycle scramble meetings, which one resident memorably described as "sounding like a drunken bluebottle". After a vigorous campaign led by Councillor Alf Hilling, the number of meetings was reduced to fourteen, for which no planning consent was necessary. Two years later an LVRPA scheme for an off-road driver training circuit and associated lazer clay pigeon shoot was rapidly withdrawn in the face of determined opposition. In 1994 the park published proposals for the Nazeing Meads area, which would have included model air sports and a festival site, but after a meeting at St. Giles' Hall it dropped these too. On a more positive note, the LVRPA's Broxbourne Lido was the nearest swimming pool to the village and when in 1996 it was threatened with closure Nazeing people were in the forefront of the successful campaign to have it refurbished and kept open.

The quieter activities of the LVRPA have brought opportunities for informal recreation. In 1978 it opened Clayton Hill Country Park, a much-needed recreational area for Nazeingbury, and later it created a superb ridge footpath from Clayton Hill to Colemans Lane and on to Fishers Green. To celebrate its 25th anniversary it planted 2,500 trees at Rusheymead. At Nazeing Meads a development much less ambitious than that envisaged in 1994 encouraged walking and benefited birds, which colonised the gravel lakes. In 2001 a new Lee Valley Walk from Bow Locks in London to Luton in Bedfordshire was under construction. The Nazeing section included wide gravel tracks to enable walkers to use paths which previously had been impassably waterlogged in winter.

Tennis and badminton

The origins of tennis in Nazeing are not easy to trace but there was certainly a Chapel club by June 1914, when the Sunday School minutes state: "Miss S. Pegrum also suggested a stall should be on the tennis field when a match was being played and the profits go to the treat fund." During the First World War the club asked to use the small schoolroom at the Chapel for a working party to make clothes for the men at the front. Dennis Mead remembered his mother playing on the courts, which were situated next to Smalldrinks on the site now occupied by Doune. Vera Coleman, who played at the club in the 1920s, thought that there were three courts and that players came from neighbouring areas and so were not necessarily attached to the Chapel. It was known as the Nazeing Lawn Tennis Club by June 1931, when *Nazeing Parish Magazine* carried a notice saying: "The above named club has been moved from Middle St. to Five Acres, the Pound, Nazeingbury."

No later reference to the club has been traced, so it was probably absorbed by the Upper Nazeing and District Lawn Tennis Club which was formed in 1929, mostly from members and friends of the choir at All

The Nazeing Lawn Tennis Club courts next to Smalldrinks. Doune was built on the site of the courts.

Saints'. Archdale Palmer was president and helped financially with setting up the courts. Arthur Hollow remembered that Col. Andrew gave permission for a court at Buttfield, which was rented at that time by Arthur's father Johnny. The vicar, James Sutherland, played, Adelaide and Harold Starling were founder members, and among the senior players whom Dennis Mead recalled were members of the Hollow, Reynolds, Sainsbury, and Starling families. This notice appeared in *Nazeing Parish Magazine* for May 1930:

Upper Nazeing and District Tennis Club

The above club will open its courts, weather permitting, on Saturday, May 3rd when four courts will be available for play. The Club will welcome both new Junior and Senior members. Owing to the great success of the Junior section last year one court has been set aside for the Junior members, and it is hoped that this section will be greatly increased this season. Hoping that we shall be favoured with a very successful year.

Harold Starling, Hon. Sec.

Probably the club folded with the onset of the Second World War, when the field where it was situated became an allotment.

Dennis Mead remembered also playing tennis on courts at Buttfield. This became impossible in the early part of the war because their surface was somewhat disturbed by bomb craters but, as Isa Lavis recalled: "With double summertime, the Church Youth Club used to play tennis several times a week on long summer evenings at Rookswood by kind permission of Capt. Palmer". Although there was no tennis club after the war, youth club members continued to play on the courts at Rookswood. The youth club flourished around 1950 and was the catalyst for several marriages. In 1952 Harold Hawkins re-formed the Church Social and Tennis Club for over-13s.

The Nazeing Badminton club was started in 1930 as a Chapel club by Dean Hubert Janische. It was part of a general move to provide recreation for the young people in the Chapel and began as a social as well as badminton club. Janische presented cups for the winners of men's and women's singles tournaments which, in the 1930s, were frequently won by Jack Pearce and Edith Judd. The club was evidently very lively since there are several reports in *Nazeing Parish Magazine* of successful socials and concerts, where club members showed talents other than on the badminton court. The edition for May 1933 reported:

On 18th of March the much looked for concert took place at the School Hall, when a large company had gathered together, in fact it seemed as though all Nazeing were gathered at the doors - as a matter of fact there was a table outside piled with tickets and the show was good.

If our young people show such talent and real cleverness, together with a wonderful memory for their parts, they will be a real help to the church in the days ahead. Thirteen is supposed to be an unfortunate number but appended are the artists who made up the cast in this splendid show:- Mr. S.G. Payne (Secretary), Mr. M.G. Coleman, Mr. B. Pegrum, Mr. C. Nash, Mr. A. Rout, Mr. M. Ogilvie, Mr. C. J. Judd, Miss L. Selway, Miss K. Judd, Mrs. Sewell, Miss K. Banks, Miss M. Ashby and Miss Gwen Enoch.

The club had a programme of matches during the winter and played at home and away to clubs at Hoddesdon, Roydon, Broxbourne, and Enfield. Some of the matches played in the early 1930s seem to have been the best of sixteen games, which on a single court would have taken about seven hours, so they may have played over a Saturday afternoon and evening, with refreshments at tea time. The more usual format of nine games, each the best of three, is the only one recorded after the war.

The club was suspended in 1939 with the advent of war but was re-formed around 1948. It was still a church club with a majority of church members on the committee, until 1968 when Rose and Norman King, stalwarts both before and after the war, retired and moved away. There were no longer enough church members to dominate the committee and so formal links with the chapel were broken, although the club has continued to play in the Chapel Hall.

The club had considerable success, at first in the local area and then in the county leagues, fielding two mixed, two men's, and two ladies' teams, making a total of some sixty matches home and away during a season. Nazeing was quite serious about its badminton but there were still annual social events, one of them a very popular "tin and bottle" tournament held at the end of the match season. Players brought a tin or bottle and were paired randomly in mixed couples for a tournament, the winners having the pick of the tins and bottles. Many visiting players will recall that for many years electricity was on a slot meter so that, if insufficient shillings had been fed into the meter before the match, the hall would be plunged into darkness, often at a crucial moment. On one occasion a rather large gentleman named Ted Allen, who played for a team in Hoddesdon, walloped the shuttle with all his might and fell backwards through the swing doors at the back of the hall. His gallant partner retrieved the shuttle when it returned and as their opponents sent it back over the net yet again, Ted emerged from the swing doors and played the next shot.

The Chapel badminton team in 1961 when they won the Hertfordshire Area League and the president's shield. Back row from the left: Robin Pallett, Ray Hutchings, Peter Wyatt, John Barrett. Front row: Paddy Hutchings, Rose King and Doreen Parratt.

Although there is only one Nazeing Badminton Club, it is not the only one to have played in the Chapel Hall, the only

337

building in the village suitable for the game. Among the other groups was one formed by a number of ladies in the 1950s which played on Friday afternoons, until the 1990s.

Football

By 1900 Association Football was well established as the most popular winter game in southern England, so it would certainly have been played in Nazeing, at least informally. The first recorded club was founded around 1904 at the Chapel by Dean Robert Davies (*Five miles from everywhere,* p145). It was called Nazeing FC and perhaps included non-Chapel players from the outset. The club played on some land farmed by Joseph Pegrum at the bottom of Langfield opposite the Crooked Billet and beside a pond. It was flat and ideal for football. Bernard Pegrum, whose memoirs of Chapel life are our main source for this early period, was told that on one occasion the visiting side from the Elephant and Castle district in London was displeased with the home referee, Ted Coleman.

> By misjudgment or bad management he blew his whistle for "time" in that part of the field which was near the pond and before anyone knew what was happening some of the visiting team seized him and threw him in the pond...

View from Middle Street of Langfield, when it was being used for football and cricket. Wheelers would be just out of the picture to the right.

He would have to go home and change and I should not think he put in an appearance at the tea at the Chapel, which invariably followed these particular matches.

In August 1924, Ted Coleman suggested at a Congregational Church meeting that

> ... as there was no probability of there being any more football or cricket played in Langfield, the shed there which was the property of the Chapel Cricket Club (now extinct) now became Chapel property and he suggested that it be sold to the highest bidder. The secretary was asked to write offering it to the Nazeing Football Club.

Langfield was no longer available because David Pegrum was beginning to develop it for housing. After that Nazeing FC became a secular organisation but its links with the Chapel were not broken entirely, as Bernard Pegrum continued to play for the club and was for thirty years its chairman, which he regarded as a great honour.

Dennis Mead thought that in the 1920s Nazeing FC played on a pitch behind the Sun and used a shed at the side of the pub for a changing room. In the 1930s the ground was situated at what was then called School Fields, behind where the telephone exchange was built later, with

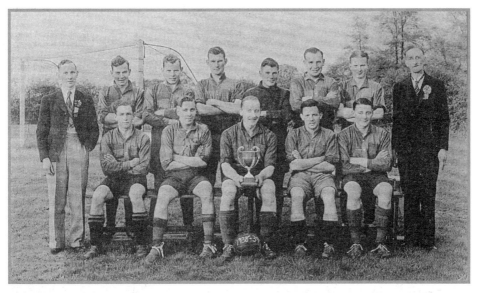

In 1938-39, Nazeing FC won the West Essex Border Cup beating Hatfield Broad Oak 5-2 in the final. Standing from the left: J Pearce, A Hollow, Les Hollow, Doug Reynolds, H Hollow, T Oakley, Peter Judd, Jimmy Brent. Seated: C Watson, L Trussell, Roy Brent, W Hollow, R Nash.

the changing rooms at various times in the outbuildings of the King Harold's Head and in a barn at Goodalls. In 1933 a parish magazine report on the wedding of Eric and Connie Reynolds stated that the bridegroom had been secretary of Nazeing FC for nine years, again suggesting that the 1924 move from Langfield marked a major break in the club's history. The Hollow, Reynolds, and Brent families were prominent in the club. Len Trussell was a player who refereed over 1,550 matches, continuing until just before his death at the age of 78 in 1999.

Dennis Mead has vague memories that during the 1939-45 war there was a temporary pitch in Laundry Lane, which sloped in both directions, and a pitch behind Black Adder Cottages where the Nazeing Horse Shows were held subsequently.

From 1959 Nazeing FC played at Bumbles Green. In the 1996-7 season the Youth Under-11 Team won the championship of the Mid-Herts Rural Minors league with an extraordinary 100 per cent record, winning all 26 games and scoring 156 goals.

Golf

In 1890, as golf was gaining in popularity among the more affluent in society, Thomas Goddard and Ralph Palmer established the first course in Nazeing, on the Common. Although the venture encountered considerable opposition at first, by 1902 the course was well-established and *Kelly's Directory* described it as "probably one of the best of the links within 20 miles of London". In 1912 the clubhouse at the corner of Betts Lane offered a large dining room, a smoking room, a ladies room, two dressing rooms, and a verandah with good views over to the course. The club rented the adjacent cottages in Betts Lane which may, after the burning down of the original dormy house in 1908, have been used for the overnight accommodation of members.

Then in 1913 came a potentially serious threat to the club. In 1907 the trustees of Nazeing Wood or Park had gained their Pyrrhic victory in the Palmer *v.* Guadagni court case about carting wood over the Common, when they won the argument but lost £440 in costs (*Five miles from everywhere*, pp155-7). Ralph Palmer paid this out of his own pocket. The intention was that gradually he should be reimbursed but, as Nazeing Wood or Park did little more than break even, after five years he was still owed £325. The golf club, an important source of revenue which brought

Above: "The 1st. Tee and Club House" at Nazeing Common Golf Club. Jimmy Savage, the professional, is addressing the ball. Below: Arthur "Tractor" Smith at Cutlands where he was Ralph Bury's tenant. Smith with Walter Samuel of Pond House complained that, due to the golf course, "we are being robbed of our very inheritance ..." (see next page).

in ten shillings a year for each member, had complained about the heavy hoofmarks of cattle and horses which were spoiling the course. The trustees therefore moved to protect the course by enclosing 75 acres of the common with a 4' 6" post and wire fence, constructed to exclude the larger animals while allowing sheep to squeeze underneath. Sheep have much shallower footprints and, as they crop the grass more closely, were a positive benefit to the course.

To justify letting to the golf club the trustees claimed that income from marking sheep and cattle was not enough to pay the expenses of managing the Common, but there was strong opposition from some of the tenants. Arthur "Tractor" Smith of Cutlands and Walter Samuel of Pond House wrote to the Board of Agriculture complaining that "...we are being robbed of our very inheritance and many others besides". It was a courageous action, for Smith's landlord was Ralph Bury and Samuel's was Ralph Palmer, both trustees.

Walter Samuel was never afraid to stand up to authority. He had brushed with Palmer a few years earlier when the parish council, of which Palmer was chairman, rejected his application for an allotment because he "is an independent occupier of some seven acres of land and building; and is not one of the labouring population referred to in the Allotments Acts".

Pond House, for many years the home of Walter Samuel. The road is officially part of Back Lane but locals know it as Ricketts Hill.

In 1905 his child was removed from his house with diphtheria, which proved at the hospital to be a mistaken diagnosis; Samuel claimed that this had caused him to lose sales of seven gallons of milk for eight days at an estimated value of £5 2s 8d and claimed compensation which, remarkably, was paid. In 1928 he complained to the parish council about an "obstruction upon the right-of-way running along the fence of a Cabbage Field towards the Sun Inn", so Archdale Palmer had a quiet word with the owner, F.W. Green, who undertook to attend to the matter personally. In 1931 the parish council arranged for Samuel to maintain the hedges on the Upper Recreation Ground in exchange for free grazing there. Mistakenly he was sent a ten shilling bill for the grazing and it was left to Palmer to apologise. There was a touching postscript to Walter Samuel's sometimes edgy relationship with the Palmers: in 1945, when Samuel was 84 years old, his brother-in-law offered to buy Pond House from Archdale Palmer who was willing to sell, but only on condition that Samuel was allowed to stay there.

Shrewdly Smith and Samuel enlisted the support of the Commons and Footpaths Preservation Society (CFPS), which found that Ralph Palmer held forty of the then 101 common rights and that

> While many of the smaller commoners were believed to resent the enclosure,
> they were unlikely to take part in the proceedings owing to the local
> influence and power of Mr. Palmer, the Chairman of the Trustees.

Palmer owned the Golf Club House and the adjacent Betts Lane cottages too, and so had a vested interest in the success of the club. The CFPS asked Essex County Council, which had bought Shottentons Farm recently and therefore had a common right, to act on behalf of the commoners. The council's officers recommended that what was undoubtedly one of the finest open spaces in the county should not be interfered with; they proposed legal proceedings against the trustees. Then Ralph Bury, a Deputy Lord Lieutenant of the county, intervened and the council dropped the matter. In 1914 club membership increased by twenty-two to 135 and the rent charged by the trustees of the Common went up to fifteen shillings per member, which brought in over £100, so suggesting that the fences had had the desired effect.

During the First World War numbers fell away greatly and, although they recovered soon afterwards, the rent reverted to and remained at ten shillings per member. The club ran at a loss, which was made up by friends, and, in 1924, asked to lease a portion of the Common rather than

343

pay rent per member. The trustees were sympathetic but had no power to grant leases of land. In 1929 membership jumped suddenly from 112 to 168, almost certainly because the club admitted women for the first time. Over the next twelve years the average membership was 145 and the club remained firmly established until forced to close when the Common was requisitioned in 1940.

Few Nazeing residents could afford the membership fees but local people were allowed to play during summer evenings when members were not using the course. Connie Cordell remembered that local lads lined up at the gate of the Common to act as caddies. Ken Judd and Dennis Mead were two of them and recalled that there used to be a caddies' match. Jack Hutchings was a green keeper at the club and his son, Dennis, was paid a shilling a round for caddying. Maurice Coleman recounted how he and other youngsters used to fish for lost golf balls from the cascade pond and sell them to the players. Enid Brent remembered that the two main fairways were cut regularly by hand mowers and that additional trimming was supplied by the sheep which wandered over the course.

Bert Coleman mowing the golf course on Nazeingwood Common. Abbot's Cottage and the Golf Clubhouse are in the background.

In 1992 golf returned to Nazeing after an interval of fifty years. This second course, like the first, had its fair share of controversy. In 1989 an application for a new 160 acre course on land between Middle Street and Back Lane was opposed by Nazeing Conservation Society and local residents and was turned down by Epping Forest Council, but the owners made a successful appeal and construction of the course went ahead. They stated at the appeal that "there was no intention of using the proposed clubhouse for purposes unrelated to golf" but in 2000 it was advertised as open to the public for Sunday lunches and special functions.

The Nazeing Golf Club features all-year-round greens, five purpose-built lakes, a driving range, and a new clubhouse built in the Essex vernacular style. An old-established hedge and a tree with a preservation order on it were removed but birds colonised the lakes and the club planted plenty of new trees, so arguably the course provided a better environment than set-aside or intensive farming would have done. The many fund-raising charity events there included an appearance by stars from TV's *London's Burning* at a golf day that raised £2,200 for the Mayor of Waltham Abbey's Charity Fund, and a charity day organised by Buckley Building Services of Middle Street which raised £5,155 for Nazeing County Primary School. Recognition from the golfing community came with the establishment of the club as a venue for the Eastern Region PGA Championship. In the year 2000 there was a nostalgic link with the past when artefacts from the old club on the Common turned up, including some clubs of Jimmy Savage, the professional. The new club was able to buy them and put them on display in the clubhouse.

Cricket

There have been at least three cricket clubs in Nazeing. The Chapel club was probably founded in the early 1900s, when the Chapel had a wealth of young men who played in the cricket and football clubs and the brass band. It had a cricket shed on Langfield but, like the Chapel football club, was no longer playing there by 1924, when the area was developed. There was also a Keysers Club that played on a field behind the Crown between the wars.

The oldest and longest lasting is Nazeing Common Cricket Club, which was still playing on the Common in 2001. It began in 1882 when the trustees of Nazeing Wood or Park gave permission to use land in

This 1940s photograph records a cricket match played during the war when younger men were away. Back row from the left: George Crowe, Sid Pearman, Jack Hutchings, "Gunner" Starling, unknown, Andrew Welch, unknown, Stan Welch. Middle row: Jim Wallace, Ted Coleman, Alec Gray, Hugh Eldred, unknown, Arthur Mead, Frank Kingman, Harry Mead, Sid Humphreys, Jim Robertson, George Mead. Seated: Johnny Hollow, Jack Challis, Alfred Eldred, Harry "Bogey" Hutchings, Arch Coleman, Billy Johnson, George Cordell, Bert Coleman, Arthur Brett.

virtually the same position as the present ground. A tent was originally used as a pavilion. The ground was part of the land ploughed up for wartime food production so until 1950, when the Common was de-requisitioned, cricket was played on a concrete pitch. A brick pavilion was built to serve this temporary pitch, and after the pitch was reinstated on the Common it was still possible to see where the doors had been repositioned in the wall facing the new pitch. At the start of the season, Geoff Blake's Land Rover had to beat a direct path across the ploughed land to the pavilion, although later a track for access to the club was formed from a gate directly opposite the Sun Inn. There was no electricity on the site of the original pavilion, so winter committee meetings were held at the Sun, and summer ones in the pavilion. John and Richard Coleman recalled that sub-committee meetings convened in the 1960s to agree the siting of trees occasioned endless discussion in ever deepening darkness. Ironically, the largest of the trees, planted at the bottom end of the pitch, is now right behind the bowler's arm. In the early 1970s a new pavilion was erected complete with electricity. After a heated debate, the parish council granted £100 towards the costs.

Nazeing Common Cricket Club has had its moments of glory. The Colemans remembered that for several years a special team came annually from the Cricketers Club in London to play at Nazeing. The team included ex-test cricketers such as Trevor Bailey, of Essex and England, and the Australians Colin McDonald and Barry Jarman. Jarman was so taken with Nazeing that he brought a touring team from Australia who asked to play at Nazeing so that they could experience genuine village cricket unknown back home. In 1968 the famous Portuguese footballer Eusebio, who was staying at The Saxon Inn for the European Cup final, joined the Nazeing cricket eleven for a bit of a lark and the crowd swelled rapidly. John Coleman and Peter Joyce were batting at the time and, when John got on the train the following morning, he was confronted with his own face staring at him from the back page of the *Daily Mail*. He snatched it out of the astonished reader's hand yelling: "That's me, that's me." Among business gentlemen travelling to the City such unseemly behaviour was just not cricket.

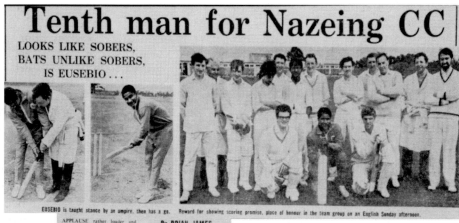

This article from the *Daily Mail* records that, in 1968, Eusebio, the famous Portuguese footballer, joined the Nazeing cricket eleven for their match against Stort. Apparently the best shots of Eusebio were those taken by the photographer – the star needed to be shown how to take his stance!

Drama and folk dancing

People in the village often got together to put on their own entertainment, as with the Badminton Club concert in 1933. In 1934 a school concert was held at the Chapel Hall to raise money for the Nazeing Council School Sports Fund, and the parish magazine reported that it

> was packed and a good programme consisting of 16 items was enjoyed. The children from the School gave the major part of the programme but some parents and friends performed a sketch and songs and Mr. Dellar gave a conjuring exhibition. The concert realised a total of £7 10s.

Children's parties with home-grown entertainment were held frequently, by organisations such as the British Legion and the Unionist Association. The Women's Institute often had a dedicated drama group, which put on well rehearsed plays and sketches.

The Nazeing Amateur Theatrical Society (NATS) in their 1952 production
Nautical Notions. **From the left: Alan Barrick, Dennis Ragg, Eric Reynolds (Neptune), Bruce Nicholls?, Jean Weare, Doreen Griffin, Jackie Price, Brenda Barrick, Pat Reynolds, Douglas Ragg (kneeling), Margaret Nicholls, Walter Chapman, George Price, Keith Ragg (crouching), Edward Brown.**

In 1949, the Nazeing Amateur Theatrical Society, commonly called the NATS, was formed. Their first show was *Cinderella*, a pantomime produced by Lilian Banks, which was staged twice at the Chapel Hall in January 1950. Paddy Hutchings, both of whose parents were involved in the production of *Cinderella*, kept a diary of this period. In July 1950 she recorded that there was a NATS general meeting at which there was a "nasty atmosphere" and a week later Lilian and David Banks and Betty Pedder resigned. The NATS continued, with the Ragg and Reynolds families prominent, but further difficulties arose when the Chapel deacons insisted on a preview of all scripts.

In October 1950 the NATS considered disbanding but decided to continue, using the Parish Hall and frequently performing in other villages including Epping Green and Roydon. Shows included a review in May 1951, *Café du Chat Noir* in November 1951, *Nautical Notions* in 1952, and *Dick Whittington* in 1954. The NATS installed free of charge a set of footlights which were available to all hirers of the Parish Hall, and received a 25 shilling reduction from their hiring fee because there were not enough chairs to meet the demand for their shows. There were, however, complaints about the inconvenience caused to other hirers by its scenery, which may have contributed to its demise in 1954 or soon afterwards. Pat Camp, née Reynolds, suggested that many of the cast, who were in their teens or early twenties, moved away on marrying.

Meanwhile Lilian Banks formed a drama group called The Footlights, some of whom had been in the original NATS *Cinderella*. She wrote and produced their material, which often consisted of three one-act plays. They continued to perform at the Chapel Hall and in December 1950 put on a show called *Christmas Cavalcade*. In the early 1950s prominent members of the cast were Jack and May Bilton, Aileen Cochran, Bernie Lanham, and Gloria King. In 1953 Phyllis Temple-Scotton and her husband, familiarly known as "Scottie", joined the Footlights; she rapidly became the leading lady, he the stage manager. In the mid-50s they put on some quite lavish productions, including *The Snow Queen* in 1957. Shirley and Michael Roos joined around this time, she to perform, while he did lighting, sound, and scenery. They remembered that the Snow Queen's costume had sewn onto it hundreds of tiny mirrors, which had been obtained from Brocket Stores, Hoddesdon. Like the NATS, the Footlights often took their productions to other villages and Mike Roos recalled what hard work it was to rig and then take down the stage for one-night or two-night stands in places like Esdale Hall, Hoddesdon, and as far away as Hunsdon. Even when the stage had been removed from the Chapel Hall in about 1959 and Lilian Banks had moved away the Footlights continued. In 1964 it put on a production of *Fools Rush in* at St. Giles', a month after the hall opened, but it seems that it folded soon afterwards.

**The Footlights Club. From the left: Pat Harknett, June Bilton, May Bilton,
unknown (partly concealed).**

Nazeing never had its own folk dance group but many people in the village belonged to the Great Parndon Folk Dance Club. It was formed in 1945 and met in a little hall near The Three Horseshoes in Great Parndon. Founder members included many local people with Nazeing connections, including the Wells family of Tylers Farm, who often held dances in their barn, the Haycocks of Broadley Common, and Geoff and Sheila Blake. The Great Parndon hall was demolished in the early 1960s and the club moved to a little hall next to the Congregational Church at Broadley Common. When this hall too was demolished, the club moved to its present venue at the Nazeing Chapel Hall but retained its original name. It was always the practice to have a fortnightly club evening, usually with records, and an open dance once or twice a year to which other clubs were invited and where there was a guest caller and live music.

Older people

The Evergreens Club was started in 1952 on the initiative of Connie Reynolds, who was secretary and treasurer. The club organised outings and entertainment for its members and an annual Christmas dinner, held in the Bumbles Green school canteen. BBC artistes gave an annual concert at the Chapel Hall to raise funds for the Evergreens; on one occasion their mandolin group broadcast on the BBC's popular *Town and Country* radio programme. In 1968 they moved to St. Giles' Hall where they continued to meet until the late 1980s.

The Evergreens was a purely social club but in 1972 Dennis Driver and Margaret Gervis, who were both parish councillors, realised that there was also a need for care in the village. Therefore they started the Nazeing Association for the Elderly and Handicapped, a voluntary association of village people who undertook visiting, gave advice about welfare options,

The Evergreens outside Ninnings where they met. Ninnings was the home of their President, Mrs Norton who is shown seated in the armchair.

351

Sometimes the Evergreens went to entertain other elderly groups, but this photo in the Chapel Hall shows them being entertained , apparently by the famous comedian Arthur Askey.

and organised outings and other entertainments. The parish council made an initial grant of £50 and its chairman commented on "the wonderful work being done by many for the elderly and handicapped". Margaret Gervis remained very active in the association, aiming to organise at least one person to be responsible for the elderly and handicapped in each ward. There were no regular meetings, apart from committee meetings, but a mini-market was always held at Nazeing Bury in June, and special events like the Christmas party and the bazaar were usually held at St. Giles'.

Other predominantly social clubs for the elderly included the Golden Club meeting fortnightly at the Bumbles Green Leisure Centre, the Tuesday Club meeting there weekly, and the Thursday Club meeting at Hyde Mead House.

The Royal British Legion and the Royal Air Force Association

At a meeting of Nazeing ex-servicemen in February 1924 Archdale Palmer explained the financial and other benefits which could be claimed from the British Legion Relief Fund (BLRF) and the United Service Fund

(USF) if a branch of the Legion were to be formed in the village. Accordingly the Nazeing branch of the British Legion was formed at a general meeting of 35 ex-servicemen held on 27th February 1925. Palmer was voted in as chairman and a joint committee was set up under the chairmanship of Major F.M. Green to administer money obtained from the BLRF and the USF. In 1926 the funds of the BLRF, the USF, and the British Legion Nazeing Branch were put into one account, although moneys used for general purposes, entertainment, and relief were kept separately in the books.

The annual subscription for British Legion members was 2s 6d and meetings were held at the council school. Poppy Day collections, originally organised by Palmer throughout Nazeing, have continued to raise considerable sums for the Legion's central funds (the total collected in 2001 was £3,174). Palmer resigned as Chairman in 1948 and, out of respect for his many active years of service, was elected president, whilst Richard Andrew took over the chairmanship. William Johnson faithfully performed the task of secretary for many years from 1927.

There were two main aspects of the committee's work. The first was the administration of relief funds for ex-service men and their families, so that the committee minutes provide a revealing insight into the hardships of Nazeing people between the wars. The committee claimed assistance on behalf of many individuals and made generous payments from their own funds, although they were careful to ensure that the money went only to "necessitous cases", whose needs included rent, vouchers for food, and help in the procuring of jobs. They granted, for example, three pounds to an unemployed ex-serviceman "for boots & clothing for his four little children ... part of this to be for cod liver oil for the baby which is ill". Sometimes they did not wait for an application but took the initiative in asking whether help was needed, as in the case of a man whose daughter had broken her arm.

In 1926, for one man who had been wounded and invalided home after four years' service, the USF made a contribution of £10 15s towards treatment in Guy's Hospital for duodenal ulcers. In addition to this, "considering the poverty of his case (Wife & 3 children. Rent of house 10s. Income 24s 6d)", the committee paid train fares for his trips to and from the hospital. He still needed help so later they paid him "10s per wk. in kind up to a period of 8 wks. provided he also applies for Parish Relief".

Even after the Second World War and the coming of the welfare state, the Legion continued to look after the needs of its members. In April 1948, aged 82 and in failing health, Archdale Palmer went to great pains to help the widow of an ex-Royal Marine who had been left with three small children. The problem was not only money but also rationing, so he established that her 24 clothing coupons would buy 5¼ yards of cloth. This was enough to make overcoats for the three children but not for her; even though she would have to wait until the new issue of coupons in August , at least she would have hers in time for winter. In May the area secretary at Cambridge sent her £2 19s 6d for the children's overcoats, and when the new coupons arrived he sent a further £3 12s 6d, which paid for her overcoat and nine pairs of stockings for the children.

Sometimes the committee approved a loan that was to be repaid within a specified time. In 1947 a payment of £4 5s was agreed for Harry Hutchings "to meet the cost of two journeys by Motor to Cambridge and back (£2 10s) and to Writtle and back (£1 15s) in connection with a complaint by the Essex War Agricultural Ex. Ctee about Mr. Hutchings' Farm of 84 acres." As a result of this complaint the "War Ag" ordered Hutchings to purchase a hydraulic plough, which was beyond his means. After careful investigation the Nazeing Branch of the British Legion negotiated from the BLRF and the USF a loan for £100, which was to be repaid within twelve months, and voted to lend him a further £25 from its own funds. The £100 was duly forthcoming but, because he obtained a cheaper tractor, Hutchings decided he would not need the extra £25. He repaid the £100 in 1948.

The committee's second main function was the organisation of entertainments for ex-servicemen, treats for the children, and fund-raising events to pay for them. They instituted an annual dinner, often held at the King Harold's Head but sometimes in other hostelries. Initially the men were expected to contribute a substantial "2s 6d or so", while the committee reserved to themselves the right to exempt anyone who could not afford to pay. Soon, however, the committee reduced the charge to two shillings and made up the difference from branch funds. Annual concerts, usually held just before Christmas in the Chapel Hall, were a major village event attracting a quarter of the population. In 1926, for example, 171 tickets were sold at a shilling each and 113 free tickets were issued, presumably to ex-servicemen and their families.

There were also whist drives and dances at the Parish Hall: it was one of these that sparked off a huge dispute. Following an event on 4th January 1936, less than two years after the hall was first licensed for dancing, the vicar, James Sutherland, lodged a complaint that made six points:

1. That intoxicants were brought into and consumed in the Hall.

2. That more than 100 persons were admitted into the Hall.

3. That a party of drunken people sought but were refused admission to the Hall.

4. That there was some boisterous horse-play in the Hall during the evening.

5. That something of a highly indecent character was found in the Hall.

6. That some of those present in the Hall were not respectable.

These complaints, the first two written and the last four oral, were brought before the Branch meeting for discussion. Tempers ran high on both sides and occasioned the writing of three letters from Sutherland and three replies from Palmer as chairman. The minutes state:

> In so far as the Vicar's last letter purported to be an answer to the Chairman's second one, it was seen that, of these four verbal complaints, one, viz. concerning an unmentionably indecent discovery in the Hall - the nature of which has never been disclosed - was withdrawn by the vicar without the slightest expression of regret.

The vicar wanted William Johnson removed from the running of such events before he would consider allowing the British Legion to hire the Parish Hall again, but the meeting was "not prepared to recommend that Mr. Johnson be sacrificed". For war veterans, "sacrificed" is an emotive word that shows the depth of feeling. The meeting regarded the vicar's demand as "...an attempt at victimisation and entirely contrary to all notions of fair play". It was resolved to ask all members present at the whist drive and dance to fill in a questionnaire as to what they knew of events on that evening and that, if these showed "...that the charges made by the Vicar were unfounded, he should be called upon to express regret for the imputations thrown upon the Branch and upon its Secretary".

When the vicar received the questionnaires and the request to eat a large slice of humble pie, he returned them unopened and unread "...as being not worth the paper they are written on". The chairman then appealed to the meeting not to "...divulge the present proceedings to any except members of the Legion, stating that all kinds of wild and irresponsible rumours and stories had become current in the village, which could do the Branch no kind of good". He added that the Bishop of Barking had approached him and had been apprised of the whole story.

Later Captain Palmer reported that he had that very morning "received two more letters from the Vicar wherein Mr. Sutherland tendered an apology and expressions of regret for his action". Evidently Palmer had drawn deeply on the diplomatic skills acquired in a lifetime of delicate negotiation, because the committee thanked him for "his untiring efforts to uphold the honour of the Branch, and at the same time, to bring the dispute with the Vicar to a satisfactory conclusion". The vicar's apology was duly accepted and at the next meeting a letter was read from him "...asking that his name should be deleted from the list of Officers of the Branch - as he had no further desire to act in the capacity of Hon. Chaplain. IT WAS UNANIMOUSLY RESOLVED that this resignation be accepted."

The episode shows clearly how customs and opinions change, so an incident that sixty years later would have been of little consequence scandalised the entire village. Almost certainly it contributed to Sutherland's keenness to transfer management of the hall to the parish council, a matter which he raised at a PCC meeting just two months afterwards. Extensive research has failed to reveal the precise nature of the "unmentionably indecent discovery".

Since 1936 the activities of the Nazeing Branch of the British Legion have been rather less controversial. Meetings were usually held at the council school until the early 1950s when, in an attempt to increase membership, the branch made strenuous efforts to get its own headquarters. Various suggestions were made, including the Land Army hostel in North Street, but they all came to nothing. In 1953 the Branch was given the use of the tea-room at the King Harold's Head, which it made into a clubroom, with billiards and other pastimes on Wednesdays and Saturdays. Meetings were held there regularly until the 1960s, when they were occasionally at the Red Lion instead. When the Red Lion closed in 1970, the meetings moved to the Crooked Billet.

The Royal Air Force Association helps former servicemen in a similar way. The inaugural meeting of the Nazeing branch was on 1st February 1950 at the Crooked Billet, where it continued to meet. Andrew Welch was the senior member, having been in the Royal Flying Corps during the

Peter Banson, with his wife Helen, ran the King Harold's Head. In 1954 he received the British Legion's highest award, the Gold Badge.

First World War. In March 2000 the Association celebrated its golden anniversary at its annual dinner and dance by exchanging the old red and blue tassels on its ceremonial flag for glittering new gold ones.

The Women's Institute

The first Women's Institute (WI) was formed in 1915 and by 1989 there were over nine thousand groups throughout the country. Nazeing has been particularly well served with WIs; at one time there were three in the village, Lower Nazeing, Upper Nazeing, and Nazeingbury.

The Nazeing WI was formed in November 1930 and for many years met in the Chapel Hall. The Upper Nazeing WI began in 1934, whereupon the Nazeing WI was renamed the Lower Nazeing WI. Aline Andrew, the first Treasurer of the Lower Nazeing WI, was also for many years a leading light in the Upper Nazeing WI, so there was some link between the two. The new institute was probably established because of rapidly growing numbers and the scattered nature of the village.

In 1937 there occurred what Archdale Palmer called an "unpleasant

357

Four ladies of Upper Nazeing Womens' Institute in the early 1930s. From the left: Ethel Eldred, May Ring, Mary Elizabeth Starling and Mrs Hutchings.

incident", which brought all his diplomatic skills into play again. The Lower Nazeing WI ran a whist drive and dance at the Parish Hall, which was the venue for ordinary meetings of the Upper Nazeing WI, and a "member of the Parish with two friends insisted on entering the Hall despite the Organiser requesting them to retire on the grounds that the hall was full". Palmer interviewed the offending party, almost certainly the president of the Upper Nazeing WI, who "expressed regret in writing, both to the Lady Organiser in question and also to the Society of which she was President". As a result of the incident Palmer gave instructions for the printing of two notices, one forbidding entry when the number had reached a hundred and one "to the hope that Dancers would refrain from smoking when actually dancing".

The experience of the British Legion and the WI shows that a whist drive and dance in Nazeing was not always the innocent pastime that it sounds. Following yet another rowdy one in 1946 the parish council resolved that in future hirers would be obliged to pay for any damage and instituted a hire charge of tuppence per chair and threepence per table.

Usually WI activities conformed more to the traditional "jam and Jerusalem" image. One typical report reads:

The monthly meeting of the Lower Nazeing WI took place in the Chapel Hall on Jan 9th 1940 at 2.30 p.m. with Mrs. Lawton in the chair. The meeting commenced with the singing of Jerusalem. The minutes of the previous meeting were read, approved and signed. Miss Griffiths who is a nurse at Tangiers told us of her life and work among the people there. Mrs. Lawton said she had wool to be knitted for navy comforts. The tea hostesses were Mrs. Eldred and Mrs. Mead. Mrs. Lawton thanked the speaker and the meeting closed with the singing of the National Anthem.

A Lower Nazeing WI programme for 1942, when Mrs. Fowler was president, included such talks as *Pitfalls of Knitting, Seasonal Operations in the Garden,* and *War-time Dressmaking,* with competitions including *Any article from odd pieces of wool* and *Best darned socks.* A register for 1952/3 shows over sixty members whereas in 1999 there were only sixteen. In the mid 1960s the venue changed from the Chapel Hall to St. Giles', where meetings continued to be held monthly.

The Upper Nazeing WI met in the Parish Hall until it was pulled down, when they moved to Dormarlyn Hall. In 1984 founder members Connie Cordell and Olive Knight were among the fifty members who celebrated the golden anniversary with a party in a marquee at the home of president Anne

Ladies of the Lower Nazeing 1963 WI drama group in the playground at the village centre (formerly Bumbles Green School). Back row, second from left is Mrs Wootten. Front row from the left May Bilton, Pat Harknett, unknown and Doris Newton.

Meering. When Dormarlyn Hall had closed, the Institute held its meetings at the Bumbles Green Leisure Centre.

The Nazeingbury WI, which was formed in 1968, met monthly in the evenings at St. Giles'. It catered for women who worked during the day or were otherwise unable to attend afternoon meetings. Together with the other Nazeing WIs and one from Roydon, it formed the Lea Group, each taking it in turns to host a show when they competed with one another for a cup. It celebrated its twenty-first anniversary in 1989 but closed soon afterwards. The changing status of women meant that the younger ones had less time for an evening commitment and that the older ones, as they had more leisure, joined one of the afternoon groups.

Activities of the Nazeing WIs ranged widely and included meetings with talks on a variety of subjects, often with demonstrations and competitions. There were fund raising events for charity and outings to gardens, craft centres, places of historic interest, and even television shows. Social activities included drama, dancing, Christmas parties, singing in choirs, and special weekends at the WI College at Denman, where members could have a break from household chores and pursue a particular subject or hobby which interested them.

Other women's meetings

A Mothers' Meeting was already part of Chapel life in 1888 but by 1930 the main meeting for women was the Women's Own, with a membership of about fifty. They were a very active village group, holding weekly meetings with a spiritual bias in the old Chapel schoolroom as well as organising outings, sales of work, and other events. Their anniversary tea, preceded by a service in the Chapel, was quite a big affair, when women from other local churches joined them. In the 1940s and 50s the meetings were still well attended but by the late 1980s numbers were dwindling, so that in the 1990s the remaining seven or eight rather elderly ladies met in one another's homes for greater comfort. When Ruth Bonnett, the minister's wife, left the village in 1998, no one could continue the running of the meeting and it closed, after having been in existence for at least seventy years.

An organisation called the Women's Fellowship was listed on the 1936 Nazeing Parish Hall Scale of Charges. Although the parish clerk thought it had ceased to function by 1938, Nancy Humphreys remembered joining just after she was married, in 1939. Perhaps it was superseded by

The Women's Fellowship and visitors c1955.

the Upper Nazeing WI, or suspended at the outbreak of war. In 1951 Harold Hawkins, the vicar, suggested the formation of a branch of the Mothers' Union but instead a Women's Fellowship for Anglican ladies was started, with Nellie Hawkins as president and Nancy's sister, Connie Cordell, as treasurer. They met monthly at All Saints' for a service, after which they adjourned to the Parish Hall for a cup of tea and some socialising. Sometimes they were joined by other groups of ladies, for example from Parndon. When St. Giles' was built the fellowship moved there and in 1978 it was renamed the Ladies' Fellowship. It continued until shortly after its 40th anniversary celebration in 1991.

The Young Wives' Group was started in 1961 by Sheila Read, the vicar's wife. For many years it remained a Church organisation but later the connection became tenuous. The "Young" slipped from its name to reflect the change in its composition but, as the Nazeing Wives' Group, it continued meeting monthly at St. Giles'.

Youth and children's groups

Before the Second World War the 3rd Waltham Abbey Scout Troop operated in Nazeing, and there was a Cub group too. Ray Hutchings remembered that he had just come up from Cubs to Scouts when he went to Scout camp and had to come home a day early because war had been declared. He thought they met in the Chapel Hall.

The present 1st Nazeing Troop was formed in 1950 when the Group Scoutmaster was "Tich" Hayes and the Scoutmaster was Mr. R. Kirby. Mrs. Knott, assisted by her husband, ran a Cub pack of about twenty. Initially they met in the garage at 78 North Street, home of First Group Chairman Harry Tulley, and then in a storeroom at the Crooked Billet. In 1957 the Troop wanted its own headquarters and the Parent Supporters' Committee was formed to raise funds for a Scout Hut. Their untiring efforts, together with support from the village in attending the many fund-raising events, enabled them to purchase a site at Perry Hill in 1963. The following year site clearance began and a dance held in St. Giles' Hall (the first booking there) raised £125. Volunteers did much of the labouring and the hut was completed in 1967. George Cohen, a member of England's 1966 World Cup winning football team, opened it at a special ceremony on 24th June. The vicar, David Read, officiated and the Girl Guides presented the Scouts with a clock and a plaque. Scouts and Cubs continued to meet in the hut and, although vandalism and diminishing numbers made the venture more difficult, in 2000 there was a tremendous response to an appeal for help.

The Girl Guides performance of *Briar Rose* in the 1960s.

Formed in 1949, the 1st Nazeing Girl Guides Company was led until 1954 by Trixie Finch (now Camp), who was assisted by Doreen King. They met on Wednesdays at the Chapel Hall and paraded alternately at Church and Chapel one Sunday a month. Their activities included taking part in District competitions, camping, and maypole and country dancing. The group was later led by Joan Noakes and her daughter Janice, and a Brownie pack was started. Although there were only a few Guides by 2000, there were two Brownie packs (7-10 years) and a group of Rainbows (5-7 years), who met at the Scout Hut.

Throughout the twentieth century there were clubs catering especially for young people in the village. Sporting activities like badminton, cricket, and tennis were often associated with the churches, which aimed to provide leisure activities and meeting places which would encourage spiritual ideals and morality. There were also Christian-based organisations like the Girls' Life Brigade, the Boys' Brigade, and Lifebuoys. For older youngsters there were youth clubs but, as active church membership declined, sports and youth clubs became secular. In 1968 part-time warden Chris Locke started Nazeing Youth Centre, funded by Essex County Council, at the old Bumbles Green School.

For nearly twenty years Smalldrinks was a popular Youth Hostel

A postcard of Smalldrinks in 1957, towards the end of its time as a Youth Hostel.

visited each year by some 2,000 hostellers, some of them from abroad. Six months after their marriage in 1937 Ronald and Karen Toettcher moved into the house. With her experience of hostelling in her native Denmark and his in southern England, they opened their home as a Youth Hostel in April 1941. Ernest Wellsman, YHA London Regions secretary, registered the first bednight. Local YHA groups in London and Essex supported enthusiastically midsummer dances in the garden, Bonfire Night parties, and other enterprises. At least one couple whose first experience of Nazeing was its Youth Hostel settled in the village later. Then in 1960, despite the efforts of neighbours and friends including an MP, this pleasant hostel, with its hospitable great open fireplaces, was forced to close and hostelling in Nazeing came to an end.

In 1967-8 the parish council installed play equipment at Bumbles Green, Pound Close, and Palmers Grove. As these locations were not ideal, in 1988 a group of mothers approached the council with a request for a children's play area near the shops. They set up SPAN (Safe Play Area for Nazeing) to raise funds for accessible and imaginative play equipment. The parish council gave them use of the recreation ground behind Elizabeth Close and a sum of money to start them off. Donations from the village totalled over £900 and the first equipment was installed in July 1989, when John Mackie performed the opening ceremony. SPAN had always envisaged that eventually the parish council would run the scheme as part of its recreational provision but some parish councillors opposed the suggestion, so when, after a lengthy debate, the council voted by six to four to take it over, the decision was greeted by relieved applause from SPAN members present. Over the next three years SPAN held events including a craft fair, a disco, and a quiz which, together with grants from the district and parish councils, raised £11,500. In 1992, having achieved its aims, the group disbanded and handed the equipment over to the parish council which continued to maintain it.

In 1965 at St. Giles' Hall Nancy Bradbury started a playgroup for the under fives, always referred to by David Read as "Mrs. Bradbury's Academy". She was assisted by Claire Gross and "Auntie Win" (Win Wiles). By the mid-1980s it had come under the management of the church and was run by Sue Oliver, later being designated a Pre-School Community Group. The Nazeing Tots Playgroup was set up in the canteen at the old Bumbles Green School in the 1960s. It transferred to a room at the Hyde Mead School in 1984, when Marion Marsh ran it.

364

Nazeing History Workshop

This began in 1993, when about twenty people responded to an article by David Pracy in *Nazeing Parish News*. Initially part of the Conservation Society, it became a separate organisation in 1996. It aimed to discover, record, and share information about the history of the village. The name was chosen to indicate the fact that members would work on different projects and share their information. Meetings were held in members' homes and other costs were also borne by individuals, so membership was free. Later a category of Associate Member, who paid a small subscription, was introduced for people who were interested in the workshop's activities but were unable to undertake research projects.

The workshop lived up to its name. Members created several databases that brought together various sources to provide detailed information about people and places in Nazeing. They published three books and many articles about specific aspects of village history. With the aid of a generous millennium grant from the parish council, the workshop published *Five miles from everywhere*, the first volume of its village history. This second volume is the culmination of nine years' hard work by all concerned.

In October 2000 members of the workshop were investigating the field below All Saints' Church when a well-intentioned but ill-informed bus driver deposited at St. Giles' some American members of the Camp family seeking the church of their Nazeing ancestors. Advised of their mistake, they made their way up Hoe Lane where they saw what appeared to be a group of farm labourers hard at work. They were surprised that English agriculture was not more mechanised and spoke to one of the "labourers", who just happened to have a database that included hundreds of pieces of information about the Camps of Nazeing. This was one of many links that the workshop's members have made with Americans and others in search of their Nazeing roots.

Special events

Royal occasions always provided a suitable excuse for the village to enjoy itself.

On Saturday 11th May 1935 celebrations for the Silver Jubilee of George V were organised by a special committee whose "indefatigable services...contributed greatly to the success of the day". They took place in the Chapel Field, where there were sports, games, and a decorated

The celebration of King George V's Silver Jubilee in 1935 on the Chapel Field.

bicycle parade for the children. 300 Jubilee beakers were purchased at a cost of fivepence each and presented to the children by Archdale Palmer. The Entertainment Committee reported a surplus of £18 12s 4d, which was "used to present a Pound of Tea to the Old Ladies over 65 years, and a ¼ Pound of Tobacco to the Old Men of the same age, both in suitable Jubilee Canisters". After this outlay there was 15s 4d left and it was decided that "a Flag Staff and Union Jack should be presented to each of the Nazeing schools". As the flags alone cost fifteen shillings, Palmer "thought he could guarantee to find monies to defray the cost of the erection of the Flag-Staffs, viz. £3-15-0". The flagstaffs were duly erected and proudly flew their Union Flags on Poppy Day 1935.

Two years later Nazeing celebrated the coronation of George VI. Again beakers were ordered, despite doubts about "the likeness of H.M. The King and the rather crooked appearance of the shield bearing the initials of the King and Queen". By then the parish council had taken over the Parish Hall and an event held there was said to have been successful, although little is recorded about it.

The wedding of Princess Elizabeth in 1947 was marked by a successful children's party organised on behalf of the Women's

Voluntary Service by Connie Reynolds and Flossie Welch. As rationing was in force, the parish council authorised its clerk to sign a docket for the allocation of food to the event.

To celebrate the coronation of Elizabeth II in 1953 the village raised £230 of which the Herts & Essex Aeroclub gave £150. It was then generously decided to divert the money to relief of the East Coast flood disaster, but a special committee raised a further £200 for a day of celebrations on Saturday 6th June at Compton's Field, where St. Giles' Hall was built later. A procession from The Crown to St. Leonards Road was followed by a full programme of events, which included a variety of sports, sideshows, dancing, and music, with teas for children and over-sixties. Although provision was prudently made for a dance at the Parish Hall and a whist drive in the Cadet Hut, the day turned out fine and concluded with a bonfire and singsong that went on until well after dark. The committee was well supported by private individuals and local organisations. Babies born in Nazeing during coronation week received a National Savings Certificate. One lasting relic of the coronation was the

Nazeing Amateur Theatrical Society's lorry float at the Coronation procession in 1953. From the left: Eric Reynolds, Pat Reynolds, George Price, Walter Chapman, Keith Ragg, Doreen Griffin, Dennis Ragg, Jean Weare, May Ragg, Edward Brown, Jackie Price and Brenda Barrick.

illuminated cross which was erected on the tower of All Saints'; it continued to be used every year at Christmas.

In 1977 a Silver Jubilee committee of representatives of various local organisations put together a wide-ranging programme of events. They included an Elderly and Handicapped Association coach trip to see the decorations in London, a party and two discos at the Scout Hut for children and young people, and a barbecue with two dance bands organised by Nazeing Conservation Society in the main barn at Harold's Park Farm; it was attended by over a thousand people. On a glorious summer's day a carnival procession travelled from Old Nazeing Road to Bumbles Green Recreation Ground, where there were various sporting events. John Gervis recalled that there was also a tea party at Nazeing Bury, following which the children joined the procession whilst their fathers slept on the lawn.

The anniversary of VE Day in 1995 saw another tea party at Nazeing Bury. Tables were set out in front of the house for one hundred guests to partake of a typical wartime tea served by ladies in headscarves. There were games for the children and a photograph exhibition for adults.

The people of Nazeing have always been willing to dig deep into their pockets for worthy causes such as village campaigns and amenities, medical facilities, and Poppy Day. Other important fundraising activities do not fall into any of these categories but are well worth a mention. In 1960-1 a procession and other events raised £694 10s 1d for World Refugee Year and in 1963 £250 was raised for the Freedom from Hunger campaign.

In 1952 Ralph Bury passed to the Coronation Committee a letter giving a detailed description of the Beating of the Bounds in 1891. The committee revived the event with all the old customs and on 16th May 1953 "some 30 men, women and children took part in various degrees", with Tom Franklin's "moving pictures" recording it. In 1981 the Nazeing Conservation Society organised a Beating of the Bounds in which almost 200 people took part. In 1983 the Church organised a similar event, and in 1988 the British Legion followed suit. One feature that seems to have been common to most of the occasions is rain, either on the day or in the preceding few months. This is not guaranteed to provide ideal conditions for walking twelve and a half miles on Nazeing's heavy clay soil. The wettest spring for many years meant that a Beating of the Bounds planned in 2000 as part of the Millennium celebrations had to be postponed from

May to October, when it was completed on a glorious autumn day just a few hours before yet another torrential downpour flooded much of the village.

In 1999 a committee called Nazeing Towards the Millennium organised a programme of events that was jointly funded by the Millennium awards, the parish council, a collection within the village, and monies raised from the events. The first event was appropriately a fireworks display held at Meridian Park on New Year's Eve 1999, when the crescendo of sound and light was much enjoyed by some 250 people. On 29th April 2000, at St. Giles' Hall, the Pavilion Players staged an Old Time Musical, followed by fish and chip supper, for members of the Association for the Elderly and Handicapped. Over the August Bank Holiday weekend, with some trepidation, members of the History Workshop laid on a village history exhibition, *Amazing Nazeing.* Photographs illustrated local happenings during the preceding one hundred years and Waltham Abbey Museum and various individuals displayed artifacts. Over 600 people attended and many memories were stirred. A village fun day on 16th September was affected by rain and a petrol strike but nevertheless some 150 children and parents participated in a variety of races, as well as the tea and refreshments from a licensed bar. As a final acknowledgement of the new millennium, the Conservation Society, with the support of the parish council, erected at Nazeingbury Parade a village sign in the form of a splendid map.

**The Nazeing History Workshop's *Amazing Nazeing*
exhibition in St Giles' Hall, August 2000.**

369

BIBLIOGRAPHY

Seventeen miles from Town, like *Five miles from everywhere*, is based on a wide range of primary and secondary sources. There are no footnotes in the book but a longer, fully sourced version of the text is available on application to Nazeing History Workshop or, for reference only, at the Essex Record Office. Copies of *Nazeing Parish Magazine*, *Nazeing Church News*, and *Nazeing Parish News* are held by Colin Dauris. Other items should be available through the public library service but, in case of difficulty, please contact Nazeing History Workshop c/o Colin Dauris, Goodalls, Middle Street, Nazeing, Essex, EN9 2LP.

Every effort has been made to trace and seek permission from copyright holders, and to acknowledge all contributions to the making of the book. We shall be glad to hear from anyone who has been inadvertently omitted.

The following are the sources, other than those listed in *Five miles from everywhere*, of which most use has been made:

PRINTED BOOKS AND NEWSPAPERS

ADSHEAD, S.D. The west Essex regional planning scheme 1933: the report prepared for the advisory joint town planning committee. J. Alexander, 1933.

CHERRY, Gordon, E. and ROGERS, Alan. Rural change and planning: England and Wales in the twentieth century. Spon, 1996.

EPPING FOREST DISTRICT COUNCIL. Draft local plan for Roydon, Waltham Abbey and Nazeing, 1983.

Epping Forest then and now, 3rd ed. After the Battle Publications, 1999.

GIBBERD, Frederick and others. Harlow: the story of a New Town. Publications For Companies, 1980.

Hertfordshire Mercury.

MUNTON, Richard. London's Green Belt: containment in practice. Allen & Unwin, 1983.

NAZEING HISTORY WORKSHOP. Publications listed on the title page verso.

NAZEING PARISH COUNCIL. Report on the Draft local plan for Roydon, Waltham Abbey and Nazeing, [1983].

TAYLOR, A.J.P. English history 1914-1945. OUP, 1975.

THOMAS, David A. Churchill the member for Woodford. F. Cass, 1995.

West Essex Gazette.

ARCHIVAL SOURCES

Essex Record Office

C/DP... Various papers related to county planning policy.

D/DU434. Papers relating to sale of Archdale Palmer's Nazeing Park estate, 1858-1945. In 2001, the Record Office had received these papers only recently and had not fully catalogued them.

Public Record Office

"New Domesday" 1910, survey for Nazeing done in 1912. Field books are IR58/37360-3 and survey maps are IR127/3/79-84. These two sources are best used together and may be seen in the map room at the P.R.O.

HLG4/7. Epping Rural District Council planning documents, 1936-43. Includes Essex County Council Town Plan, 1939.

Private documents

Nazeing Parish Council and Parish Meeting minutes 1894-1992.

Nazeing Parochial Church Council minutes, 1922-1999.

Nazeing School logbooks 1878-1970.

British Legion, Nazeing Branch minutes 1924-1970.

Nazeing Congregational Church meeting minutes 1914-1982

APPENDIX 1

NAZEING ROAD NAMES

In 1956 the builder of Langley Green named it without reference to Nazeing Parish Council or Epping and Ongar Rural District Council. The parish council declared it "essential that traditional local names and places should be preserved when naming new roads", and most names given subsequently were at its suggestion. A catalogue of individual house and field names would warrant a volume to itself, something that Nazeing History Workshop hopes to produce eventually. Meanwhile this list gives the origin of all village road names and, where possible, their first known date of use.

Name	Date	Origin
Allmains Close	1921	From the neighbouring common right house.
Banes Down	1961	From the eighteenth-century landowner Thomas Bane, who gave his name to a nearby field.
Back Lane		Ancient name describing the *bæck,* or back-shaped spur of land, leading to Upper Town and All Saints' Church.
Barnard Acres	1979	From two nineteenth-century landlords, father and son, who owned land nearby.
Barnfield Close	1947	Field name.
Belchers Lane	1923	From the common right farm-house now at the end of a road that formerly ran through to Middle Street. Known in the 19th century as Brewhouse Lane after the brewery at the King Harold's Head.
Betts Lane		Lane to Betses land, before 1732.
Blackadder Cottages	1939	In 1931, E.R. Boswall built himself a detached house in Nazeing Road called Blackadder, said to have been named from a property in Scotland. The cottages were built soon after.
Bumbles Green Lane		Called Galley Hill Lane until 1912 and later. Unofficially known for much of the twentieth century as Pig Lane, from Emily Hampton's famous Tottie. Galley sometimes derives from Gallows.
Buttondene Crescent	1939	Developed by a builder named Arthur Button.
Carthagena Estate		Distant parts of villages were often given fanciful names of foreign places to indicate their remoteness. Portobello and Carthagena locks on the Lea were named after naval objectives on the coast of Colombia in the War of Jenkins's Ear (1739-40). Hence Carthagena Estate.

Cemetery Lane	1891	Possibly the intended site of a seventeenth-century Baptist cemetery, although the earliest written mention traced so far is the 1891 census, which refers to a cottage "Near the Cemetery".
Colemans Lane	1896	Known in 1600 as Coldhams Lane, from the field next to it. The change was perhaps because the Coleman family name was common in the village.
Common Road	1796	Originally just a track, it became the main road when William Palmer diverted the old road that ran past his newly-built Nazeing Park.
Council Houses, Long Green	1921	The dwellings were built on a field called Carters Mead, which would have made a pleasant name for the new development. Instead they were given their prosaically descriptive name.
Crooked Way	1939	Presumably because it is near the Crooked Billet.
Crownfield	1969	The land between the river and Keysers Estate was always known as Crownfield, although this development was built on only a very small triangle of it
Elizabeth Close	1976	Named not as a patriotic Silver Jubilee gesture but after Mrs Compton, the builder's wife.
Great Meadow	1970	Field name.
Green Lane	1962	Presumably from its character when not being devastated by gravel lorries. Formerly known as Occupation Lane, a name given to roads primarily intended for the use of the occupier.
Highland Road	1926	Perhaps because it leads to the high land at Maplecroft.
Hoe Lane	1947	An ancient name describing the *hoo,* or heel-shaped spur of land leading to Nazeing Church. The upper part from Tinkers Lane was known c1920 as the Church Hill. The lower part was known c1900 as High Street and between the wars as Greenleaves Road. What we know as Hoe Lane was defined by Epping RDC in 1947.
Hoecroft	1963	On the site of Hoecroft, a detached house built in 1938.
Hyde Mead	1958	Field name.
John Eliot Close	1970	From the 17th-century "Apostle to the Indians" who was one of Nazeing's most notable emigrants to America.
Keysers Road	1934	From the family which held the farm in the sixteenth and seventeenth centuries, and gave its name to the whole estate.

Lake Road	1934	Origin uncertain. The road now overlooks the gravel lakes but it is unlikely that they had been formed when it was built. John Lake was the tenant farmer at Nazeing Bury in the eighteenth century but there is no obvious reason why he rather than any of the previous or later tenants should have given his name to the road.
Langfield Close	1956	Field name that gave its name to the whole estate.
Langley Green	1956	Reason uncertain. See introduction above.
Laundry Lane		The laundry to the Bury family's estate was situated at Laundry Cottage in the nineteenth century, but the road is much older than that.
Maplecroft Lane	1954	From the common right house to which it leads. Formerly Occupation Lane (North Street). Curiously, this Occupation Lane was known locally as Snakes Lane and the present-day Green Lane as Snakey Lane – whether by coincidence or some so far untraced link is unclear. Green Lane is dead straight, so the name is more likely to relate to the reptile than to the route.
Mayflower Close	1975	From the nearby common right house which the Ashby family, who lived there, had so named by 1923.
Meadgate Road		The road leading to Nazeing Mead, formerly Sedge Green Lane or Hedge Green Lane.
Middle Street		Very ancient descriptive name.
Nazeing New Road	1947	Descriptive. Known until 1947 as Broxbourne New Road.
Nazeing Road / Old Nazeing Road	1947	The original road to Broxbourne. Old Nazeing Road was often known as "the road to Keysers" or a similar phrase until named officially.
North Street / Pecks Hill	1921	Originally the whole road from Nazeingbury crossroads to Sedge Green was called Pecks Hill. It is not known for certain why the lower part was renamed. One possibility is that in the 1920s residents of the new houses there felt that they were some way from the sharp hill that gave the road its original name. In 1947 Epping RDC recommended that the whole thing should be called North Street but this did not happen, so now the two parts have different names.
Nursery Road		Originally Maddox Mead, a version of the ancient field name Nattox Mead. Had been given its present name by the 1920s, when houses and nurseries were built on the land sold off by Walter Benjafield.

Old House Lane	1925	From the common right house to which it leads.
Palmers Grove	1951	From Archdale Palmer, who died in 1950.
Paynes Lane		In the nineteenth century the road to Paynes Farm became the main access to Langridge Farm, formerly approached via St Leonards Road and Colemans Lane.
Perry Hill		Ancient name taken from the pear orchard that was at its summit in the fourteenth century.
Pound Close	1948	From the pound that formerly stood near the crossroads.
Riverside Avenue	1927	Descriptive.
Sedge Green		Probably the mediaeval name for the area. Greens were very small commons.
Shooters Drive	1931	The plans for Langfield Hill, the house built by David Pegrum for Arthur May in 1926, show that the original intention was for the road to be called Lanercost Road, after a village in Cumbria. The reason for the change and the significance of the new name are unknown.
St Leonards Road	1947	From the nearby house. Between the wars, the stretch near Nazeingbury crossroads was known as Pound Road and the remainder as Bury Road.
Sunnyside	1970	From the Victorian house formerly on the site.
Tatsfield Avenue	1928	Originally Tratt's Field, from the Trott family which owned it in the seventeenth century.
Tatsford Villas	1924	As above. The exact relationship between Tatsfield and Tatsford is far from clear, but certainly goes back well before the twentieth century.
Tinkers Lane	1920	In 1838 it was part of Hoe Lane.
Tovey Close	1979	From King Canute's standard-bearer, Tovi, who is said to have brought the Holy Cross from Montacute in Somerset to Waltham in 1035.
Waltham Road	1923	The road to Waltham Abbey and therefore descriptive. Formerly known as Nazeing Long Green, a name that is still used for the council houses.
Western Road	1927	Presumably from its situation on the western side of the Langfield development.
Wheelers Close	1965	From the neighbouring common right house.
Whitehall Close	1963	From the farm of which it was once a part.

APPENDIX 2

SALE OF ARCHDALE PALMER'S NAZEING PARK ESTATE, 1924-1945

The lot number is the one given in the 1924 sale catalogue.

* = sitting tenant.

LOT	DESCRIPTION	PURCHASER	£	DATE
1	Whitehall Farm	David Pegrum	1775	10.11.24
1	(part) Whitehall Cottage	Langham King *	300	21.05.24
2	Brewitts Farm (Part)	J.T. Chapple	1800	15.07.24
	"	Aline Andrew	1080	31.07.24
3	Lodge Farm	D.H. Graham	4500	9.10.24
4	Belchers Farm	Walter Hargreaves	3700	5.11.24
5	Teys Farm	"	"	"
6	The Rookery, St Leonards Road	H.H. Watts	260	28.08.24
7	Garlands Field, St Leonards Road	E Fowler	800	20.08.24
8	Brook Cottage, Middle Street	George Sinclair *	1550	24.06.24
9	Mansion House Farm	"	"	"
10	Two cottages [Bentons Farm]	Frederick W. Green	760	29.09.24
11	Grassland, Bumbles Green	Annie Louisa Fink	660	21.08.24
12	Hawthorn & Callis Cottages	"	"	"
13	Cottage, Nazeing Gate	"	"	"
14	Grassland, Dobbs Weir	Walter Benjafield	1200	29.12.30
15	Grassland, Nazeing Marsh	14th Epping Forest BP Scout Gp.	1200	1936
16	Grassland, Nazeing New Rd.	E. H. Co-op. Society	1200	24.12.25
	" (part)	Herbert Edward Hughes	200	9.08.28
	" (part)	Judd & Coleman	800	1931-3

OTHER SALES

Collyers, including Golf House	Frederick W. Green *	5000	14.01.24
The Old Mill House	Annie & Adelaide Savage *	475	22.04.24
Burnt Hall	W.A. Pulham *	425	2.06.24
Heather/Vine/Clematis Cottage	Frederick W. Green	320	29.09.24
Four cottages near Golf House	Frederick W. Green	350	9.10.24
Profits Hill Cottages	Maggie Taylor	725	1925
Nazeing Park	Walter Hargreaves *	8800	30.10.25
Hubbards	Mina Norris	400	31.10.25
Ravens	Jane Jeffrey *	350	5.01.31
Kingswood Chase	Frederick J. Jacobs *	1250	14.10.37
Pond House	George H. Whitbread	500	1945

INDEX

The dates in the index are accurate according to the information available to us. A few may be wrong by one year.